Managing
RAID
on
LINUX

Related titles from O'Reilly

Learning Red Hat Linux

Linux Device Drivers

Linux in a Nutshell

Linux Network Administrator's Guide

Building Secure Servers with Linux

LPI Linux Certification in a Nutshell

Running Linux

Understanding the Linux Kernel

Unix Power Tools

Also available

The Linux Web Server CD Bookshelf

Managing
RAID
on
LINUX

Derek Vadala

O'REILLY®

Beijing · Cambridge · Farnham · Köln · Paris · Sebastopol · Taipei · Tokyo

Managing RAID on Linux
by Derek Vadala

Published by O'Reilly & Associates, Inc., 1005 Gravenstein Highway North, Sebastopol, CA 95472.

O'Reilly & Associates books may be purchased for educational, business, or sales promotional use. Online editions are also available for most titles (*safari.oreilly.com*). For more information, contact our corporate/institutional sales department: (800) 998-9938 or *corporate@oreilly.com*.

Editor:	Andy Oram
Production Editor:	Claire Cloutier
Cover Designer:	Emma Colby
Interior Designer:	David Futato

Printing History:

December 2002:   First Edition.

ISBN: 1-56592-730-3

[M]

Table of Contents

O'REILLY BOOK REGISTRATION

Register your book with O'Reilly by completing this card and receive a **FREE** copy of our latest catalog. Or register online at **register.oreilly.com** and, in addition to our catalog, we'll send you email notification of new editions of this book, information about new titles, and special offers available only to registered O'Reilly customers.

Which book(s) are you registering? Please include title and ISBN # (above bar code on back cover)

Title	ISBN #
Title	ISBN #
Title	ISBN #

Name	Company/Organization

Address

City	State	Zip/Postal Code	Country

Telephone	Email address

www.oreilly.com

Part #10326

Preface

Linux has come a long way in the last decade. No longer relegated to the world of hobbyists and developers, Linux is ubiquitous and is quickly taking hold of enterprise and high-performance computing. Established corporations such as IBM, Hewlett-Packard, and Sun Microsystems have embraced Linux. Linux is now used to produce blockbuster motion pictures, create real-time models of worldwide weather patterns, and aid in scientific and medical research. Linux is even used on the International Space Station.

Linux has accomplished this because of a vast, and seemingly tireless, network of developers, documenters, and evangelists who share the common mantra that software should be reliable, efficient, and secure as well as free. The hard work of these individuals has propelled Linux into the mainstream. Their focus on technologies that allow Linux to compete with traditional operating systems certainly accounts for a large part of the success of Linux.

This book focuses on using one of those technologies: RAID, also known as a Redundant Array of Inexpensive Disks. As you will find out, RAID allows individuals and organizations to get more out of their hardware by increasing the performance and reliability of their data. RAID is but one component of what makes Linux a competitive platform.

Overview of the Book

Here is a brief overview of the contents of this book.

Chapter 1, *Introduction*, provides a quick overview of RAID on Linux, including its evolution and future direction. The chapter briefly outlines the RAID levels and identifies which are available under Linux through hardware or software.

Chapter 2, *Planning and Architecture*, helps you determine what type of RAID is best suited for your needs. The chapter focuses on the differences between hardware and software RAIDs and discusses which is the best choice, depending on your budget and long- and short-term goals. Also included is a discussion of PC hardware relevant to building a RAID system: disk protocols, buses, hard drives, I/O channels, cable types and lengths, and cases.

If you decide on a software RAID, then Chapter 3, *Getting Started: Building a Software RAID*, outlines the necessary steps in getting your first array online.

Chapter 4, *Software RAID Reference*, contains all the command-line references for the RAID utilities available under Linux. It also covers the RAID kernel parameters and commands related to array and disk management.

Chapter 5, *Hardware RAID*, covers RAID controllers for Linux. Chapter 5 also covers some widely available disk controllers and discusses driver availability, support, and online array management.

Chapter 6, *Filesystems*, offers a roundup of the journaling filesystems available for Linux, including ext3, IBM's JFS, ReiserFS, and Silicon Graphics's XFS. The chapter covers installation and also offers some performance tuning tips.

Chapter 7, *Performance, Tuning, and Maintenance*, covers a range of topics that include monitoring RAID devices, tuning hard disks, and booting from software RAID.

Appendix A, *Additional Resources*, lists online resources, mailing lists, and additional reading.

Appendix B, *Hardware RAID Controller Vendors*, offers information about RAID vendors.

A Note About Architecture

In the interest of appealing to the widest audience, this book covers i386-based systems. Software RAID does work under other architectures, such as SPARC, and I encourage you to use them. Support for hardware RAID controllers varies between architectures, so it's best to contact vendors and confirm hardware compatibility before making any purchases.

Kernels

Using RAID on Linux involves reconfiguring and modifying the Linux kernel. In general, I prefer to use monolithic kernels instead of modules, whenever possible. While kernel modules are quite useful for home desktop systems and notebooks, they aren't the best choice for servers and production systems. The choice between the two types of kernel is ultimately up to the user. Many users prefer modules to statically compiled kernel subsystems.

In order to maintain consistency, I had to settle on specific kernels that are used in the examples found throughout this book. It's inevitable that between the time of this writing and the release of the book, newer kernels will become available. This should not pose any problem for users working with newer kernels. This book uses kernels 2.4.18, 2.2.20, and 2.0.39, and focuses specifically on the 2.4 kernel.

LILO

Throughout this book, I focus on LILO when discussing boot loaders. I know that there are many other options available (GRUB, for example), but LILO has worked reliably with Linux's RAID capabilities, and some of the newer choices are not quite compatible yet.

Prompts

There are a number of command output listings throughout this book. The commands in these sections start with a prompt (either $ or #) that indicates whether the command should be executed by a normal user or whether it should be run as *root*.

```
$ less /etc/raidtab
# vi /etc/raidtab
```

For example, in the preceding code, the $ prompt indicates that the first command can be run as a normal user. By default, any user can view, but not modify, the file */etc/raidtab*. To edit that file, however, you need *root* access (as the # prompt denotes).

Conventions Used in This Book

The following typographical conventions are used in this book.

Italic
> Used for file and directory names, programs, commands, command-line options, hostnames, usernames, machine names, email addresses, pathnames, URLs, and new terms.

Constant width
> Used for variables, keywords, values, options, and IDs. Also used in examples to show the contents of files or the output from commands.

Constant width italic
> Used for text that the user is to replace with an actual value.

These icons signify a tip, suggestion, or general note.

 These icons indicate a warning or caution.

Comments and Questions

Please address comments and questions concerning this book to the publisher:

O'Reilly & Associates, Inc.
1005 Gravenstein Highway North
Sebastopol, CA 95472
(800) 998-9938 (in the U.S. or Canada)
(707) 829-0515 (international/local)
(707) 829-0104 (fax)

To comment or ask technical questions about this book, send email to:

bookquestions@oreilly.com

O'Reilly has a web site for this book, where they'll list examples, errata, and any plans for future editions. The site also includes a link to a forum where you can discuss the book with the author and other readers. You can access this site at:

http://www.oreilly.com/catalog/mraidlinux/

For more information about books, conferences, Resource Centers, and the O'Reilly Network, see the O'Reilly web site at:

http://www.oreilly.com

Acknowledgments

Many people helped with the writing of this book, but the greatest credit is owed to Andy Oram, my editor. It was his early interest in my original proposal that started this project, and his suggestions, criticism, and raw editorial work turned this text from a draft into an O'Reilly book. I'm also indebted to many people at O'Reilly, for all their hard work on the numerous tasks involved in producing a book.

Neil Brown, Nick Moffitt, Jakob Oestergaard, and Levy Vargas reviewed the final draft for technical errors and provided me with essential feedback. Their insight and expertise helped make this book stronger. Many others helped review various bits of material along the way, including Joel Becker, Martin Bene, Danny Cox, Jim Ford, Corin Hartland-Swann, Dan Jones, Eyal Lebedinsky, Greg Lehey, Ingo Molnar, and Benjamin Turner.

Thanks to all the filesystem developers who offered me feedback on Chapter 6: Stephen C. Tweedie, Seth Mos, Steve Lord, Steve Best, Theodore Ts'o, Vladimir V. Saveliev, and Hans Reiser. My appreciation also goes out to all the vendors who provided me with software, equipment, and comments: Thomas Bayens, Chin-Tien Chu, and Thomas Hall at IBM; Angelina Lu and Deanna Bonds at Adaptec; Craig Lyons and Daron Keith at Promise; James Evans at LSI Logic; Pete Kisich, Kathleen Paulus, and Adam Radford at 3ware; Joey Lai at Highpoint Technologies; Mathilde Kraskovetz at Mandrake; and Harshit Mehta at SuSE.

Thanks to my family and friends, who provided support and countless favors while I was writing this book, especially Dallas Wisehaupt, Philippe Stephan, Stephen Fisher, Trevor Noonan, Carolyn Keddy, Erynne Simpson, David Perry, Benjamin Richards, Matthew Williams, Peter Pacheco, Eric Bronnimann, Al Lenderink, Ben Feltz, and Erich Bechtel.

I owe special thanks to Craig Newmark, Jim Buckmaster, Jeff Green, and the entire staff of Craigslist.org for graciously providing me with office space and Internet access during my many excursions to San Francisco. Their hospitality directly resulted in the writing of Chapter 2. And finally, thanks especially to Eric Scheide, who encouraged me to write the original proposal for this book, gave me my first job as a Unix system administrator, and didn't argue as I slowly retired Ultrix and Solaris machines in favor of Linux.

## CHAPTER 1

Introduction

Every system administrator sooner or later realizes that the most elusive foe in sustaining reliable system performance is bandwidth. On one hand, network connectivity provides a crucial connection to the outside world through which your servers deliver data to users. This type of bandwidth, and its associated issues, is well documented and well studied by virtually all system and network administrators. It is at the forefront of modern computing, and the topic most often addressed by both non-technical managers and the mainstream media. A multitude of software and documentation has been written to address network and bandwidth issues. Most administrators, however, don't realize that similar bandwidth problems exist at the bus level in each system you manage. Unfortunately, this internal data transfer bottleneck is more sparsely documented than its network counterpart. Because of its second stage coverage, many administrators, users, and managers are left with often perplexing performance issues.

Although we tend to think of computers as entirely electronic, they still rely on moving parts. Hard drives, for example, contain plates and mechanical arms that are subject to the constraints of the physical world we inhabit. Introducing moving parts into a digital computer creates an inherent bottleneck. So even though disk transfer speeds have risen steadily in the past two decades, disks are still an inherently slow component in modern computer systems. A high-performance hard disk might be able to achieve a throughput of around 30 MB per second. But that rate is still more than a dozen times slower than the speed of a typical motherboard—and the motherboard isn't even the fastest part of the computer.

There is a solution to this I/O gap that does not include redefining the laws of physics. Systems can alleviate it by distributing the controllers' and buses' loads across multiple, identical parts. The trick is doing it in a way that can let the computer deal seamlessly with the complex arrangement of data as if it were one straightforward disk. In essence, by increasing the number of moving parts, we can decrease the bottleneck. *RAID (Redundant Array of Independent Disks)* technology attempts to reconcile this gap by implementing this practical, yet simple, method for swift, invisible data access.

Simply put, RAID is a method by which many independent disks attached to a computer can be made, from the perspective of users and applications, to appear as a single disk. This arrangement has several implications.

- Performance can be dramatically improved because the bottleneck of using a single disk for all I/O is spread across more than one disk.

- Larger storage capacities can be achieved, since you are using multiple disks instead of a single disk.

- Specific disks can be used to transparently store data that can then be used to survive a disk failure.

RAID allows systems to perform traditionally slow tasks in parallel, increasing performance. It also hides the complexities of mapping data across multiple hard disks by adding a layer of indirection between users and hardware.

RAID can be achieved in one of two ways. Software RAID uses the computer's CPU to carry out RAID operations. Hardware RAID uses specialized processors, on disk controllers, to manage the disks. The resulting disk set, colloquially called an array, can provide various improvements in performance and reliability, depending on its implementation.

The term RAID was coined at Berkeley in 1988 by David A. Patterson, Garth A. Gibson, and Randy H. Katz in their paper, "A Case for Redundant Arrays of Inexpensive Disks (RAID)." This and subsequent articles on RAID have come to be called the "Berkeley Papers." People started to change the "I" in RAID from "inexpensive" to "independent" when they realized, first, that disks were getting so cheap that anyone could afford whatever they needed, and second, that RAID was solving important problems faced by many computing sites, whether or not cost was an issue. Today, the disk storage playing field has leveled. Large disks have become affordable for both small companies and consumers. Giant magnetic spindles have been all but eliminated, making even the largest-drives (in terms of capacity) usable on the desktop. Therefore the evolution of the acronym reflects the definition of RAID today: several independent drives operating in unison. However, the two meanings of the acronym are often used interchangeably.

RAID began as a response to the gap between I/O and processing power. Patterson, Gibson, and Katz saw that while there would continue to be exponential growth in CPU speed and memory capacity, disk performance was achieving only linear increases and would continue to take this growth curve for the foreseeable future. The Berkeley Papers sought to attack the I/O problem by implementing systems that no longer relied on a *Single Large Expensive Disk (SLED)*, but rather, concatenated many smaller disks that could be accessed by operating systems and applications as a single disk.

This approach helps to solve many different problems facing many different organizations. For example, some organizations might need to deal with data such as newsgroup postings, which are of relatively low importance, but require an extremely large amount of storage. These organizations will realize that a single hard drive is grossly inadequate for their storage needs and that manually organizing data is a futile effort. Other companies might work with small amounts of vitally important data, in a situation in which downtime or data loss would be catastrophic to their business. RAID, because of its robust and varying implementations, can scale to meet the needs of both these types of organizations, and many others.

RAID Terminology

One of the most confusing parts of system administration is its terminology. Misnomers often obscure simple topics, making it hard to search for documentation and even harder to locate relevant software. This has unfortunately been the case with RAID on Linux, but Linux isn't specifically to blame. Since RAID began as an open specification that was quickly adopted and made proprietary by a multitude of value-added resellers and storage manufacturers, it fell victim to mismarketing. For example, arrays are often referred to as metadevices, logical volumes, or volume groups. All of these terms mean the same thing: a group of drives that behave as one—that is, a RAID or an array. In the following section, we will introduce various terms used to describe RAID.

RAID has the ability to survive disk failures and increase overall disk performance. The RAID levels described in the following section each provide a different combination of performance and reliability. The levels that yield the most impressive performance often sacrifice the ability to survive disk failures and vice versa.

Redundancy

Redundancy is a feature that allows an array to survive a disk failure. Not all RAID levels support this feature. In fact, although the term RAID is used to describe certain types of non-redundant arrays, these arrays are not, in fact, RAID because they do not support any data redundancy.

Despite its redundant capabilities, RAID should never be used as a replacement for reliable backups. RAID does not protect your data in the event of a fire, natural disaster, or user error.

Mirroring

Two basic forms of redundancy appear throughout the RAID specification. The first is accomplished with a process called *disk mirroring*, shown in Figure 1-1. Mirroring replicates data onto every disk in the array. Each member disk contains the same data and has an equal role in the array. In the event of a disk failure, data can be read from the remaining disks.

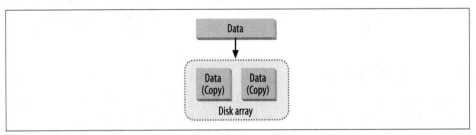

Figure 1-1. Disk mirroring writes a copy of all data to each disk.

Improved read performance is a by-product of disk mirroring. When the array is operating normally, meaning that no disks have failed, data can be read in parallel from each disk in the mirror. The result is that reads can yield a linear performance based on the number of disks in the array. A two-disk mirror could yield read speeds up to two times that of a single disk. However, in practice, you probably won't see a read performance increase that's quite this dramatic. That's because many other factors, including filesystem performance and data distribution, also affect throughput. But you can still expect read performance that's better than that of a single disk.

Unfortunately, mirroring also means that data must be written twice—once to each disk in the array. The result is slightly slower write performance, compared to that of a single disk or nonmirroring array.

Parity

Parity algorithms are the other method of redundancy. When data is written to an array, recovery information is written onto a separate disk, as shown in Figure 1-2. If a drive fails, the original data can be reconstructed from the parity information and the remaining data. You can find more information on how parity redundancy works in Chapter 2.

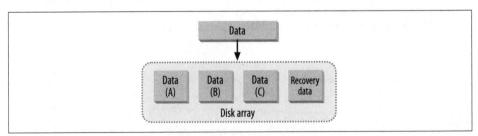

Figure 1-2. Parity redundancy is accomplished by storing recovery data on specified drives.

Degraded

Degraded describes an array that supports redundancy, but has one or more failed disks. The array is still operational, but its reliability and, in some cases, its performance, is diminished. When an array is in *degraded mode*, an additional disk failure usually indicates data loss, although certain types of arrays can withstand multiple disk failures.

Reconstruction, resynchronization, and recovery

When a failed disk from a degraded array is replaced, a recovery process begins. The terms *reconstruction*, *resynchronization*, *recovery*, and *rebuild* are often used interchangeably to describe this recovery process. During recovery, data is either copied verbatim to the new disk (if mirroring was used) or reconstructed using the parity information provided by the remaining disks (if parity was used). The recovery process usually puts an additional strain on system resources. Recovery can be automated by both hardware and software, provided that enough hardware (disks) is available to repair an array without user intervention.

Whenever a new redundant array is created, an initial recovery process is performed. This process ensures that all disks are synchronized. It is part of normal RAID operations and does not indicate any hardware or software errors.

Striping

Striping is a method by which data is spread across multiple disks (see Figure 1-3). A fixed amount of data is written to each disk. The first disk in the array is not reused until an equal amount of data is written to each of the other disks in the array. This results in improved read and write performance, because data is written to more than one drive at a time. Some arrays that store data in stripes also support redundancy through disk parity. RAID-0 defines a striped array without redundancy, resulting in extremely fast read and write performance, but no method for surviving a disk failure. Not all types of arrays support striping.

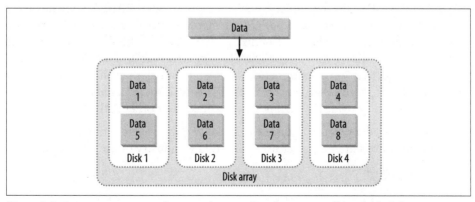

Figure 1-3. Striping improves performance by spreading data across all available disks.

Stripe-size versus chunk-size

The *stripe-size* of an array defines the amount of data written to a group of parallel disk blocks. Assume you have an array of four disks with a stripe size of 64 KB (a common default). In this case, 16 KB worth of data is written to each disk (see Figure 1-4), for a total of 64 KB per stripe. An array's *chunk-size* defines the smallest amount of data per write operation that should be written to each individual disk. That means a striping array made up of four disks, with a chunk-size of 64 KB, has a stripe-size of 256 KB, because a minimum of 64 KB is written to each component disk. Depending on the specific RAID implementation, users may be asked to set a stripe-size or a chunk-size. For example, most hardware RAID controllers use a stripe-size, while the Linux kernel uses a chunk-size.

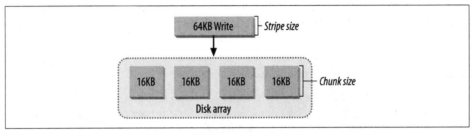

Figure 1-4. Stripe-size defines the size of write operations.

The RAID Levels: An Overview

Patterson, Gibson, and Katz realized that different types of systems would inevitably have different performance and redundancy requirements. The Berkeley Papers provided specifications for five levels of RAID, offering various compromises between performance and data redundancy. After the publication of the Berkeley Papers, however, the computer industry quickly realized that some of the original levels failed to provide a good balance between cost and performance, and therefore weren't really worth using.

RAID-2 and RAID-3, for example, quickly became useless. RAID-2 implemented a read/write level *error correction code* (*ECC*) that later became a standard firmware feature on hard drives. This development left RAID-2 without any advantage in redundancy over other RAID levels. The ECC implementation now required unnecessary overhead that hurt performance. RAID-3 required that all disks operate in lockstep (all disk spindles are synchronized). This added additional design considerations and did not provide any significant advantage over other RAID levels.

RAID has changed a great deal since the Berkeley Papers were written. While some of the original levels are no longer used, the storage industry quickly made additions to the original specification. This book will cover all of the RAID levels available to Linux users, but will not cover obsolete implementations like RAID-2 and RAID-3. Below you will find a concise overview of each RAID level. Chapter 2 covers each of the RAID levels in more detail, including hybrid arrays that are built by combining multiple RAID levels.

RAID-0: Striping

RAID-0 is also known as *striping* because data is interleaved across all drives in the array. Each block of data is written in round-robin fashion to array disks until the write operation is complete. Data is read in the same fashion. Since data transfer is constantly shifted to a new disk, bottlenecks associated with reading and writing data to a single disk are alleviated and performance dramatically improves. Striping was not part of the original RAID specification and, technically speaking, is not a RAID because it provides no mechanism for data redundancy. Nonetheless, the concept of striping is also found in other RAID levels. For example, RAID-4 and RAID-5 (described below) use a combination of striping and recovery algorithms to achieve improvements in performance while still offering redundancy.

RAID-1: Mirroring

RAID-1 (*mirroring*) stores an exact replica of all data on a separate disk or disks. This practice provides complete data redundancy in the event of a disk failure. However, because data must be written to disk more than once, there is a write performance hit, which increases as you add disks. On the other hand, read operations can be done in parallel so that read performance improves (compared to that of a single disk), depending on the number of disks in the mirror.

RAID-4: Dedicated Parity

RAID-4 works similarly to striping. However, a dedicated drive is used to store parity information. Every time data is written to an array disk, an algorithm generates recovery information that is written to a specially flagged *parity drive*. In the event of single disk failure, the algorithm can be reversed and missing data can be automatically generated, based on the remaining data and the parity information.

RAID-5: Distributed Parity

RAID-5 is similar to RAID-4, except that the parity information is spread across all drives in the array. This helps reduce the bottleneck inherent in writing parity information to a single drive during each write operation.

Linear Mode

Linear mode, also called append mode, writes data to a single array disk until it is full. Once the disk is full, data is written to the next disk in the array until all disks are full. This provides an easy way to use disks of different sizes in an array, so that no space is ever wasted. Like striping, linear mode is not technically a RAID, because no redundancy is provided. It was also not present in the original RAID specification. For clarity, I will use the term linear mode, rather than append mode, throughout the rest of the book.

Disk spanning

The term linear mode is unique to the Linux kernel's implementation of RAID. Most hardware RAID vendors use the term *disk spanning*, or simply *spanning*, to refer to this type of end-to-end disk arrangement. The terms *disk concatenation* or *concatenated disks* are also used.

JBOD (Just a Bunch Of Disks)

JBOD refers to the single-disk operating mode that many hardware RAID controllers support. With JBOD mode, the controller is able to circumvent RAID firmware and treat a single hard disk as a normal disk controller would. This is useful when you have disks that you want to configure without RAID support, but that you want to connect to a RAID controller. If your controller does not support JBOD, then you would need to use a standard disk controller to connect non-RAID disks, resulting in additional hardware spending and the use of another expansion slot.

I have seen some instances where the term JBOD is used interchangeably with terms like linear mode, disk spanning, and concatenation. When I use it throughout this book, I mean it in the context described here: a standalone disk connected to a RAID controller.

RAID on Linux

It's important to understand that when I refer to a RAID array, I'm talking about a block device and not a filesystem. You could think of the relationship between the two much in the same way you might think of the relationship between a house and its foundation. If the foundation is weak, the house will eventually collapse. The filesystem, which represents the house in my analogy, is built on top of a block device. Normally, a block device is a single hard disk, but RAID introduces another layer (see Figure 1-5). RAID groups many block devices into a single virtual device.

This means that Linux interacts with an array through a single block device having a single major and minor number. Physically, the array device points to many different physical disks, each with their own major and minor numbers. Programmers might

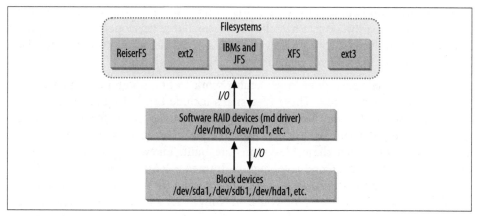

Figure 1-5. Filesystems are built on block devices; RAID introduces an intermediary layer.

think of this model the same way they think of an array data type, hence the use of the word "array" in the RAID acronym.

Each piece of hardware connected to a Linux system is assigned a major and minor number. The major number refers to a specific group of hardware (such as small computer systems interface, or SCSI, disks), while the minor uniquely identifies each installed piece of hardware within the group (for example, each individual SCSI disk). Since RAID is merely an intermediary layer, and because it works just like any other block device, you can build any type of filesystem on top of it. When working with Linux's RAID implementation, you can even build arrays on top of other arrays, or use other types of storage management like Logical Volume Management (LVM).

The Linux device names for accessing software RAID devices are designated *md*. While you might assume that *md* stands for metadevice, that's incorrect (although the abbreviation is used that way by many people). The *md* in Linux software RAID actually refers to the kernel subsystem that handles arrays: the *multiple devices* driver. */dev/md[0-255]* represents the default block devices used for accessing software RAID on Linux, allowing a total of 256 software RAID devices on a single Linux system.

RAID under Linux is available as part of the kernel. The kernel supports five different RAID levels: linear mode, striping (RAID-0), mirroring (RAID-1), RAID-4, and RAID-5. The RAID subsystem can be compiled statically into the kernel or used as a loadable module. Chapter 3 covers software RAID implementation under Linux. If you are already familiar with RAID from an architectural standpoint, you can skip ahead to Chapter 3 and start rebuilding your kernel.

With the popularity of Linux increasing daily, many manufacturers have begun to release Linux drivers for hardware RAID cards and offer full-scale technical support for such RAID cards. Many of these companies have gone one step further and released drivers that are open source (*http://opensource.org*). Some companies that have not been kind enough to release drivers have still released technical information about their hardware that has allowed open source developers to write drivers. This growing industry support allows Linux, and open source, to more effectively compete with commercial systems and legacy operating systems.

Linux professionals have done considerable work to bring high-performance, open source filesystems to Linux. These filesystems include IBM's Journaled File System (JFS), ext3, SGI's XFS, and ReiserFS. However, improving the performance and reliability of a filesystem can be a wasted effort if equal consideration is not given to the block devices on which these filesystems are built. Likewise, you'd be foolish to spend your time building a reliable, high-performance RAID system without considering the filesystem that you are going to use. In fact, in many cases, limitations of filesystems like ext2 will prevent you from fully realizing the potential of a RAID device. Chapter 6 provides a brief overview of some high-performance filesystems.

Hardware Versus Software

Although RAID is built directly into the Linux kernel, some users might find it advantageous to buy custom drive controllers that have built-in RAID capabilities. Some users might even find it worthwhile to purchase custom RAID systems that have been preconfigured. The choice between using software (kernel-based) or hardware (controller-based) RAID or buying a turnkey RAID solution can be difficult, but this book will help you determine which option is best suited for your needs.

## CHAPTER 2

Planning and Architecture

Choosing the right RAID solution can be a daunting task. Buzzwords and marketing often cloud administrators' understanding of RAID technology. Conflicting information can cause inexperienced administrators to make mistakes. It is not unnatural to make mistakes when architecting a complicated system. But unfortunately, deadlines and financial considerations can make any mistakes catastrophic. I hope that this book, and this chapter in particular, will leave you informed enough to make as few mistakes as possible, so you can maximize both your time and the resources you have at your disposal. This chapter will help you pick the best RAID solution by first selecting which RAID level to use and then focusing on the following areas:

- Hardware costs
- Scalability
- Performance and redundancy

Hardware or Software?

RAID, like many other computer technologies, is divided into two camps: hardware and software. Software RAID uses the computer's CPU to perform RAID operations and is implemented in the kernel. Hardware RAID uses specialized processors, usually found on disk controllers, to perform array management functions. The choice between software and hardware is the first decision you need to make.

Software (Kernel-Managed) RAID

Software RAID means that an array is managed by the kernel, rather than by specialized hardware (see Figure 2-1). The kernel keeps track of how to organize data on many disks while presenting only a single virtual device to applications. This virtual device works just like any normal fixed disk.

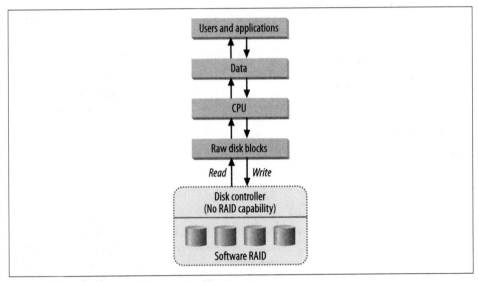

Figure 2-1. Software RAID uses the kernel to manage arrays.

Software RAID has unfortunately fallen victim to a FUD (fear, uncertainty, doubt) campaign in the system administrator community. I can't count the number of system administrators whom I've heard completely disparage all forms of software RAID, irrespective of platform. Many of these same people have admittedly not used software RAID in several years, if at all.

Why the stigma? Well, there are a couple of reasons. For one, when software RAID first saw the light of day, computers were still slow and expensive (at least by today's standards). Offloading a high-performance task like RAID I/O onto a CPU that was likely already heavily overused meant that performing fundamental tasks such as file operations required a tremendous amount of CPU overhead. So, on heavily saturated systems, the simple task of calling the *stat** function could be extremely slow when compared to systems that didn't have the additional overhead of managing RAID arrays. But today, even multiprocessor systems are both inexpensive and common. Previously, multiprocessor systems were very expensive and unavailable to typical PC consumers. Today, anyone can build a multiprocessor system using affordable PC hardware. This shift in hardware cost and availability makes software RAID attractive because Linux runs well on common PC hardware. Thus, in cases when a single-processor system isn't enough, you can cost-effectively add a second processor to augment system performance.

Another big problem was that software RAID implementations were part of proprietary operating systems. The vendors promoted software RAID as a value-added

---

* The *stat(2)* system call reports information about files and is required for many commonplace activities like the *ls* command.

incentive for customers who couldn't afford hardware RAID, but who needed a way to increase disk performance and add redundancy. The problem here was that closed-source implementations, coupled with the fact that software RAID wasn't a priority in OS development, often left users with buggy and confusing packages.

Linux, on the other hand, has a really good chance to change the negative perceptions of software RAID. Not only is Linux's software RAID open source, the inexpensive hardware that runs Linux finally makes it easy and affordable to build reliable software RAID systems. Administrators can now build systems that have sufficient processing power to deal with day-to-day user tasks and high-performance system functions, like RAID, at the same time. Direct access to developers and a helpful user base doesn't hurt, either.

If you're still not convinced that software RAID is worth your time, then don't fret. There are also plenty of hardware solutions available for Linux.

Hardware

Hardware RAID means that arrays are managed by specialized disk controllers that contain RAID firmware (embedded software). Hardware solutions can appear in several forms. RAID controller cards that are directly attached to drives work like any normal PCI disk controller, with the exception that they are able to internally administer arrays. Also available are external storage cabinets that are connected to high-end SCSI controllers or network connections to form a *Storage Area Network (SAN)*. There is one common factor in all these solutions: the operating system accesses only a single block device because the array itself is hidden and managed by the controller.

Large-scale and expensive hardware RAID solutions are typically faster than software solutions and don't require additional CPU overhead to manage arrays. But Linux's software RAID can generally outperform low-end hardware controllers. That's partly because, when working with Linux's software RAID, the CPU is much faster than a RAID controller's onboard processor, and also because Linux's RAID code has had the benefit of optimization through peer review.

The major trade-off you have to make for improved performance is lack of support, although costs will also increase. While hardware RAID cards for Linux have become more ubiquitous and affordable, you may not have some things you traditionally get with Linux. Direct access to developers is one example. Mailing lists for the Linux kernel and for the RAID subsystem are easily accessible and carefully read by the developers who spend their days working on the code. With some exceptions, you probably won't get that level of support from any disk controller vendor—at least not without paying extra.

Another trade-off in choosing a hardware-based RAID solution is that it probably won't be open source. While many vendors have released cards that are supported under Linux, a lot of them require you to use closed-source components. This means that you won't be able to fix bugs yourself, add new features, or customize the code to meet your needs. Some manufacturers provide open source drivers while providing only closed-source, binary-only management tools, and vice versa. No vendors provide open source firmware. So if there is a problem with the software embedded on the controller, you are forced to wait for a fix from the vendor—and that could impact a data recovery effort! With software RAID, you could write your own patch or pay someone to write one for you straightaway.

RAID controllers

Some disk controllers internally support RAID and can manage disks without the help of the CPU (see Figure 2-2). These RAID cards handle all array functions and present the array as a standard block device to Linux. Hardware RAID cards usually contain an onboard BIOS that provides the management tools for configuring and maintaining arrays. Software packages that run at the OS level are usually provided as a means of post-installation array management. This allows administrators to maintain RAID devices without rebooting the system.

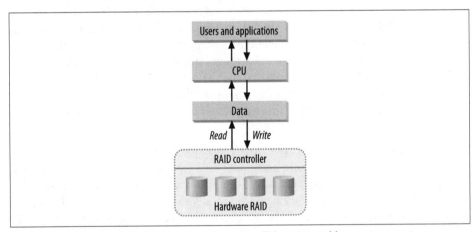

Figure 2-2. Disk controllers shift the array functions off the CPU, yielding an increase in performance.

While a lot of card manufacturers have recently begun to support Linux, it's important to make sure that the card you're planning to purchase is supported under Linux. Be sure that your manufacturer provides at least a loadable kernel module, or, ideally, open source drivers that can be statically compiled into the kernel. Open source drivers are always preferred over binary-only kernel modules. If you are stuck using a binary-only module, you won't get much support from the Linux community because without access to source code, it's quite impossible for them to diagnose interoperability problems between proprietary drivers and the Linux kernel. Luckily, several vendors either provide open source drivers or have allowed kernel hackers to develop their own. One shining example is Mylex, which sells RAID controllers. Their open source drivers are written by Leonard Zubkoff* of Dandelion Digital and can be managed through a convenient interface under the */proc* filesystem. Chapter 5 discusses some of the cards that are currently supported by Linux.

Outboard solutions

The second hardware alternative is a turnkey solution, usually found in outboard drive enclosures. These enclosures are typically connected to the system through a standard or high-performance SCSI controller. It's not uncommon for these specialized systems to support multiple SCSI connections to a single system, and many of them even provide directly accessible network storage, using NFS and other protocols.

These outboard solutions generally appear to an operating system as a standard SCSI block device or network mount point (see Figure 2-3) and therefore don't usually require any special kernel modules or device drivers to function. These solutions are often extremely expensive and operate as black box devices, in that they are almost always proprietary solutions. Outboard RAID boxes are nonetheless highly popular among organizations that can afford them. They are highly configurable and their modular construction provides quick and seamless, although costly, replacement options. Companies like EMC and Network Appliance specialize in this arena.

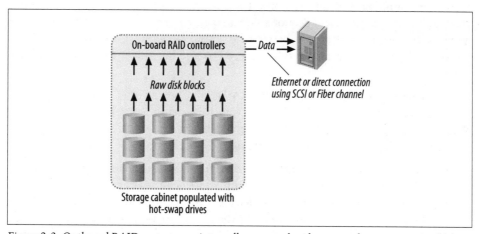

Figure 2-3. Outboard RAID systems are internally managed and connected to a system to which they appear as a single hard disk.

---

* Leonard Zubkoff was very sadly killed in a helicopter crash on August 29, 2002. I learned of his death about a week later, as did many in the open source community. I didn't know Leonard personally. We'd had only one email exchange, earlier in the summer of 2002, in which he had graciously agreed to review material I had written about the Mylex driver. His site remains operational, but I have created a mirror at *http:// dandelion.cynicism.com/*, which I will maintain indefinitely.

If you can afford an outboard RAID system and you think it's the best solution for your project, you will find them reliable performers. Do not forget to factor support costs into your budget. Outboard systems not only have a high entry cost, but they are also costly to maintain. You might also consider factoring spare parts into your budget, since a system failure could otherwise result in downtime while you are waiting for new parts to arrive. In most cases, you will not be able to find replacement parts for an outboard system at local computer stores, and even if they are available, using them will more than likely void your warranty and support contracts.

I hope you will find the architectural discussions later in this chapter helpful when choosing a vendor. I've compiled a list of organizations that provide hardware RAID systems in the Appendix. But I urge you to consider the software solutions discussed throughout this book. Administrators often spend enormous amounts of money on solutions that are well in excess of their needs. After reading this book, you may find that you can accomplish what you set out to do with a lot less money and a little more hard work.

Storage Area Network (SAN)

SAN is a relatively new method of storage management, in which various storage platforms are interconnected on a separate, usually high-speed, network (see Figure 2-4). The SAN is then connected to local area networks (LANs) throughout an organization. It is not uncommon for a SAN to be connected to several different parts of a LAN so that users do not share a single path to the SAN. This prevents a network bottleneck and allows better throughput between users and storage systems. Typically, a SAN might also be exposed to satellite offices using wide area network (WAN) connections.

Many companies that produce turnkey RAID solutions also offer services for planning and implementing a SAN. In fact, even drive manufacturers such as IBM and Western Digital, as well as large network and telecommunications companies such as Lucent and Nortel Networks, now provide SAN solutions.

SAN is very expensive, but is quickly becoming a necessity for large, distributed organizations. It has become vital in backup strategies for large businesses and will likely grow significantly over the next decade. SAN is not a replacement for RAID; rather, RAID is at the heart of SAN. A SAN could be comprised of a robotic tape backup solution and many RAID systems. SAN uses data and storage management in a world where enormous amounts of data need to be stored, organized, and recalled at a moment's notice. A SAN is usually designed and implemented by vendors as a top-down solution that is customized for each organization. It is therefore not discussed further in this book.

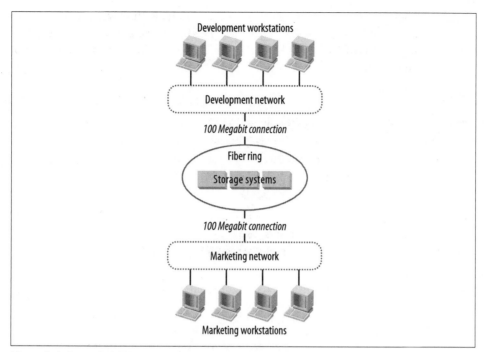

Figure 2-4. A simple SAN arrangement.

The RAID Levels: In Depth

It is important to realize that different implementations of RAID are suited to different applications and the wallets of different organizations. All implementations revolve around the basic levels first outlined in the Berkeley Papers. These core levels have been further expanded by software developers and hardware manufacturers. The RAID levels are not organized hierarchically, although vendors sometimes market their products to imply that there is a hierarchical advantage. As discussed in Chapter 1, the RAID levels offer varying compromises between performance and redundancy. For example, the fastest level offers no additional reliability when compared with a standalone hard disk. Choosing an appropriate level assumes that you have a good understanding of the needs of your applications and users. It may turn out that you have to sacrifice some performance to build an array that is more redundant. You can't have the best of both worlds.

The first decision you need to make when building or buying an array is how large it needs to be. This means talking to users and examining usage to determine how big your data is and how much you expect it to grow during the life of the array.

Table 2-1 briefly outlines the storage yield of the various RAID levels. It should give you a basic idea of how many drives you will need to purchase to build the initial array. Remember that RAID-2 and RAID-3 are now obsolete and therefore are not covered in this book.

Table 2-1. Realized RAID storage capacities

RAID level	Realized capacity
Linear mode	$DiskSize_0+DiskSize_1+...DiskSize_n$
RAID-0 (striping)	TotalDisks * DiskSize
RAID-1 (mirroring)	DiskSize
RAID-4	(TotalDisks-1) * DiskSize
RAID-5	(TotalDisks-1) * DiskSize
RAID-10 (striped mirror)	NumberOfMirrors * DiskSize
RAID-50 (striped parity)	(TotalDisks-ParityDisks) * DiskSize

 Remember that you will eventually need to build a filesystem on your RAID device. Don't forget to take the size of the filesystem into account when figuring out how many disks you need to purchase. ext2 reserves five percent of the filesystem, for example. Chapter 6 covers filesystem tuning and high-performance filesystems, such as JFS, ext3, ReiserFS, XFS, and ext2.

The "RAID Case Studies: What Should I Choose?" section, later in this chapter, focuses on various environments in which different RAID levels make the most sense. Table 2-2 offers a quick comparison of the standard RAID levels.

Table 2-2. RAID level comparison

	RAID-1	Linear mode	RAID-0	RAID-4	RAID-5
Write performance	Slow writes, worse than a standalone disk; as disks are added, write performance declines	Same as a standalone disk	Best write performance; much better than a single disk	Comparable to RAID-0, with one less disk	Comparable to RAID-0, with one less disk for large write operations; potentially slower than a single disk for write operations that are smaller than the stripe size
Read performance	Fast read performance; as disks are added, read performance improves	Same as a standalone disk	Best read performance	Comparable to RAID-0, with one less disk	Comparable to RAID-0, with one less disk

Table 2-2. RAID level comparison (continued)

	RAID-1	Linear mode	RAID-0	RAID-4	RAID-5
Number of disk failures	N-1	0	0	1	1
Applications	Image servers; application servers; systems with little dynamic content/updates	Recycling old disks; no application-specific advantages		Same as RAID-5, which is a better alternative	File servers; databases

RAID-0 (Striping)

RAID-0 is sometimes referred to simply as striping; it was not included in the original Berkeley specification and is not, strictly speaking, a form of RAID because there is no redundancy. Under RAID-0, the host system or a separate controller breaks data into blocks and writes it to different disks in round-robin fashion (as shown in Figure 2-5).

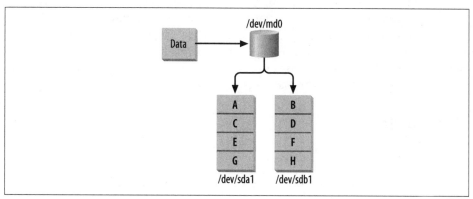

Figure 2-5. RAID-0 (striping) writes data consecutively across multiple drives.

This level yields the greatest performance and utilizes the maximum amount of available disk storage, as long as member disks are of identical sizes. Typically, if member disks are not of identical sizes, then each member of a striped array will be able to utilize only an amount of space equal to the size of the smallest member disk. Likewise, using member disks of differing speeds might introduce a bottleneck during periods of demanding I/O. See the "I/O Channels" and "Matched Drives" sections, later in this chapter, for more information on the importance of using identical disks and controllers in an array.

In some implementations, stripes are organized so that all available storage space is usable. To facilitate this, data is striped across all disks until the smallest disk is full. The process repeats until no space is left on the array. The Linux kernel implements stripes in this way, but if you are working with a hardware RAID controller, this behavior might vary. Check the available technical documentation or contact your vendor for clarification.

Because there is no redundancy in RAID-0, a single disk failure can wipe out all files. Striped arrays are best suited to applications that require intensive disk access, but where the potential for disk failure and data loss is also acceptable. RAID-O might therefore be appropriate for a situation where backups are easily accessible or where data is available elsewhere in the event of a system failure—on a load-balanced network, for example.

Disk striping is also well suited for video production applications because the high data transfer rates allow tremendous source files to be postprocessed easily. But users would be wise to keep copies of finished clips on another volume that is protected either by traditional backups or a more redundant RAID architecture. Usenet news sites have historically chosen RAID-0 because, while data is not critical, I/O throughput is essential for maintaining a large-volume news feed. Local groups and backbone sites can keep newsgroups for which they are responsible on separate fault-tolerant drives to additionally protect against data loss.

Linear Mode

Linux supports another non-RAID capability called linear (or sometimes append) mode. Linear mode sequentially concatenates disks, creating one large disk without data redundancy or increased performance (as shown in Figure 2-6).

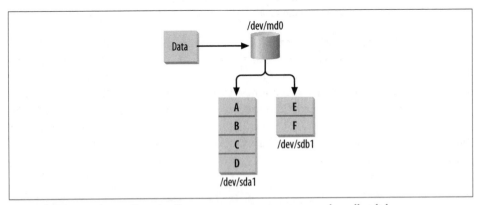

Figure 2-6. Linear (append) mode allows users to concatenate several smaller disks.

Linear arrays are most useful when working with disks and controllers of varying sizes, types, and speeds. Disks belonging to linear arrays are written to until they are full. Since data is not interleaved across the member disks, parallel operations that could be affected by a single disk bottleneck do not occur, as they can in RAID-0. No space is ever wasted when working with linear arrays, regardless of differing disk sizes. Over time, however, as data becomes more spread out over a linear array, you will see performance differences when accessing files that are on different disks of differing speeds and sizes, and when you access a file that spans more than one disk.

Like RAID-0, linear mode arrays offer no redundancy. A disk failure means complete data loss, although recovering data from a damaged array might be a bit easier than with RAID-0, because data is not interleaved across all disks. Because it offers no redundancy or performance improvement, linear mode is best left for desktop and hobbyist use.

Linear mode, and to a lesser degree, RAID-0, are also ideal for recycling old drives that might not have practical application when used individually. A spare disk controller can easily turn a stack of 2- or 3-gigabyte drives into a receptacle for storing movies and music to annoy the RIAA and MPAA.

RAID-1 (Mirroring)

RAID-1 provides the most complete form of redundancy because it can survive multiple disk failures without the need for special data recovery algorithms. Data is mirrored block-by-block onto each member disk (see Figure 2-7). So for every N disks in a RAID-1, the array can withstand a failure of N-1 disks without data loss. In a four-disk RAID-1, up to three disks could be lost without loss of data.

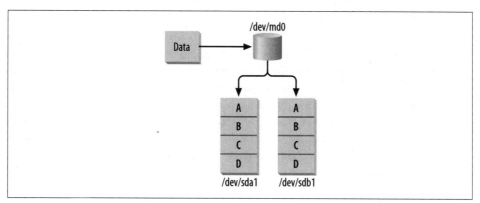

Figure 2-7. Fully redundant RAID-1.

As the number of member disks in a mirror increases, the write performance of the array decreases. Each write incurs a performance hit because each block must be written to each participating disk. However, a substantial advantage in read performance is achieved through parallel access. Duplicate copies of data on different hard drives allow the system to make concurrent read requests.

For example, let's examine the read and write operations of a two-disk RAID-1. Let's say that I'm going to perform a database query to display a list of all the customers that have ordered from my company this year. Fifty such customers exist, and each of their customer data records is 1 KB. My RAID-1 array receives a request to retrieve these fifty customer records and output them to my company's sales engineer. The drives in my array store data in 1 KB chunks and support a data throughput of 1 KB at a time. However, my controller card and system bus support a data throughput of 2 KB at a time. Because my data exists on more than one disk drive, I can utilize the full potential of my system bus and disk controller despite the limitation of my hard drives.

Suppose one of my sales engineers needs to change information about each of the same fifty customers. Now we need to write fifty records, each consisting of 1 KB. Unfortunately, we need to write each chunk of information to both drives in our array. So in this case, we need to write 100 KB of data to our disks, rather than 50 KB. The number of write operations increases with each disk added to a mirror array. In this case, if the array had four member disks, a total of 4 KB would be written to disk for each 1 KB of data passed to the array.

This example reveals an important distinction between hardware and software RAID-1. With software RAID, each write operation (one per disk) travels over the PCI bus to corresponding controllers and disks (see the sections "Motherboards and the PCI Bus" and "I/O Channels," later in this chapter). With hardware RAID, only a single write operation travels over the PCI bus. The RAID controller sends the proper number of write operations out to each disk. Thus, with hardware RAID-1, the PCI bus is less saturated with I/O requests.

Although RAID-1 provides complete fault tolerance, it is cost-prohibitive for some users because it at least doubles storage costs. However, for sites that require zero downtime, but are willing to take a slight hit on write performance, mirroring is ideal. Such sites might include online magazines and newspapers, which serve a large number of customers but have relatively static content. Online advertising aggregators that facilitate the distribution of banner ads to customers would also benefit from disk mirroring. If your content is nearly static, you won't suffer much from the write performance penalty, while you will benefit from the parallel read-as-you-serve image files. Full fault tolerance ensures that the revenue stream is never interrupted and that users can always access data.

RAID-1 works extremely well when servers are already load-balanced at the network level. This means usage can be distributed across multiple machines, each of which supports full redundancy. Typically, RAID-1 is deployed using two-disk mirrors. Although you could create mirrors with more disks, allowing the system to survive a multiple disk failure, there are other arrangements that allow comparable redundancy and read performance and much better write performance. See the "Hybrid Arrays" section, later in this chapter. RAID-1 is also well suited for system disks.

RAID-4

RAID-4 stripes block-sized chunks of data across each drive in the array marked as a data drive. In addition, one drive is designated as a dedicated parity drive (see Figure 2-8).

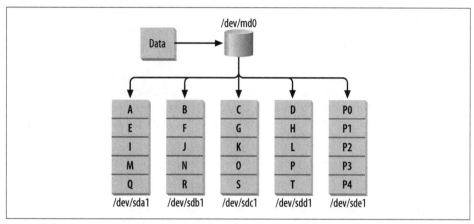

Figure 2-8. RAID-4 stripes data to all disks except a dedicated parity drive.

RAID-4 uses an exclusive OR (XOR) operation to generate checksum information that can be used for disaster recovery. Checksum information is generated during each write operation at the block level. The XOR operation uses the dedicated parity drive to store a block containing checksum information derived from the blocks on the other disks.

In the event of a disk failure, an XOR operation can be performed on the checksum information and the parallel data blocks on the remaining member disks. Users and applications can continue to access data in the array, but performance is degraded because the XOR operation must be called during each read to reconstruct the missing data. When the failed disk is replaced, administrators can rebuild the data from the failed drive using the parity information on the remaining disks. By sequentially performing an XOR on all parallel blocks and writing the result to the new drive, data is restored.

Although the original RAID specification called for only a single dedicated parity drive in RAID-4, some modern implementations allow the use of multiple dedicated parity drives. Since each write generates parity information, a bottleneck is inherent in RAID-4.

XOR

The exclusive OR (XOR) is a logical operation that returns a TRUE value if and only if one of the operands is TRUE. If both operands are TRUE, then a value of FALSE is returned.

```
p   q   p XOR q
-----------------------
T   T   F
T   F   T
F   T   T
F   F   T
```

When a parity RAID generates its checksum information, it performs the XOR on each data byte. For example, a RAID-5 with three member disks writes the byte 11011011 binary to the first disk and the byte 01101100 to the second disk. The first two bytes are user data. Next, a parity byte of 10110111 is written to the third disk. If a byte is lost because of the failure of either the first or the second disk, the array can perform the XOR operation on the other data byte and the parity information in order to retrieve the missing data byte. This holds true for any number of data bytes or, in our case, disks.

Placing the parity drive at the beginning of an I/O channel and giving it the lowest SCSI ID in that chain will help improve performance. Using a dedicated channel for the parity drive is also recommended.

It is very unlikely that RAID-4 makes sense for any modern setup. With the exception of some specialized, turnkey RAID hardware, RAID-4 is not often used. RAID-5 provides better performance and is likely a better choice for anyone who is considering RAID-4. It's prudent to mention here, however, that many NAS vendors still use RAID-4 simply because online array expansion is easier to implement and expansion is faster than with RAID-5. That's because you don't need to reposition all the parity blocks when you expand a RAID-4.

Dedicating a drive for parity information means that you lose one drive's worth of potential data storage when using RAID-4. When using N disk drives, each with space S, and dedicating one drive for parity storage, you are left with (N-1) * S space under RAID-4. When using more than one parity drive, you are left with (N-P) * S space, where P represents the total number of dedicated parity drives in the array.

RAID-5

RAID-5 eliminates the use of a dedicated parity drive and stripes parity information across each disk in the array, using the same XOR algorithm found in RAID-4 (see

Figure 2-9). During each write operation, one chunk worth of data in each stripe is used to store parity. The disk that stores parity alternates with each stripe, until each disk has one chunk worth of parity information. The process then repeats, beginning with the first disk.

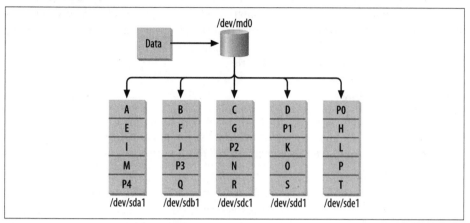

Figure 2-9. RAID-5 eliminates the dedicated parity disk by distributing parity across all drives.

Take the example of a RAID-5 with five member disks. In this case, every fifth chunk-sized block on each member disk will contain parity information for the other four disks. This means that, as in RAID-1 and RAID-4, a portion of your total storage space will be unusable. In an array with five disks, a single disk's worth of space is occupied by parity information, although the parity information is spread across every disk in the array. In general, if you have N disk drives in a RAID-5, each of size S, you will be left with (N-1) * S space available. So, RAID-4 and RAID-5 yield the same usable storage. Unfortunately, also like RAID-4, a RAID-5 can withstand only a single disk failure. If more than one drive fails, all data on the array is lost.

RAID-5 performs almost as well as a striped array for reads. Write performance on full stripe operations is also comparable, but when writes smaller than a single stripe occur, performance can be much slower. The slow performance results from prereading that must be performed so that corrected parity can be written for the stripe. During a disk failure, RAID-5 read performance slows down because each time data from the failed drive is needed, the parity algorithm must reconstruct the lost data. Writes during a disk failure do not take a performance hit and will actually be slightly faster. Once a failed disk is replaced, data reconstruction begins either automatically or after a system administrator intervenes, depending on the hardware.

RAID-5 has become extremely popular among Internet and e-commerce companies because it allows administrators to achieve a safe level of fault-tolerance without sacrificing the tremendous amount of disk space necessary in a RAID-1 configuration or suffering the bottleneck inherent in RAID-4. RAID-5 is especially useful in production environments where data is replicated across multiple servers, shifting the internal need for disk redundancy partially away from a single machine.

Hybrid Arrays

After the Berkeley Papers were published, many vendors began combining different RAID levels in an attempt to increase both performance and reliability. These hybrid arrays are supported by most hardware RAID controllers and external systems. The Linux kernel will also allow the combination of two or more RAID levels to form a hybrid array. In fact, it allows any combination of arrays, although some of them might not offer any benefit. The most common types of hybrid arrays, summarized in the following sections, are covered in this book.

RAID-10 (striping mirror)

The most widely used, and effective, hybrid array results from the combination of RAID-0 and RAID-1. The fast performance of striping, coupled with the redundant properties of mirroring, create a quick and reliable solution—although it is the most expensive solution.

A striped-mirror, or RAID-10, is simple. Two separate mirrors are created, each with a unique set of member disks. Then the two mirror arrays are added to a new striped array (see Figure 2-10). When data is written to the logical RAID device, it is striped across the two mirrors.

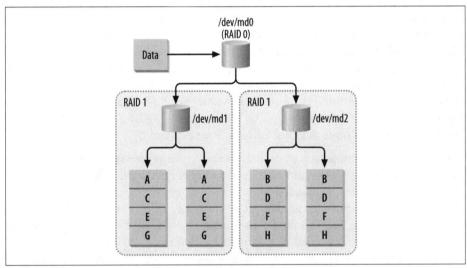

Figure 2-10. A hybrid array formed by combining two mirrors, which are then combined into a stripe.

Although this arrangement requires a lot of surplus disk hardware, it provides a fast and reliable solution. I/O approaches a throughput close to that of a standalone striped array. When any single disk in a RAID-10 fails, both sides of the hybrid (each mirror) may still operate, although the one with the failed disk will be operating in degraded mode. A RAID-10 arrangement could even withstand multiple disk failures on different sides of the stripe.

When creating a RAID-10, it's a good idea to distribute the mirroring arrays across multiple I/O channels. This will help the array withstand controller failures. For example, take the case of a RAID-10 consisting of two mirror sets, each containing two member disks. If each mirror is placed on its own I/O channel, then a failure of that channel will render the entire hybrid array useless. However, if each member disk of a single mirror is placed on a separate channel, then the array can withstand the failure of an entire I/O channel (see Figure 2-11).

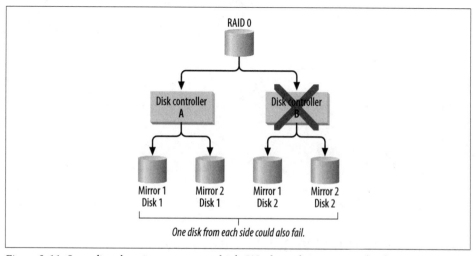

Figure 2-11. Spreading the mirrors across multiple I/O channels increases redundancy.

While you could combine two stripes into a mirror, this arrangement offers no increase in performance over RAID-10 and does not increase redundancy. In fact, RAID-10 can withstand more disk failures than what many manufacturers call RAID-0+1 (two stripes combined into a mirror). While it's true that a RAID-0+1 could survive two disk failures within the same stripe, that second disk failure is trivial because it's already part of a nonfunctioning stripe.

I've mentioned earlier that vendors often deviate from naming conventions when describing RAID. This is especially true with hybrid arrays. Make sure that your controller combines mirrors into a stripe (RAID-10) and not stripes into a mirror (RAID-0+1).

RAID-50 (striping parity)

Users who simply cannot afford to build a RAID-0+1 array because of the enormous disk overhead can combine two RAID-5 arrays into a striped array (see Figure 2-12). While read performance is slightly lower than a RAID-0+1, users will see increased write performance because each side of the stripe is made up of RAID-5 arrays, which also utilize disk striping. Each side of the RAID-50 array can survive a single disk failure. A failure of more than one disk in either RAID-5, though, would result in failure of the entire RAID-50.

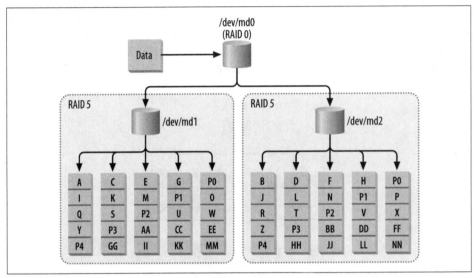

Figure 2-12. A hybrid array formed by combining RAID-5 arrays into a striped array.

RAID Case Studies: What Should I Choose?

Choosing an architecture can be extremely difficult. Trying to connect a specific technology to a specific application is one of the hardest tasks that system administrators face. Below are some examples of where RAID is useful in the real world.

Case 1: HTTP Image Server

Because RAID-1 supports parallel reads, it makes a great HTTP image server. Companies that sell products online and provide product photos to web surfers could use RAID-1 to serve images. Images are static content, and in this scenario, they will likely be read quite a bit more than they will be written. Although new product photos are frequently added, they are written to disk only once by a web developer, whereas they are viewed thousands of times by potential customers. Parallel read performance on RAID-1 helps facilitate the large number of hits, and the write performance loss with RAID-1 is largely irrelevant because writes are infrequent in this case. The redundancy aspect of RAID-1 also ensures that downtime is minimal in the event of a disk failure, although parallel read performance will be temporarily lost until the drive can be replaced. Using a hot-spare, of course, ensures that performance is affected for only a brief time.

Case 2: Usenet News

Striped arrays are clearly the best candidate for Internet news servers. Extremely fast read and write times are required to keep up with the enormous streams of data that a typical full-feed news server experiences. In many cases, the data on a news partition is inconsequential. Lost articles are frequent, even in normally operating feeds, and complete data loss usually means that only a few days' articles are lost.

Administrators could configure a single news server with both a striped array and mirrored array, as shown in Figure 2-13. The striped array could house newsgroups that are of no consequence and could easily withstand a day's worth of article loss without users complaining. Newsgroups that are read frequently, as well as local groups and system partitions, could be housed on the RAID-1 array. This would make the machine redundant in case of a disk failure.

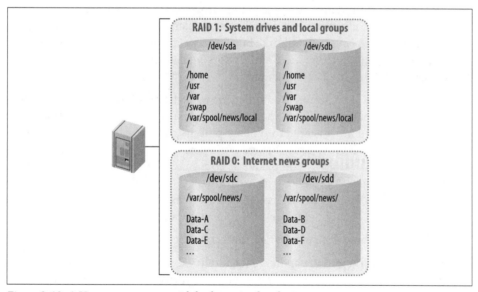

Figure 2-13. A Usenet news server with both a striped and mirror array.

Case 3: Home Use (Digital Audio, Video, and Images)

With the increasing capacity and availability of digital media, users will find it difficult to contain their files on a single hard disk. Linear mode and RAID-0 arrays provide a good storage architecture for storing MP3 audio, video, and image files. Often, these files are burned to CD or are easily replaceable, so the lack of redundancy in linear mode and RAID-0 can be overlooked. Users can opt to make backups of files that are either important or hard to replace.

A quick trip to a surplus warehouse or .COM auction might get you a supply of older, cheap hard disks that can be combined into a linear array. If you can find matched disks, then RAID-0 will work well in this case. A mix of different drives can be turned into a linear mode array. Both of these methods are perfect for home use because they maximize what might have become old and useless storage space and turn it into usable disk space.

Case 4: The Acme Motion Picture Company

People who produce motion pictures are faced with many storage problems. Accommodating giant source files, providing instant access to unedited footage, and storing a finished product that could easily exceed hundreds of gigabytes are just a few of the major storage issues that the film and television industries face.

Film production workstations would benefit greatly from RAID-5. While RAID-0 might seem like a good choice because of its fast performance, losing a work-in-progress might set work back by days, or even weeks. By using RAID-5, editors are able to achieve redundancy and see an improvement in performance. Likewise, RAID-1 might seem like a good choice because it offers redundancy without much of a performance hit during disk failures. But RAID-1, as discussed earlier, leads to an increase only in read performance, and editors will likely be writing postproduced clips often until the desired cut is achieved.

Source files and finished scenes would benefit most from RAID-1 setups. Workstations could read source files from these RAID-1 servers. Parallel reads would allow editors and production assistants to quickly pull in source video that could then be edited locally on the RAID-5 array, where write performance is better than on RAID-1. When a particular scene is completed, it could then be sent back to the RAID-1 array for safekeeping. Although write performance on RAID-1 isn't as fast as on RAID-5, the redundancy of RAID-1 is essential for ensuring that no data is ever lost. Reshooting a scene could be extremely costly and, in some cases, impossible.

Figure 2-14 shows how different RAID arrays could be used in film production.

Striping might also be a good candidate for film production workstations. If cost is a consideration, using RAID-0 will save slightly on drive costs and will outperform RAID-5. But a drive failure in a RAID-0 workstation would mean complete data loss.

Case 5: Video on Demand

This scenario offers the same considerations as Case 1, the site serving images. RAID-1, with multiple member disks, offers great read performance. Since writes aren't very frequent when working with video on demand, the write performance hit is okay.

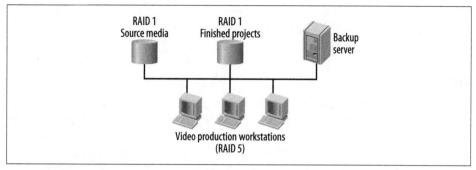

Figure 2-14. Workstations with RAID-5 arrays edit films while retrieving source films from a RAID-1 array. Finished products are sent to another RAID-1 array.

Disk Failures

Another benefit of RAID is its ability to handle disk failures without user intervention. Redundant arrays can not only remain running during a disk failure, but can also repair themselves if sufficient replacement hardware is available and was preconfigured when the array was created.

Degraded Mode

When an array member fails for any reason, the array is said to have gone into *degraded mode*. This means that the array is not performing optimally and redundancy has been compromised. Degraded mode therefore applies only to arrays that have redundant capabilities. A RAID-0, for example, has only two states: operational and failed. This interim state, available to redundant arrays, allows the array to continue operating until an administrator can resolve the problem—usually by replacing a failed disk.

Hot-Spares

As I mentioned earlier, some RAID levels can replace a failed drive with a new drive without user intervention. This functionality, known as *hot-spares*, is built into every hardware RAID controller and standalone array. It is also part of the Linux kernel. If you have hardware that supports hot-spares, then you can identify some extra disks to act as spares when a drive failure occurs. Once an array experiences a disk failure, and consequently enters into degraded mode, a hot-spare can automatically be introduced into the array. This makes the job of the administrator much easier, because the array immediately resumes normal operation, allowing the administrator to replace failed drives when convenient. In addition, having hot-spares decreases the chance that a second drive will fail and cause data loss.

Hot-spares can be used only with arrays that support redundancy: mirrors, RAID-4, and RAID-5. Striped and linear mode arrays do not support this feature.

Hot-Swap

All of the RAID levels that support redundancy are also capable of *hot-swap*. Hot-swap is the ability to removed a failed drive from a running system so that it can be replaced with a new working drive. This means drive replacement can occur without a reboot. Hot-swap is useful in two situations. First, you might not have enough space in your cases to support extra disks for the hot-spare feature. So when a disk failure occurs, you may want to immediately replace the failed drive in order to bring the array out of degraded mode and begin reconstruction. Second, although you might have hot-spares in a system, it is useful to replace the failed disk with a new hot-spare in anticipation of future failures.

Replacing a drive in a running system should not be attempted on a conventional system. While hot-swap is inherently supported by RAID, you need special hardware that supports it. This technology was originally available only to SCSI users through specially made hard drives and cases. However, some companies now make hot-swap ATA enclosures, as well as modules that allow you to safely hot-swap normal SCSI drives. For more information about hot-swap, see the "Cases, Cables, and Connectors" section, later in this chapter, and the "Managing Disk Failures" section in Chapter 7.

 Although many people have successfully disconnected traditional drives from running systems, it is not a recommended practice. Do this at your own risk. You could wipe your array or electrocute yourself.

Hardware Considerations

Whether you choose to use kernel-based software RAID or buy a specialized RAID controller, there are some important decisions to make when buying components. Even if you plan to use software RAID, you will still need to purchase hard drives and disk controllers. The first step is to determine the ultimate size of your array and figure out how many drives are necessary to accommodate all the space you need, taking into account the extra space required by the level of RAID you choose. Don't forget to factor the eventual need for hot-spares into your plan.

Choosing the right components can be the hardest decision to make when building a RAID system. If you're building a production server, you should naturally buy the best hardware you can afford. If you're just experimenting, then use whatever you have at your disposal, but realize that you may have to shell out a few dollars to make things work properly.

Several factors will ultimately affect the performance and expandability of your arrays:

- Bus throughput
- I/O channels
- Disk protocol throughput
- Drive speed
- CPU speed and memory

Computer architecture is a vast and complicated topic, and although this book covers the factors that will most drastically impact array performance, I advise anyone who is planning to build large-scale production systems, or build RAID systems for resale, to familiarize themselves thoroughly with all of the issues at hand. A complete primer on computer architecture is well beyond the scope of this book. The "Bibliography" section of the Appendix contains a list of excellent books and web sites for readers who wish to expand their knowledge of computer hardware.

One essential concept that I do want to introduce is the *bottleneck*. Imagine the filtered water pitchers that have become so omnipresent over the last ten years. When you fill the chamber at the top of the pitcher with ordinary tap water, it slowly drips through the filter into another cache, from which you can pour a glass of water. The filtering process distributes water at a rate much slower than the pressure of an ordinary faucet. The filter has therefore introduced a bottleneck in your ability to fill your water glass, although it does provide some benefits. A more expensive filtration system might be able to yield better output and cleaner water. A cheaper system could offer quicker filtration with some sacrifices in quality, or better quality at a slower pace.

In computing, a bottleneck occurs when the inadequacies of a single component cause a slowdown of the entire system. The slowdown might be the result of poor system design, overuse, or both. Each component of your system has the potential to become a bottleneck if it's not chosen carefully. As you will learn throughout this chapter, some bottlenecks are simply beyond your control, while others begin to offer diminishing returns as you upgrade them.

An Organizational Overview

All systems are built around a motherboard. The motherboard integrates all the components of a computer by providing a means through which processors, memory, peripherals, and user devices (monitors, keyboards, and mice) can communicate. Specialized system controllers facilitate communication between these devices. This group of controllers is often referred to as the motherboard's *chipset*. In addition to facilitating communication, the chipset also determines factors that affect system expandability, such as maximum memory capacity and processor speed.

When an application needs data, the CPU first checks to see if the data is stored in memory. If the data is no longer in memory, the CPU asks the chipset to request the information from disk. The chipset sends a request to the *data bus*, where it is picked up by the appropriate disk controller and sent across the *disk bus* to the drive containing the data. The drive sends the information back to the controller card, which in turn passes it back to the CPU and main memory. Figure 2-15 illustrates the connections between various components of a modern PCI motherboard.

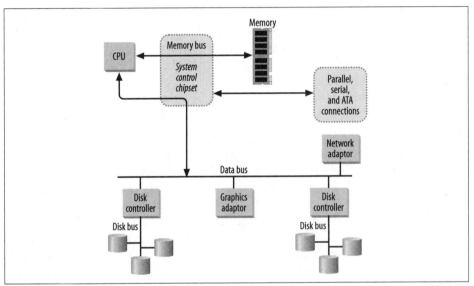

Figure 2-15. When disk I/O occurs, data travels over both the data bus and the disk bus, each a potential bottleneck.

The BIOS

Another important component of every computer system is the BIOS (basic input/output software). The BIOS is a chip on the motherboard that contains a simple set of drivers and instructions. When a machine is turned on, the software stored in the BIOS chip is loaded and executed. The BIOS has basic control over system components: hard disks, CD-ROMs, monitors, keyboards, etc. The BIOS looks for a particular disk sector and executes the program it finds there, usually an operating system. This is sometimes referred to as the *bootstrap* process.

The speeds of the data and disk buses have a direct impact on system performance, and each bus can become a bottleneck. While it's easy to add new disk controllers to a system, thereby increasing the overall number of disk buses, and consequently increasing the overall disk bus throughput, you only have one motherboard to work with. So choosing the right one for your application is essential.

Motherboards and the PCI Bus

Motherboards provide a way to interconnect the various components that make up a computer (memory, processors, and peripherals). Every motherboard has separate buses for communicating between these varied components. Disk controllers and, in turn, hard disks, communicate with the CPU and memory using the I/O bus, also called the data bus. The I/O bus is a standard interface through which peripheral cards (disk controllers, graphics adapters, network cards, etc.) can interface between peripherals (hard disks, monitors, Ethernet networks, etc.) and the CPU and memory.

The Peripheral Component Interconnect (PCI) bus is the most common data bus available today. In recent years, it has usurped the ubiquity of the now outdated Industry Standard Architecture (ISA) bus. Although ISA motherboards are still common, new motherboard purchases typically use the PCI bus. For backward compatibility, the PCI bus can handle ISA peripheral cards through the use of bridging, and many PCI motherboards provide an ISA slot for use with legacy cards.

Bus-width and bus-speed

The speed of the I/O bus is determined by two factors: *bus-width* and *bus-speed*. Bus-width describes how many bytes of data can be sent down the bus at a time. Bus-speed specifies how many times per second data can be transferred through the bus. Bus-width is measured in bits, and all motherboards support bus-widths in multiples of bytes. ISA motherboards support bus-widths of 8 and 16 bits (1 or 2 bytes), and modern PCI motherboards support bus-widths of up to 64 bits, or 8 bytes.

Bus-speed is measured by the number of *clock cycles* that can occur each second. Manufacturers now use the term Front Side Bus when referring to bus-speed. ISA boards run at 8.33 MHz, or 8.33 million clock cycles per second. The first PCI boards ran at 33.33 MHz, or 33.33 million clock cycles per second. A PCI motherboard with a 32-bit bus-width (4 bytes), operating at 33 MHz, has a maximum I/O throughput of 133.33 MB/s (4 bytes per cycle * 33.33 million cycles per second = 133.33 megabytes per second). Newer and faster PCI boards can operate at speeds of up to 533 MHz. Table 2-3 shows the various I/O throughputs of typical motherboards as a factor of bus-width and bus-speed.

Table 2-3. I/O bus throughput

Bus type	Width (bits)	Clock cycles (MHz)	Data throughput (MB/s)
ISA (XT)	8	8.33	8.33
ISA (AT)	16	8.33	16.66
PCI	32	33.33	133.33
PCI	64	66.66	533.33

The data throughput of your motherboard is the first bottleneck to consider when building a RAID system. If you are planning to use three SCSI cards, each with an advertised speed of 80 MB/s, you should quickly realize that a standard 32-bit PCI motherboard running at 33 MHz will become a bottleneck. The aggregate speed of your SCSI controllers (80 MB/s * 3 = 240 MB/s) is more than the overall speed of your I/O bus (133.33 MB/s).

64-Bit Motherboards

While some motherboards are advertised as having 64-bit PCI slots, usually only one or two of the PCI slots are usable by 64-bit PCI cards. Fortunately, many 64-bit cards can fit into 32-bit slots and operate in 32-bit mode. However, using 64-bit cards in 32-bit mode wastes their capability—they can operate at only half of their potential speed. So when choosing a 64-bit motherboard, be certain that it has enough 64-bit slots to meet your needs.

Not all motherboards are created equal. Be certain to check the manufacturer's specification when deciding which one to purchase, making careful note of the bus-width and bus-speed. Remember that all the expansion cards, including the graphics card, share the overall speed of the I/O bus. If you have a board that supports an overall bus throughput of 533 MB/s, then installing several high-end SCSI cards, a graphics adapter, and a network card might cause a bottleneck on the data bus. So for production file servers, it might make sense to configure a system without video (you could use the *console on serial port* features of Linux). Like most other aspects of technology, you should expect to see faster motherboards in the near future. Although 128-bit boards might be a year or two off, manufacturers are constantly working to increase the bus-speed.

In the same way that disks constantly fall behind the curve of storage needs, the I/O bus is always behind the curve when compared to the speed at which the CPU and main memory can interact. So the I/O bus will almost always become the most significant bottleneck on any motherboard. In response to this problem, it is common for high-end server boards to offer dedicated buses for one or more PCI slots. Some even offer a separate bus for each PCI slot, which allows you to place a RAID or SCSI card on its own I/O bus, separating other peripherals such as network and graphics cards. Using one of these dual-bus motherboards can effectively double the combined overall speed of your I/O bus.

I/O Channels

An I/O channel represents a single chain of devices attached to your machine, either internally or externally. Internal I/O channels are typically connected to a controller card (or to the motherboard) by ribbon cable. (Ribbon cables are flat cables, usually gray or blue, that interconnect hard drives and disk controllers inside a computer case.) Externally, you might connect drives or peripheral devices to a controller card using SCSI cables. The more identical, parallel I/O channels you have available for your array, the better performance you can expect out of it, as long as you are careful to identify and eliminate other bottlenecks.

The most common instance of parallel and identical I/O channels is the typical PC motherboard. Almost all i386-based motherboards include two onboard ATA/IDE disk controllers (see Figure 2-16).

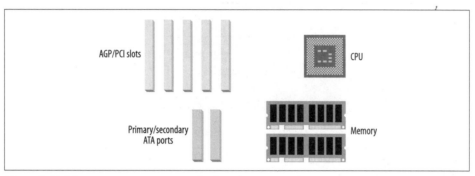

AGP/PCI slots

CPU

Primary/secondary
ATA ports

Memory

Figure 2-16. Major components on a motherboard.

When I say *identical*, I mean that each channel you select for use in your array supports the same architecture and protocols. *Parallel* means that each channel in the array can accept requests simultaneously. While you could theoretically use two different types of I/O channels in the same RAID array, you'd be wasting the performance of the faster channel because the faster chain needs to operate at slower rate in order to stay at the same pace as the other channels in the array. It's generally not a good idea to mix different iterations of the same disk protocol because their speeds vary.

It's also a bad idea to mix different disk protocols, such as SCSI and ATA, even though software RAID, in particular, allows both of these arrangements. The same is true for mixing hard drives of differing speeds, but I'll cover that issue in more detail in the "Choosing Hard Drives" section, later in this chapter.

In general, it is good practice to keep only one incarnation of any disk protocol on a single I/O channel. That might mean connecting devices such as CD-ROM drives and scanners, which operate at much slower speeds than current hard disks, on separate controllers. It is advisable to purchase a cheaper, slower controller to connect these devices, keeping them out of any I/O channel that contains faster devices that belong to an array.

For example, many SCSI controllers contain two separate, parallel channels that are not identical: a compact, high-density, 68-pin connector used to connect hard drives (wide SCSI) and a larger, low-density 50-pin connector often intended to connect

CD-ROM drives (see Figure 2-17). While both of these channels can be used in parallel, pairing them is a bad choice for RAID, because by combining the use of two channels in a single RAID array, we lose the performance associated with wide SCSI. Many cards, for example, provide two internal connectors: one that supports a 50-pin fast SCSI chain and another that supports a high-density 68-pin wide SCSI chain. If you are using the AT attachment (ATA), it's wise to connect your CD-ROM drive to a separate ATA controller when possible. ATA is discussed in the "Disk Access Protocols" section, later in this chapter.

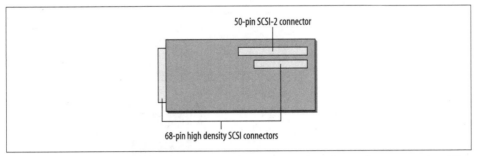

Figure 2-17. An SCSI controller with one external connector and two internal connectors (one 50-pin and one 68-pin).

It's also important to realize that while most SCSI cards provide external connectors, they are merely an extension of an internal channel. Therefore, the internal and external chains on a SCSI card do not operate in parallel. Space on your motherboard can quickly become scarce, and you might find that a single controller card with multiple I/O channels works better for you. Several manufacturers of SCSI cards make high-end versions of their consumer-grade cards that provide multiple distinct I/O channels. You might be able to get two or three I/O channels on a single PCI card.

You can also increase I/O bandwidth through a combination of two types of upgrades: buying high-density cards and adding several of them to your system to take advantage of the extra channels (see Figure 2-18).

Most hardware RAID cards are also available in models with multiple channels (see Figure 2-19). Some support as many as six separate channels on a single card, and most allow you to manage cards as a whole, so you can include devices connected to separate cards in the same array and manage them through a single interface. The number of cards that you can put in a single system is limited only by the number of slots available on your motherboard, but remember to consider the throughput of the motherboard when purchasing controller cards. Typical motherboards have a data bus throughput limit of 133 MB/s (32-bit) or 533 MB/s (64-bit). Adding three multichannel SCSI controllers that support speeds of 160 MB/s each would saturate the data bus on a heavily used system. Remember that network and graphics cards also use bandwidth on the I/O bus. Also recall that some high-end motherboards support dedicated PCI slots that can help avoid these problems.

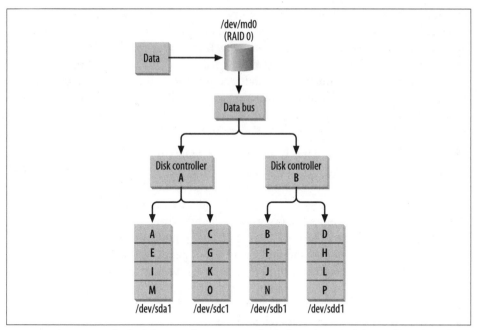

Figure 2-18. Using multiple disk controllers increases both throughput and the total number of usable drives.

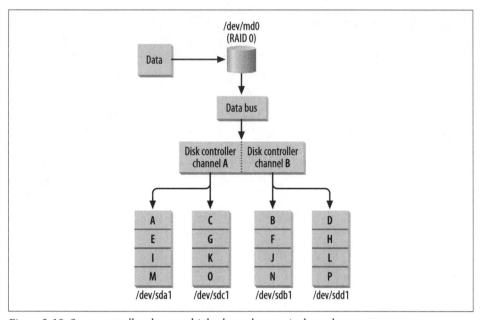

Figure 2-19. Some controllers have multiple channels on a single card.

When using more than one I/O channel, it's advisable to alternate between channels when adding disks to an array. That will help you to avoid overloading a single I/O channel. You typically don't need to worry about how you physically arrange your disks or how your hardware (or Linux) detects them. Just make certain that you balance them as equally as possible between each available channel. When you create the array, disks can be added in an arbitrary order so that their physical location can be taken into account. This process might be facilitated through a configuration file, command-line utility, GUI management package, or BIOS utility. I'll cover this process in more detail when I explain how to create new arrays in Chapters 3 and 4 (for software RAID) and in Chapter 5 (for hardware RAID).

There may also be some situations when it is necessary to use drives with slightly different performance. Let's say, for example, that you have a few ultra-wide SCSI drives from an assortment of different manufacturers. Since not all drives, regardless of protocol, are exactly the same, you will see slightly different speeds from each. In this case, it's best to arrange the drives so that the slowest has the smallest SCSI ID number and is closest to the controller. Likewise, the fastest should be placed farthest from the controller and should be set to the highest SCSI ID number. This will help to alleviate the performance differences. Users who are planning to create a linear mode array using several different drive sizes should arrange drives with this methodology in mind. This methodology may also be helpful for users who simply cannot afford to purchase new, matched drives.

Disk Access Protocols

The disk protocol of the hardware you choose has a tremendous impact on the performance and scalability of your array. Each protocol has its own hard limits on the maximum throughput of each I/O channel and the maximum number of devices you can attach to a single channel. So the disk protocol you select will have a direct impact on the maximum size of your array.

Although we traditionally think of RAID in terms of high-end SCSI systems, today it's not uncommon for consumer-marketed systems to come equipped with support for RAID on non-SCSI disks. In fact, Linux software RAID can support either SCSI or ATA devices as part of an array (see the following section). The kernel will even let you mix these protocols within a single RAID device, although that arrangement isn't recommended. (See the "Matched drives" section, later in this chapter, as well as the previous section, "I/O Channels.") Software RAID under Linux does not rely on the underlying disk architecture to work, so there is no reason why an array could not be built using a Firewire (IEEE 1394), Fiber-channel, or other disk architecture developed in the future, as long as you can find hardware and device drivers to support the architecture as a standalone device.

ATA (used interchangeably with the acronym IDE) and SCSI are discussed in detail throughout this book because they are the most common disk protocols in use today. ATA is a part of every modern motherboard, and SCSI is the most common choice for large servers.

The AT Attachment (ATA) and Integrated Disk Electronics (IDE)

Integrated disk electronics, or *IDE*, has had many incarnations and many names since its introduction in 1986. Originally, hard drives were small enough, in both size and capacity, to fit directly onto disk controllers. As storage requirements grew, manufacturers realized that housing drives on controller cards was an inefficient use of space. Soon drives and controllers became separate entities, connected by ribbon cable. This meant that drives could grow in size without interfering with the expandability of the motherboard. It was common for these integrated controller cards to make adjacent slots on the motherboard inaccessible. Manufacturers eventually decided that portions of the controller could be housed directly on the drives and that creating a standard drive interface would allow for both expandability and portability. Originally called IDE in several proprietary implementations, a standardized version called the *AT Attachment*, or *ATA*, was eventually ratified (although many people still use the terms IDE and ATA interchangeably). This new disk interface was called the AT Attachment because it was introduced with the ISA (AT) motherboard. It quickly grew in popularity, and today the ATA interface is the most widely deployed consumer disk interface. Figure 2-20 shows the ATA interface.

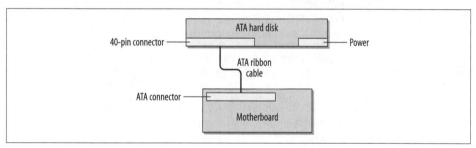

Figure 2-20. The ATA interface separated the drive and the controller.

ATA has evolved a great deal since its introduction. Its performance and scalability have improved over time. Table 2-4 outlines the various iterations of ATA.

Table 2-4. Overview of IDE/ATA types

ATA type	Maximum throughput (MB/s)	Common names
ATA-1	8.3	ATA, IDE, Fast ATA
ATA-2	16.66	EIDE, Fast ATA-2
ATA-3	16.66	Ultra DMA, Ultra ATA
ATA-4	33.33	Ultra ATA/33
ATA-5	66.66	Ultra ATA/66
ATA-6	100	Ultra ATA/100
ATA-7	133.33	Ultra ATA/133

Many of the names associated with various iterations of ATA represent departures from the ATA specification by a single manufacturer. Enhanced IDE (EIDE), for example, was an attempt by Western Digital to increase its market share by offering enhancements to the original ATA (ATA-1) specification before ATA-2 was ratified. This created a rash of vendor-enhanced ATA-compatible interfaces, resulting in many puzzling names. In general, ATA devices are compatible between iterations, but mixing old and new drives, like mixing different disk protocols, usually results in performance problems.

Master and slave

ATA devices have only two configuration settings: *master* and *slave*. Despite the unfortunate nomenclature, both drives can operate independently once the system initializes, although drives operating in slave mode won't perform as well. A single ATA disk operating as master on a dedicated channel will yield the best performance. So it's always recommended that you use only one disk per channel when working with ATA and RAID.

Only the master device can be used as a boot device, but you can use the master device from any ATA channel for booting. So on a standard system with two on-board ATA controllers, you have a maximum of two boot devices and a total of four ATA devices. Most users place their primary hard disk on the first interface and a CD-ROM drive on the second, so that either can be used as a boot device.

A simple jumper on the back of the drive determines whether an ATA device is operating in master or slave mode. Some devices also have a third setting called *cable select*. This jumper allows the system to determine which device is master or slave by its position on the cable. The first ATA device found on the cable is flagged as the master device and the second becomes the slave device. Unfortunately, many users report strange behavior when using this feature, such as disappearing drives or devices that won't boot properly. Because it's easy to manually set the devices, I recommend always setting up devices as master and slave and never using cable select.

Direct memory access (DMA)

Modern ATA devices support an I/O method called *direct memory access (DMA)* that allows two devices on the same channel to transfer data without direct CPU intervention. Using DMA relieves a lot of pressure on your CPU during array reconstruction, when large amounts of data need to be transferred between two drives. Sometimes DMA is not enabled by default. Chapter 7 discusses how to enable this feature and fine-tune ATA disks.

The drawbacks of ATA

By far the biggest drawback of ATA is its real limit of two devices per channel and its usable limit of one device per channel when performance is an issue. This limit hinders the scalability of any RAID built with ATA, in terms of performance and maximum storage. In fact, this limitation might be the determining factor in choosing SCSI over ATA. While most motherboards come with two onboard ATA controllers, the four-disk maximum (which really translates into two RAID disks) associated with a two-channel ATA system will likely warrant adding a low-end SCSI card or additional ATA controller.

Unlike SCSI, ATA does not support detached operations—a process that allows a disk controller to detach from the bus in between I/O requests so that the CPU can access another controller. In addition, drives connected to an ATA interface cannot, generally, interact with each other without CPU intervention. ATA does, however, have a simpler command set than SCSI, which helps decrease latency.

Using an ATA RAID controller should improve your performance a bit by offloading some of the load from the CPU and onto the controller. While ATA supports only two devices per channel, many of the ATA RAID cards available also provide built-in ATA controllers, so that you can add additional drives. For example, Promise Technologies and 3ware both sell controllers with more than two channels. The problem is fitting them all in a single case.

ATA, because of its ubiquity, might be the best solution for users who are unsure about building a RAID and want to test its effectiveness. It's also ideal for users who are on a budget or who simply do not need the best performance and reliability. Administrators who are considering software RAID might find it useful to experiment with some spare ATA drives; they're easy to come by.

SCSI

The *Small Computer Systems Interface*, or *SCSI*, has been around much longer than ATA, but has traditionally been priced out of consumer reach. This changed in 1986 with the introduction of the Apple Macintosh II, which came standard with an SCSI controller, but no hard disk. The following year, Apple introduced the Mac SE and the Mac II, both available with optional internal hard disks.[*]

Bus-width and signaling rates

SCSI, like the data bus of a motherboard, is defined by both a bus-width and a *signaling rate* (sometimes called the *clock rate*). Increasing either of these parameters increases the overall throughput of the SCSI bus. Bus-width is either *narrow* (8-bit) or *wide* (16-bit). As with motherboards, the bus-width determines how many bytes of data can be transmitted during each clock cycle. Bus-width also determines the number of devices that can be connected to a single SCSI bus. Narrow buses can handle eight devices and wide buses can handle sixteen. This gives each bus type 7 and 15 usable devices respectively (one device number is reserved for the controller).

[*] Thanks to *http://www.apple-history.com* for the time line.

The signaling rate measures how many times a second data can be pushed through the SCSI bus. Signaling rates are measured in megahertz. The first implementation of SCSI, also called SCSI-1, had a bus-width of 8 bits and a signaling rate of 5 MHz. One byte of data, transmitted five million times per second across the SCSI bus, gave SCSI-1 a data throughput of 5 MB/s. Since SCSI-1, more signaling rates have been added to the SCSI specification. *Fast SCSI* defined a 10 MHz signaling rate (yielding a 10 MB/s transfer rate) and from there, *Ultra SCSI* (20 MHz), *Ultra2 SCSI* (40 MHz), and *Ultra3 SCSI* (80 MHz) were eventually defined and implemented.

Although SCSI is governed by the American National Standards Institute (ANSI), some manufacturers, throughout SCSI's evolution, did not want to wait for newer and faster SCSI protocols to be standardized. In an attempt to gain market share, many SCSI manufacturers have prematurely released their own prestandardized implementations. The result, as with ATA, was a deviation in naming among manufacturers, although incompatibility was rare and today is generally a nonissue. Table 2-5 shows the various implementations of SCSI and their maximum data throughput rates.

Table 2-5. Overview of SCSI data throughput

Names	Bus width	Signaling rate (MHz)	Maximum data throughput (MB/s)
SCSI-1, SCSI, Narrow SCSI	8	5	5
Fast SCSI, Fast-Narrow SCSI	8	10	10
Fast Wide SCSI	16	10	20
Ultra SCSI	8	20	20
Ultra Wide SCSI	16	20	40
Ultra2 SCSI, Ultra2 Narrow SCSI	8	40	40
Ultra2 Wide SCSI	16	40	80
Ultra3 SCSI, Ultra 160 SCSI	16	80	160

There is already talk of yet higher signaling rates for SCSI. A wide bus with a signaling rate of 160 MHz, yielding a throughput of 320 MB/s, is currently under development. It is likely to be commonplace within the next year.

Transmission types

The final difference between SCSI implementations is found in the type of cabling used to interconnect devices. *Single-ended (SE)* devices transmit information over single wires. Using single wires for transmission on the disk bus limits the maximum cable length of the disk bus. It also limits the maximum data throughput because error correction requires a pair of wires for each signal.

Differential SCSI transmits information over a pair of wires, which requires more expensive cables, but solves the performance and cable length limitations imposed by single-ended SCSI. The first standard, *high-voltage differential (HVD)*, provided a faster disk bus and used an extremely high voltage. HVD also allowed a maximum cable length of 25 meters, compared with the 6-meter maximum of SE devices. However, manufacturing controllers and devices that supported HVD dramatically increased hardware costs. The drastic increase in voltage means that a separate chip was required to regulate the voltage of the SCSI bus. It also made HVD and SE incompatible, requiring older devices to be replaced or connected to a separate controller. Because of these limitations, HVD is extremely uncommon today, especially in the consumer market, although it is used in some specialized RAID systems.

Shortly afterward, *low-voltage differential (LVD)* devices were introduced. LVD devices provided an increased maximum throughput like HVD, but limited the overall cable length to 12 meters. However, LVD also dramatically decreased hardware costs when compared to HVD. By lowering the voltage of the SCSI bus, LVD allowed a single chip to control both the SCSI devices and the voltage. This decrease in voltage also allowed LVD and SE to coexist on the same bus. LVD is now the standard and is supported by all recent SCSI devices.

SCSI Versus ATA

Overall, SCSI is a much better choice than ATA, both as a standalone and as part of an array. It allows more devices per channel and provides higher throughput. It also has a much larger command set, compared to ATA, which translates into better performance and increased reliability. The only major drawback of SCSI is price. SCSI drives and controllers are generally more expensive, with SCSI drives typically costing two or three times as much per megabyte as their ATA equivalents. (Although today, some mid-range motherboards are available with built-in SCSI controllers at little extra cost.) If you plan to use external SCSI devices, you will need to spend extra money on cabling and external disk enclosures. On the other hand, ATA does not support external devices at all, so its expandability is limited.

Speed

In the past, SCSI outperformed ATA by leaps and bounds, but ATA has caught up substantially in recent years. Today, ATA disks perform as well as SCSI disks, so speed isn't as much of a factor as it was just three or four years ago. But, with SCSI, you can populate an I/O channel with enough devices to fully utilize the entire pipe. With ATA, you are really limited to one device per channel if you want decent performance from that device, and that's not enough to utilize the full pipe when working with the most recent ATA specifications.

High-end SCSI drives have data throughputs of about 40 MB/s. When using Ultra 160 SCSI, you would need three or four drives on a single chain to take full advantage of your bandwidth. ATA drives operate at much slower speeds, so if you were using Ultra ATA/100, you could not possibly populate a single channel with enough drives to take full advantage of your I/O pipe, even if you put two devices on the same channel. The "Choosing Hard Drives" section, later in this chapter, discusses hard disk bottlenecks in more detail.

Configuration

Many people complain about the complexities and pitfalls of SCSI termination. But it's really quite simple. The beginning and end of every SCSI chain must be terminated. Figure 2-21 illustrates termination on a controller to which only internal devices are connected. The controller card is usually the last device on a channel and comes with built-in termination enabled.

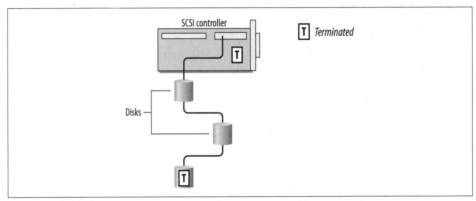

Figure 2-21. Modern controller cards provide onboard termination.

If you plan to use both internal and external devices on the same chain, then you will need to terminate the external portion of the chain. Figure 2-22 shows how to terminate a controller with both internal and external devices. Depending on your controller, you might also need to disable the controller's termination in the SCSI BIOS, although many cards automatically do this once devices are connected to the external connector.

As shown in Figure 2-23, the same methodology applies if you are using only external devices.

Finally, specifications dictate that any unused connections on an internal cable appear after the last SCSI device on that chain. In practice, this recommendation is often ignored, and many users report no errors when breaking this rule. I have never had problems using cables with more connectors than drives internally. Caveat emptor.

Likewise, there are quite a number of reports about using autotermination of SCSI chains. Autotermination is built into controllers and disks. If you experience problems, you may wish to manually disable autotermination (which is a controller BIOS

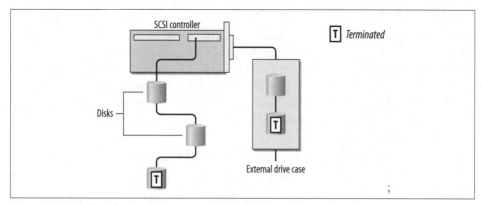

Figure 2-22. The last device on an external SCSI chain must be terminated.

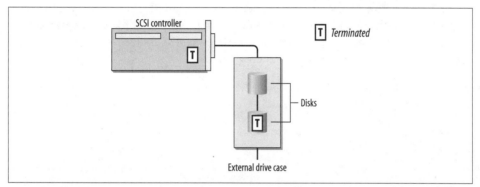

Figure 2-23. When using only external devices, the last disk on the chain and the SCSI card are terminated.

setting or a jumper on your hard disk) and actively terminate the chain at both ends. You can purchase terminators from the vendor who provides your SCSI cables, or even from a local computer store.

Growth

SCSI certainly has a much better upgrade path than ATA. Device-per-channel limits make SCSI much easier to deal with when you need to increase the size of an array. If you're on a budget, you might find it worthwhile to purchase an expensive SCSI controller, along with drives that are one or two technologies behind the current trends. Buying the latest and greatest SCSI card will increase the final price of a system by only a few hundred dollars. Buying the most cutting-edge disks, on the other hand, will affect system price by a few hundred dollars per drive. So while you can save costs by purchasing older drives initially, you won't have to discard your SCSI controller if you decide to upgrade to faster drives a few months later. Scaling back the original drive purchase initially might even place a hardware RAID controller within your budget.

Summary of SCSI versus ATA

SCSI supports more devices than ATA (although configuring many devices can be a challenge for many users and administrators). ATA is in more widespread use than SCSI, and that might make it easier to get hold of enough hardware to build a decent array. Some naysayers argue that SCSI is more confusing than ATA because SCSI users are faced with termination and drive placement considerations. Others are quick to point out the autodetection and block addressing problems with which ATA users must contend.

ATA can access only one device at a time, meaning that the benefits of parallel I/O under RAID are wasted. SCSI can address multiple devices concurrently and does not require the CPU to manage I/O, leaving more processing power for users and applications.

Table 2-6 summarizes the differences between ATA and SCSI. I think you will find that ATA is a cheap and usable way to quickly build arrays for both desktops and low-usage production systems, but that SCSI is the best choice for large systems and applications that require extremely intense I/O.

Table 2-6. The differences between SCSI and ATA

Feature	SCSI	ATA
Device limit	7 or 15 per channel	2 per channel
Maximum cable length	12 meters	~.5 meters
External devices	Yes	Not without special hardware
Termination required	Yes	No
Device ID	Yes	No (master/slave only)
Extra CPU load	No	Yes
Concurrent device access	Yes	No
Cost/availability	Expensive; need to add on	Cheap; built into most motherboards

I have excluded data throughput differences between SCSI and ATA from Table 2-6 because throughput with each protocol is typically limited by disk rather than by channel. Both SCSI and ATA will perform roughly equally in single-disk operations (assuming that similar specifications are compared). That being the case, SCSI supports many drives per channel, whereas ATA supports only one, from a usability standpoint. Thus, with SCSI, it's a lot easier to use the bandwidth you have available, while with ATA, it's really not possible.

Other Disk Access Protocols

Because RAID is oblivious to the hardware and disk architecture on which it is built, you can use any disk protocol that the Linux kernel supports to build an array. Indeed, if a newer, faster, and more reliable disk protocol (such as Serial ATA) were released this year or the next, it would only increase the usefulness of RAID. Furthermore, if a breakthrough in solid-state media happened in the next few years, these devices could also be grouped into arrays. While disk capacities and throughputs continue to increase, they nonetheless continue to fall behind the curve of increasing user needs.

Choosing Hard Drives

Hard drives represent the most challenging bottleneck in data storage. Unlike disk controllers, motherboards, and other components that make up a system, hard drives are unique because they contain mechanical components. This presents a complicated problem for engineers because the moving parts of hard drives limit the speed at which data can be stored and retrieved. Whereas memory and controllers, for example, are completely electronic and can operate at close to light speed, hard drives are much slower.

In general, it's a good idea to use the same disks in an array whenever possible. But using identical disks might not be an option all the time. Disks are made of several parts that affect their overall performance. If a situation arises in which you are forced to mix different disks, then you will want to know how to best evaluate a new disk to ensure that it will function appropriately when added to an array.

Platters, tracks, sectors, and cylinders

Two mechanical parts that affect performance are found on every hard drive. Inside each drive are magnetic *platters*, or disks, that store information. The platters, of which most common hard disks have several, sit on top of each other, with a minimum of space between each platter. They are bound by a spindle that turns them in unison. The surface of each platter (they are double-sided) has circular etchings called *tracks*, similar to a phonograph record, with the important difference being that tracks on a hard disk are concentric circles, while a record has a single spiral track.

Each track is made up of *sectors* that can store data (see Figure 2-24). The number of sectors on each track increases as you get closer to the edge of a platter. Sectors are generally 512 bytes in size, with some minor deviation that depends on the manufacturer.

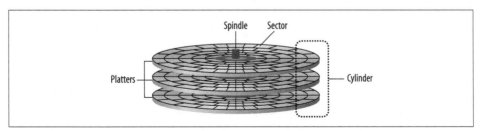

Figure 2-24. The surface of a hard disk platter.

The speed at which these disks spin affects how fast information can be read. The *rotation rate*, or *spin rate*, of a hard disk is measured in *revolutions per minute (RPM)*. Modern drives operate at speeds equal to or greater than 5400 RPM, with 7200 RPM being the most common consumer rotation rate. Drives operating at 7200 RPM are able to rotate through an entire track of data 120 times per second (7200 revolutions per minute / 60 seconds = 120 rotations per second). Most ATA drives spin at one of these rates, depending on the price of the drive. Older drives have slower spin rates. Faster SCSI drives, like those found in high-end servers or workstations, typically spin at rates of 10,000 RPM or higher.

Actuator arm

The second analog bottleneck is the *actuator arm*. The actuator arm sits on top of, or below, a platter and extends and retracts over its surface. At the end of the arm is a *read-write head* that sits a microscopic distance from the surface of the platter. The actuator arm extends across the radius of a platter so that different tracks can be accessed (see Figure 2-25). As the disk spins, the read-write head can access information on the current track without moving. When the end of the track is reached, it might seem logical for the actuator arm to move to the next track and continue writing. However, this would greatly increase the time needed to read or write data because the actuator arm moves much more slowly than the disk spins. Instead, data is written to the same track on the platter sitting directly above or below the current platter. A group of tracks, on different platters, that are the same distance from the spindle are called *cylinders*. Since the actuator arm moves every read-write head in unison, the read-write is already positioned to continue I/O. During a write, if there is no free space left on the current cylinder, the actuator arm moves the read-write heads to another track, and I/O resumes.

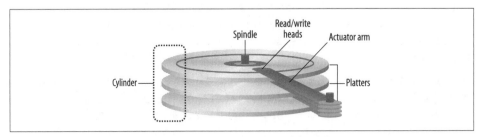

Figure 2-25. Actuator arms move heads across the surface of the disk.

When data is read or written along a single cylinder, and then along adjacent tracks, I/O is extremely fast. This is called *sequential access* because data is read from the drives in a linear fashion. When data is spread out among various tracks, sectors, and cylinders, the actuator arm must move frequently over the platters to perform I/O. This process is called *random access* and is much slower than sequential access.

Think again about the single spiral track of a phonographic record. That design makes records well suited for sequential data access, or audio playback. But it also makes random access impossible, hence the concentric circle design of hard disk platters, which are well suited for both types of data access.

 RAID helps eliminate the analog bottlenecks present in hard disks. By striping data across multiple disks, RAID can circumvent the slow analog parts of hard disks.

Maximum data throughput

Unfortunately, hard disk throughput is difficult to measure consistently. The way data is arranged on the drive can affect performance. Data that is spread across many different parts of the disk takes more time to access than data that is grouped together, because the actuator arm has to move more frequently. The *average seek time* of a hard disk is a measurement of the time it takes for the actuator arm to position itself on a new cylinder or track. Once the actuator arm arrives at a new track, it must wait until the proper sector spins into place. The time it takes for the sector and the actuator arm to line up is called *latency*.

In addition to the rotation rate, average seek time and latency, hard disks also come equipped with a *data buffer*. Similar to cache memory on a processor, the data buffer allows a disk to anticipate and cache I/O, increasing the overall throughput of the drive. When selecting hard disks, the rotation rate, average seek time, and data buffer size are all important factors. Smaller seek times mean faster throughput, while higher rotation rates and larger data buffers also increase data throughput.

Doing the math to determine the maximum data throughput of a hard drive you're considering can be tedious. Therefore, manufacturers usually advertise the overall throughput of a drive in easy-to-understand terms. The throughput of a hard disk over time is measured in megabytes per second and is found in the technical documentation for each hard disk model. Unfortunately, there is no standard for measuring this value. Therefore, the name that references it can vary from vendor to vendor. IBM calls this measure the *sustained data rate*, whereas Seagate calls it the *average formatted transfer rate*. I'll use the term *transfer rate* throughout the rest of this book.

Hard disks are also capable of occasionally reaching speeds well beyond their sustained data rates. These increased speeds generally last only for a fraction of a second. This additional benchmark is known as the *burst rate*. Burst rate speeds are usually achieved only when the data bus is idle. If a system is idle most of the time and large chunks of data are written intermittently, you will see throughputs at the burst rate more often than on a busy system. It is also unlikely that these user-friendly measurements will be printed anywhere on the product packaging, so if you plan to buy drives off the shelf, be sure to check the manufacturers' web sites first.

Matched drives

Because different hard disks have different seek times, rotation rates, data buffers, and latency, they also have different data rates. Like mixing disk protocols, using hard drives of varying speeds can hinder array performance. The high performance of fast drives might be wasted while waiting for data from slower disks. Although the performance bottleneck is not as drastic when compared to mixing different SCSI implementations, you should still try to use *matched drives* (drives that are all the same model) whenever possible.

Hard disks also vary slightly in size. Although two disks from different vendors might both be advertised as 18 GB (gigabytes), the formatted capacity may vary slightly. If this occurs, you will need to take extra care when configuring disks to ensure that partitions for any arrays other than linear mode or RAID-0 are exactly the same size. Also note that some disk partitioning tools provide an option to create a partition using the rest of any available disk space. Be careful when choosing this option, as using it on different disks could result in partitions that vary in size.

During the life of your array, it's possible that even if you have taken great pains to make sure that all your disks are matched, you may be forced to introduce a disk that is slightly different. For example, what happens if a disk fails and your vendor no longer makes the drives with which you built the array? In that case, you might have no choice but to use a different drive because the cost of upgrading all the disks might be too high. Keeping spare disks on hand in anticipation of a failure is advisable whenever financially possible.

Cases, Cables, and Connectors

Just because you decide to build a software RAID or use an internal disk controller does not mean you need to fit all your drives into a single server or desktop case. In fact, you can chain as many devices as you want to your Linux system, keeping in mind the limits on devices per channel. Remember that ATA is limited to 2 devices per channel, whereas SCSI is limited to 7 or 15 devices per channel.

By housing drives in external cases and connecting them to the external port's disk controller, you can create a formidable storage device. Putting disks in different cases will not cause a noticeable performance hit. However, don't forget that there are maximum cable lengths between devices on individual channels. ATA has a cable length limit of about .5 meters. The cable length limits of an SCSI channel depend on the specific SCSI protocol and transmission type (see Table 2-7).

Table 2-7. SCSI cable length limits

SCSI type	Maximum data throughput (MB/s)	Maximum cable length (meters)
SCSI-1, SCSI, Narrow SCSI	5	6[a]
Fast SCSI, Fast Narrow SCSI	10	3[a]
Fast Wide SCSI	20	3[a]
Ultra SCSI	20	3[a]
Ultra Wide SCSI	40	3[a]
Ultra2 SCSI, Ultra2 Narrow SCSI	40	12[b]
Ultra2 Wide SCSI	80	12[b]
Ultra3 SCSI, Ultra 160 SCSI	160	12[b]

[a] Single-ended
[b] Low voltage differential

The cable length limit applies to the total number of devices on a single channel, including external devices. Remember to take into account not only the cable connecting your controller to the external casing, but also the internal ribbon cable found inside the external case. In the rare situation that you are working with HVD SCSI, remember that it has a maximum cable length of 25 meters, regardless of the SCSI implementation it uses.

Cables come in two types: cheap and expensive. I strongly recommend that you spare no expense when purchasing cables. I've seen countless system administrators drive themselves insane diagnosing an SCSI performance problem only to later realize that they've bought poor quality cables that could not handle the data load. This mantra applies when using both internal and external cabling. Controller card manufacturers often bundle an internal ribbon cable with new controller cards (unless you buy an OEM version). Use these cables at your own risk; their quality varies greatly between manufacturers. It's probably best to find a good source of reliable cables and use them in all your systems, even when cables come bundled with cases or controllers.

Finding the correct external drive cases can be difficult, especially when working with the latest SCSI protocols. Make sure that the connectors match your card, or you will have to buy an expensive converter cable that can hinder performance. It's also important to make sure that the case is rated for the protocol you are using. Some cases may come equipped with the proper external connectors, but the internal cable might be rated for an older SCSI implementation.

Drives come in two sizes: 3.5" and 5.25". The 5.25" drives can only be placed in 5.25" bays. These drive bays are usually external, meaning that a plastic piece on the front of the case can be removed to expose the drive. 5.25" bays are full-height (3.25"). Full-height (5.25") drives are uncommon in today's PC market. You might find very large-capacity drives that have this form factor, but most disks are half-height (1.625") and have a width of 3.25". These smaller drives can be housed in 5.25" drive bays by using extension brackets that are usually bundled with cases. They can also be housed in 3.25" bays, which might be external or internal. When buying cases, external bays refer to spots that can be accessed without opening the case. Internal bays refer to drive mounts that can be accessed only when the case is opened.

Connectors

ATA cables use a standard 40-wire, 40-pin ribbon cable, while Ultra ATA (speeds of 33 MB/s and above) uses a 40-pin, 80-wire cable (as shown in Figure 2-26). The connectors and cables might look identical, but you must use the 80-wire with Ultra ATA disks. Be sure to check the specifications when purchasing cables.

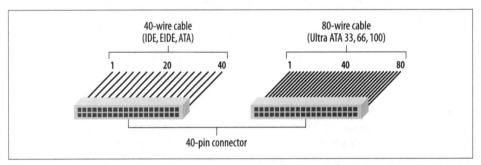

Figure 2-26. ATA cables all have the same 40-pin connectors, but Ultra AT (speeds greater than 33 MB/s) require newer 80-wire cables.

SCSI cables are much more confusing because SCSI cables have undergone more transformations than ATA cables. In most cases, you will be using a 68-pin ribbon cable for internal devices. Just make sure it's rated for the bandwidth you're using. Older external connectors have some variation (see Figure 2-27), but in most cases, 68-pin *high-density (HD)* connectors are used. However, newer 68-pin *very high-density (VHD)* connectors are making their way into the market. Decreasing the size of external connectors has made it easier for SCSI controller manufacturers to house multiple channels on a single card.

If you have different connectors on your controller card and your case, it's easy to find cables that can accommodate you. Check out *http://www.scsipro.com* for custom SCSI cables.

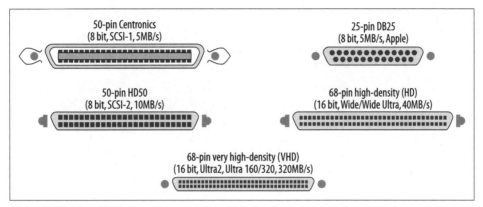

Figure 2-27. Most SCSI controllers use 68-pin high-density connectors for external connections. You may encounter some older connectors as well.

Single connector attachment (SCA)

To facilitate hot-swap disks, IBM introduced the single connector attachment (SCA) for SCSI hard disks. SCA integrates data transfer, power, and configurable options (such as SCSI ID) on a single 80-pin connector, as shown in Figure 2-28. Drives are plugged into an SCA backplane that is then connected to the SCSI bus (usually via SCSI ribbon cable) and the power supply. SCA drives are mounted in trays that slide into the backplane and lock into place, leaving the other side of the disk tray accessible from the outside of the case. These features make it easy to swap disks by eliminating the need to power down the system and dismantle the case.

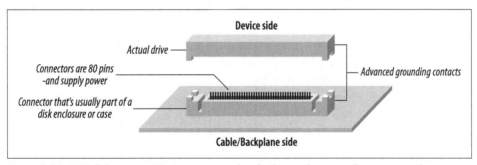

Figure 2-28. SCA disks use an 80-pin connector that facilitates data transfer, power, and configuration parameters.

Since its inception, SCA has been adopted by several manufacturers, and SCA-2 is the current implementation standard. SCA drives tend to be slightly more expensive than standard drives. Cases with SCA backplanes also run on the expensive side, but SCA is a necessity for any system that needs hot-swap capability because SCA is designed to allow power-on disk swapping. Recently, SCA chassis that fit into standard desktop cases have surfaced. Enlight Corporation (*http://www.enlightcorp.com*) man-ufactures a module that fits into three 5.25" drive bays. It supports up to five SCA disks and connects to an internal SCSI controller. Rackmount case makers also tend to sell custom drive cases that come equipped with an SCA backplane.

Individual adapter modules that allow the use of a single SCA disk with standard 68-pin SCSI cabling and power supply connection are also readily available. I've had mixed results using them, ranging from problem-free performance to SCSI channels running at less than optimal speeds. You will probably also have mixed results, but they do offer a pretty cheap way to get SCA functionality, especially on systems with only a couple of disks. Most cases support a minimum of five or six disks and are very pricey.

Power

Finally, make sure you have an adequate power supply in all your cases, whether they are dedicated drive cases or contain a system and disks. Most cases provide just enough internal power connectors so that the power supply cannot be overloaded. You can purchase power splitters if you run out of connectors, but remember that overloading a power supply can lead to fried hardware. If you find that you have more peripherals than power, you should considering upgrading your power supply. Most cases can be custom ordered with power supplies of up to 450 watts for a mini-mum of extra cash.

Making Sense of It All

In the final section of this chapter, I'd like to present an example RAID system that I built using parts available at most decent computer stores and online retailers.

The system in question was designed to replace a medium-volume web server that hosts content for video game enthusiasts. The original server was homegrown and quickly became inadequate as the site grew in popularity and moved out of its owner's workplace into a collocation facility. Connecting the system to a larger net-work pipe solved many of its initial problems, but eventually, the hardware itself became overworked.

The site is mostly static, except for a few moderators who post new articles and reviews each day. It's essential that the site have a 24×7 uptime, so RAID-0 is out of the question. And with my budget, RAID-1 wouldn't work either, because the site frequently distributes large video clips and demos of upcoming games. I simply couldn't afford the extra disks RAID-1 would require. That left RAID-5 as the best option.

In building the new RAID system, I needed to select a motherboard first because the old 32-bit PCI board was causing most of the performance problems on the original server. Because I was interested in high performance, I chose a motherboard that had two 64-bit PCI slots. Each of these 64-bit slots had a dedicated data bus with a throughput of 533 MB/s. (Remember that 64-bit PCI boards run at 66 MHz [66.6 million cycles per second * 8 bytes per cycle = 533 MB/s]). The remaining expansion slots are 32-bit and share a data bus with a throughput of 133 MB/s. The 32-bit bus wouldn't be used for anything except a low-end video card (for local administration), although in the future, a network card might be installed so that the system could be connected to a private administrative network.

In the first 64-bit PCI slot, I installed a high-speed networking card, which should alleviate any networking bottlenecks that the site was experiencing when it was using a 100-megabit Ethernet card. In the second slot, I installed a quad-channel Ultra SCSI 160 controller, giving me to a total disk bus throughput of 480 MB/s (3 * 160 MB/s). The unused bandwidth would help ensure that I didn't saturate the 533 MB/s data bus, while allowing for occasional burst rates that exceed the specifications of my disks and controller.

I found some reasonably priced hard disks that supported a sustained data rate of 40 MB/s and purchased a few external cases. Therefore, I didn't need to worry about cramming everything into a single desktop case. I knew that even the biggest desktop cases house only 7 or 8 disks, and that wouldn't allow me to take full advantage of my controller (480 MB/s ÷ 40 MB/s = 12 disks). After doing some thinking, I decided to purchase twelve drives, and I connected three of them to each controller channel. The drives are housed in the external cases I bought, externally connected to individual channels.

Although the average disk throughput was 40 MB/s, the manufacturer's specifications indicate that burst rates higher than that are common. Because I was using RAID-5, I could configure the array so that the system alternated between SCSI channels during I/O operations. That would help offset the potential for bottlenecks on an individual channel when the disks burst higher than 40 MB/s.

Once all the equipment (see Figure 2-29) was connected, I was left with three drives on each channel, with an aggregate disk bus throughput of 480 MB/s. That left some overhead on my data (PCI) bus to be safe, but didn't waste much of its potential, since I expected the disks would often outperform the 40 MB/s data rate by a small amount. I didn't need to worry about the graphics adapter or network cards interfering with disk throughput, either, because they were installed on separate data buses.

Hardware is always changing and the equipment you buy doesn't always meet your expectations, so it's always a good idea to do research before building or purchasing any system.

As an example of what can go wrong, a former collegue recently told me that he had to argue with his vendor in order to get a system with multiple SCSI backplanes. He had ordered a dual-channel RAID controller in a rackmount case with eight hard disks. But the vendor had designed the system so that there was only a single SCA

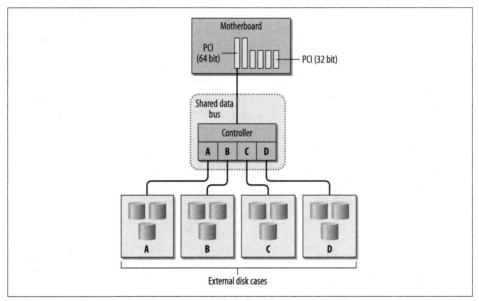

Figure 2-29. My web server contains a quad-channel SCSI controller. Three disks are connected to each channel.

backplane. This meant that all of his data would be travelling over a single SCSI channel and that the second channel would be wasted. The vendor offered the option of adding an external disk-only case for the second channel, but my colleague found that unfeasible due to the the high price of server colocation it added. In the end, my collegaue had to swap his components into a new case with two back-planes. The vendor ate the cost, but it took an extra week to get the system online.

Also, remember compatibility issues. I recommend checking relevant mailing lists and web sites to make certain that your disk controllers will work properly with your motherboard and network controller.

## CHAPTER 3

Getting Started: Building a Software RAID

Before plunging into this chapter, you should be familiar with the process of building and installing a new kernel. If you have never done this before, I strongly suggest that you read Brian Ward's "The Linux Kernel HOWTO" (*http://www.tldp.org/ HOWTO/Kernel-HOWTO.html*), which is available at any Linux Documentation Project mirror and is likely included with your distribution. If you prefer books to online documentation, then I'd recommend you pick up a copy of *Running Linux* (O'Reilly). Chapter 7 of that book offers an excellent tutorial on managing the kernel. To become comfortable installing a new kernel, I suggest you make some simple changes first.

A good start would be to eliminate some loadable modules from your kernel and include those subsystems statically. Most distributions set up major system peripherals as loadable modules, rather than compiling them statically into the kernel. Network drivers are a good example of kernel subsystems that are often installed, by default, as loadable modules. The sheer number of available network hardware configurations makes this the only efficient way to circulate network-enabled Linux distributions. So, in order to maintain compatibility with as many systems as possible, distributors such as Red Hat, Mandrake, and SuSE automatically load modules appropriate to your system at boot time, while installing a stock kernel with support for loadable modules. Using modules also helps conserve system memory by reducing the size of the running kernel. Modules can be unloaded when they are no longer needed, freeing up additional system resources.

While this is a completely viable way to set up a Linux machine, I tend to feel that a monolithic kernel, a kernel without modules, is more appropriate for system stability and is essential for servers. Loadable modules leave room for uncertainty during system initialization and are therefore best left to desktop machines and novices. Since servers typically perform specific and dedicated services, a monolithic kernel suits them best. Once you are comfortable recompiling the kernel and reconfiguring your boot manager, you can begin adding support for RAID.

This chapter will guide you through implementing a software RAID by explaining how to:

- Enable kernel RAID features
- Download and install software RAID utilities
- Partition hard disks
- Create an array

Kernel Configuration

Software RAID support must be enabled in the kernel before you can create any arrays. This generally means recompiling your kernel, configuring your boot loader (such as LILO or GRUB) to load the new kernel, and, finally, restarting the system with the new kernel.

A Brief History Lesson

Although kernels prior to 2.0.35 shipped with some RAID support, it wasn't until the release of 2.0.35 that support for RAID-1, RAID-4, and RAID-5 became available. The *multiple devices (md)* driver that provides kernel RAID support is currently at version 0.90. The latest stable kernels in the 2.0 and 2.2 series ship with an outdated version (0.36) of the software RAID driver. Patches for the 0.90 code are available for these older kernels (see the sections below on "Kernel 2.2" and "Kernel 2.0"). Kernels prior to 2.0.35 ship with version 0.35 of the *md* driver and should not be used, except if you absolutely have to keep them in operation for legacy reasons.

The 0.90 code was finally merged with the kernel source tree during the 2.3 development phase, so 2.4 ships with the latest RAID code. So will all subsequent stable and development kernels. In general, it's best to run at least a 2.4 series kernel when using software RAID, or a 2.2 kernel with the proper RAID patches applied. Using the old 0.36 driver is not recommended.

Along with drivers to provide software RAID for Linux, a set of utilities for managing, configuring, and tuning software arrays has emerged. These utilities, collectively called the *RAID Tools* (*raidtools* is the package name), are maintained by Ingo Molnar and Erik Troan of Red Hat and are now included with many major distributions. Molnar also served as the primary developer and maintainer of the software RAID subsystem from version 0.36 through 0.90's integration into the stable kernel tree. Today, he shares that responsibility with Neil Brown, a software engineer at the University of New South Wales. Brown also contributed many performance and reliability-related patches before becoming an official maintainer. In August 2001, Brown began work on his own software RAID utilities for Linux. His *multiple devices administration (mdadm)* program is a great alternative to the slightly aging *raidtools*. Both packages are covered in this book. I recommend using *mdadm* when possible.

Many other programmers have contributed to the *md* driver since its original development. Marc Zyngier wrote the original implementations of linear mode and RAID-0, along with the predecessor to *raidtools*. Miguel de Icaza helped develop the first implementation of RAID-1 and wrote the first version of *raidtools*. Gadi Oxman wrote the first 0.90 implementation of RAID-5.

Kernel 2.4

As of version 2.4, software RAID has its own subsection in the kernel configuration (in previous versions, options were found under the Block Devices submenu). The Multi-device Support (RAID and LVM) submenu contains all the configuration options for software RAID. The first option, CONFIG_MD, is a configuration switch that reveals options for RAID and Logical Volume Management (LVM). After selecting CONFIG_MD, choose CONFIG_BLK_DEV_MD, which allows the kernel to address multiple physical devices through a single logical device (see Figure 3-1). CONFIG_BLK_DEV_MD provides the foundation for the *md* driver and needs to be enabled on every system that uses software RAID, regardless of which RAID level is implemented.

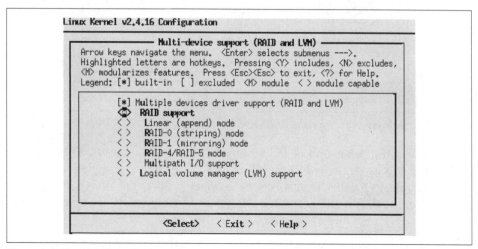

Figure 3-1. Enabling kernel RAID support.

In order to successfully build a software RAID device, one of the available RAID levels must also be enabled. The following kernel directives enable support for specific RAID levels:

```
CONFIG_MD_LINEAR
CONFIG_MD_RAID0
CONFIG_MD_RAID1
CONFIG_MD_RAID5
```

CONFIG_MD_LINEAR and CONFIG_MD_RAID0 enable support for the non-RAID methods of disk grouping supported by the Linux kernel. CONFIG_MD_RAID1 provides support for data redundancy through disk mirroring. Finally, CONFIG_MD_RAID5 enables support for both RAID-4 and RAID-5 layouts. The choice between using RAID-4 or RAID-5 is made later, when creating an array. If you plan to experiment with more than one of the available RAID levels, or if you are still unsure which RAID level you plan to implement, you can enable all four levels, rather than compiling a separate kernel for each (Figure 3-2) or recompiling your kernel each time you wish to experiment with another level. This is extremely useful during testing. When you're ready to go into production, simply rebuild the kernel with only the RAID levels you need. RAID support is also available as loadable kernel modules.

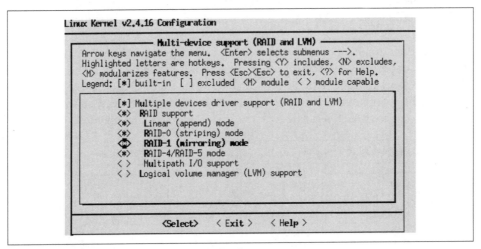

Figure 3-2. Enable support for specific RAID levels.

You will also notice an option for Multipath I/O support (CONFIG_MD_MULTIPATH). This newer feature of the *md* driver allows the addressing of a single physical disk using multiple I/O paths (controllers or channels). So if one I/O path becomes unavailable, the disk is still accessible. Multipath I/O support is not covered in this book.

Once you have added the desired options to your kernel configuration, compile the new kernel with support for software RAID.

```
# make dep
# make bzImage
```

The new kernel should be located at *.../arch/i386/boot/bzImage* (for i386-based systems), under the kernel source directory. If you are using a non-Intel machine, look for the compiled kernel image in the directory that is appropriate for your architecture (*.../arch/sparc/boot/* on SPARC systems, for example).

Installing the new kernel

Linux kernels are traditionally stored in the */boot* directory (usually a dedicated partition) or occasionally in the *root* directory. Copy the new kernel to the */boot* directory, or to the directory where you normally keep your kernels, if you have a nonstandard situation. The following example works on i386-based systems.

```
# cp arch/i386/boot/bzImage /boot/bzImage.raid
# cp System.map /boot/
```

You can name the kernel anything you like, but I find it helpful to name it something descriptive. Others prefer to include the version number in the filename. Next, add an entry for the RAID-enabled kernel to the boot loader configuration.

On systems using the Linux Loader (LILO), */etc/lilo.conf* contains information about which kernel image is loaded during the system initialization. LILO users might add the following entry to */etc/lilo.conf*:

```
image=/boot/bzImage.raid
 label=linux-raid
 read-only
 root=/dev/sda1
```

Make sure that you enter the correct *root* device, if it is not */dev/sda1*. Either place this stanza before all the others listed in */etc/lilo.conf*, or use the default global keyword to specify which kernel to boot (see the *lilo.conf* manual page for further details). You can also simply select the Linux-raid kernel from the LILO prompt during startup and avoid changing the default.

```
# lilo
Added linux-raid *
Added linux-orig
# shutdown -r now
```

You can also use *lilo -R* to specify which kernel to load when the system restarts (after you run *lilo* to rebuild the boot sector). In the following example, the Linux-raid kernel will be loaded the next time the system restarts, even though it is not the default kernel listed in */etc/lilo.conf*.

```
# lilo
Added linux-raid
Added linux-orig *
# lilo -R linux-raid
# shutdown -r now
```

lilo -R works for only one subsequent reboot. So, once you are satisfied with the new kernel, remember to change the default in */etc/lilo.conf* or rearrange the stanzas.

Some distributions are beginning to use the Grand Unified Bootloader (GRUB) instead of LILO. GRUB users can add lines like the following to their */boot/grub/ grub.conf* file:

```
title Linux RAID (2.4.18)
     root (hd0,0)
     kernel /bz.2418 ro root=/dev/sda2
```

This entry will load the kernel found at */boot/bz.2418* on the first hard disk (*hd0,0*) using a *root* device of */dev/sda2*, mounted initially as read-only. By default, GRUB will boot the first entry it finds in *grub.conf*, so you could either place the lines above as the first entry or change the default parameter to reflect the correct kernel.

System initialization

When the system restarts, a message indicates that the *md* driver has initialized. Each RAID level compiled into the kernel is listed, along with information about the driver. On a system with support for all available RAID levels, the following message should appear:

```
md driver 0.90.0 MAX_MD_DEVS=256, MD_SB_DISKS=27
linear personality registered
raid0 personality registered
raid1 personality registered
raid5 personality registered
```

If your system boots faster than you can read the messages, use the *dmesg* command to examine boot messages after the system has initialized. *dmesg* displays the kernel ring buffer, allowing users to examine important kernel messages that they might have missed during kernel initialization. The kernel ring buffer stores, in memory, messages about the current state of the running kernel. Some distributions are already preconfigured to dump these messages to a file after the system boots, but you can simply redirect the output to a file (dmesg > boot.messages) or pipe it into a pager (dmesg | less) at your whim. Messages returned by *dmesg* might look a little bit different from their appearance while the system is booting, but the same information is there:

```
# dmesg | grep md
md: linear personality registered as nr 1
md: raid0 personality registered as nr 2
md: raid1 personality registered as nr 3
md: raid5 personality registered as nr 4
md: multipath personality registered as nr 7
md: md driver 0.90.0 MAX_MD_DEVS=256, MD_SB_DISKS=27
```

When the *md* driver initializes, its version is displayed (0.90.0, in this case). MAX_MD_ DEVS indicates that the number of RAID devices is limited to 256 (with devices files named */dev/md[0-255]*), and MD_SB_DISKS indicates that each software array is limited to 27 member disks. However, by building hybrid arrays, users can move well beyond this limit. Hardware limitations will become an issue long before you reach the limits of the *md* driver.

The kernel also registers each RAID level, or personality. In this case, the kernel contains support for linear mode, RAID-0, RAID-1, and RAID-4/5. If RAID support was compiled as loadable kernel modules, these initialization messages will not appear, but you should see them later in your system logs when those modules are inserted. These messages will be reported (like all *md* driver messages), using the kern facility, starting at the info level.

Please note that as the system remains running, the kernel ring buffer will begin to expunge old messages. So be certain to examine it soon after booting if you need to view information generated by the boot process. Most distributions are also preconfigured to place this information in */var/log/messages* after the system boots. Please be aware that some distributions also come configured with an */etc/syslogd.conf* that generates a misnamed file called */var/log/boot.log*, using the log facility local7. This file (and any files generated using local7) contains messages from system initialization scripts (*rc*), not kernel initialization messages. Kernel messages are captured by *klogd* and dumped to *syslogd* once *klogd* has executed. In most default configurations, you will find messages about the *md* driver in */var/log/messages*, including those dumped from the kernel ring buffer by *klogd*. Chapter 7 covers system logging and the *md* driver in further detail.

If RAID-5 is supported, the kernel will also optimize the XOR routines used for parity checksum in a RAID-5. A message indicating that the test was performed is displayed, along with its results:

```
raid5: measuring checksumming speed
   8regs     :  1835.600 MB/sec
   32regs    :   871.600 MB/sec
   pIII_sse  :  2021.200 MB/sec
   pII_mmx   :  2277.200 MB/sec
   p5_mmx    :  2386.000 MB/sec
raid5: using function: pIII_sse (2021.200 MB/sec)
```

Since different i386-based processor architectures implement different ways to perform the necessary XOR operations, Linux needs to determine which one is the most efficient for a particular system in advance. Notice that in this example, the fastest checksum operation was not chosen. On systems that support Streaming SIMD Extensions (SSE), that choice is selected because of its ability to circumvent the L2 cache and perform operations in parallel (see */usr/src/linux/include/asm-i386/xor.h*). This functionality improves the performance of checksum operations. Information about checksum algorithms is also recorded in the kernel ring buffer.

After the system restarts, examining */proc/mdstat* will also show that the RAID subsystem was successfully initialized with support for linear mode, RAID-0, RAID-1, and RAID-4/5.

```
# cat /proc/mdstat
Personalities : [linear] [raid0] [raid1] [raid5]
read_ahead not set
unused devices: <none>
```

See the section "Examining Arrays Using /proc/mdstat," later in this chapter, for more information.

Patching Older Kernels

Working with 2.0.X and 2.2.X kernels can be extremely confusing because of the layout and documentation for the available patches. Most people have a lot of trouble sifting through all the old and erroneous information relating to these kernel versions and their RAID implementations. While RAID support is included with 2.0.X and 2.2.X series kernels, the most recent drivers are not distributed with the kernel source code, and patches should be applied when possible. There are also known problems with RAID-5 on 2.2 and 2.0 kernels, so if you want to use RAID-5, you should upgrade to at least a 2.4 kernel.

Kernel 2.2

When working with 2.2 series kernels, I strongly recommend that you upgrade to the latest RAID code (0.90). The 0.90 code is available as a patch to the kernel and should be applied before any attempt to build new arrays. As a general principle, you should always be working with version 0.90 (or later) of the RAID code. You can examine the file *.../linux/include/linux/md.h* to determine which version of the RAID code is present on 2.0 and 2.2 series kernels. Version information is located near the beginning of the file:

```
[...]
#define MD_MAJOR_VERSION            0
#define MD_MINOR_VERSION            36
#define MD_PATCHLEVEL_VERSION       6
[...]
```

This 2.2 kernel has version 0.36.6 of the RAID subsystem; therefore, a patch should be applied. If *.../linux/include/linux/md.h* is either empty or missing, your kernel is probably already patched to version 0.90. Instead, check the file *.../linux/include/linux/raid/md.h* for the version information. Note the extra subdirectory named *raid* in the path. As the size of RAID code grew, a subdirectory was created to better organize its components.

Patches for the 2.2 kernel are available at *http://people.redhat.com/mingo/raid-patches/*. A patch for the most recent sublevel release of 2.2, as well as patches for a few prior 2.2 sublevel releases, should be available at this site. Grab the one for the specific sublevel release with which you are working. If a patch for that particular sublevel release is unavailable, I recommend upgrading to the most recent 2.2 release and using the matching RAID patch.

For example, if you are working with kernel 2.2.20, download the patch *http://people.redhat.com/mingo/raid-patches/raid-2.2.20-A0*. Apply the *raid-2.2.20-A0* patch to your 2.2.20 kernel, using the *-p1* flag to indicate that you are in the *root* directory of the source tree:

```
# cd /usr/src/linux-2.2.20
# patch -s -p1 < /usr/src/patches/raid-2.2.20-A0
```

Passing the *-s* flag to *patch* invokes quiet mode. If *patch* is successful, no output it returned. If an error was encountered, then *patch* will output a list of reject files that contain more detailed information about the errors. If you encounter errors, it's possible that a faulty, or untested, patch was released. Try throttling your kernel backward one revision (to 2.2.19, in this case), download a new patch, and reapply it. When the problem is eventually corrected, you can safely upgrade and repatch. You can, alternatively, examine the reject files and attempt to manually fix problems that *patch* encounters. If you choose not to use quiet mode, then *patch* will return a list of files that have been successfully patched, in addition to the names of any reject files generated.

Remember that new patch files and kernels are released often, so the filenames used throughout this book may differ slightly from the ones you encounter when downloading patches. The locations of important kernel patches will also inevitably change as kernel maintainers change employers and as subsystems change maintainers.

When working with kernel patches, it's a good idea to apply them to a clean, unpatched kernel. Moshe Bar has written an excellent article for *BYTE* magazine that explains the implications of kernel source trees and applying patches to clean kernels (*http://www.byte.com/documents/s=2470/byt1012259408690/0204_bar.html*).

As in 2.4 kernels, RAID support must be enabled during kernel configuration of 2.2 kernels. During this earlier phase of RAID development, the RAID subsystem did not have its own submenu. Instead, RAID configuration options were put in the Block Devices submenu. Simply enable Multiple Devices Driver Support (CONFIG_BLK_DEV_MD) and at least one RAID level (see Figure 3-3).

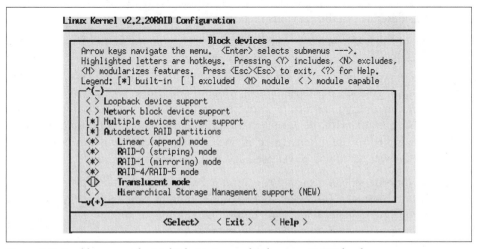

Figure 3-3. Enable support for Multiple Devices and at least one RAID level.

If you plan to experiment with different RAID levels, simply enable all of them. Under 2.2, the various RAID levels can also be built as loadable kernel modules. You might also notice some other options that provide additional features. The first, Autodetect RAID Partitions (CONFIG_AUTODETECT_RAID), allows the kernel to automatically activate arrays when the system boots. Originally, RAID devices were started either manually at the command line or by system initialization (*rc*) scripts.

Autodetection examines the RAID superblock (see "The RAID Superblock" section, later in this chapter) on hard disks to determine which disks are members of arrays and then to activate them. It is safe to leave RAID autodetection enabled. On newer kernels, autodetection is standard and therefore no longer appears as an option.

Translucent Mode (CONFIG_MD_TRANSLUCENT) and Hierarchical Storage Management Support (CONFIG_MD_HSM) were experimental options that appeared in the 2.2 kernel, but were never developed. They no longer appear in later kernels and should be disabled when working with any kernel that advertises them as features.

Kernel 2.0

As I've mentioned several times earlier in this chapter, kernels earlier than 2.2 are best not used for software RAID. Software RAID under 2.0 kernels is especially confusing. Patch files are no longer maintained, older utilities are needed to manage devices, and both patches and tools are kept in an area of *kernel.org* that is not maintained. So it's best to avoid using software RAID with 2.0 kernels, unless there are extenuating circumstances. If you must work with a 2.0 kernel, I strongly recommend upgrading to the latest kernel prior to using software RAID. Usable patches are available only for kernels newer than 2.0.35. It's a bad idea to even attempt using a kernel older than this.

Download the most recent 2.0 kernel patch from *ftp://ftp.kernel.org/pub/linux/ daemons/raid/alpha/*. Notice that this directory contains files for both 2.0 and 2.2 kernels. Use only 2.0 kernel patches from this directory. (Patches for 2.2 should be obtained as described in the previous section, "Kernel 2.2.")

Note, though, that if you were using kernel 2.0.39, you would need to download *raid0145-19990824-2.0.37.gz*. As of this writing, no patches specific to kernels later than 2.0.37 were available. The 2.0.37 patch should apply without severe problems. But if you find yourself in a situation in which a patch doesn't match your kernel sublevel version, or if you encounter problems while patching or compiling a 2.0 kernel, you should work with the kernel that matches the most recent patch. At worst, you will be forced to use a kernel that is one or two sublevel revisions behind, and eventually a newer patch will be released and you can upgrade.

To be on the safe side, I'm going to unroll a 2.0.37 kernel and apply this patch, rather than risk using a 2.0.39 kernel that might present problems during compilation or at runtime.

```
# cd /usr/src/linux-2.0.37
# patch -s -p1 < /usr/src/patches/raid0145-19990824-2.0.37
```

With 2.0.37, the patch returns no errors. A 2.0 kernel using the 0.90 RAID subsystem is now ready for compilation. Enable RAID features under the Floppy, IDE, and other block devices submenu during configuration (see Figure 3-4). First, enable Multiple Devices Support (CONFIG_BLK_DEV_MD) and then any RAID you need. It is safe to leave Autodetect RAID Partitions (CONFIG_AUTODETECT_RAID) activated, but leave Translucent Mode (CONFIG_MD_TRANSLUCENT) and Hierarchical Storage Management Support (CONFIG_MD_HSM) disabled (see the previous section, "Kernel 2.2").

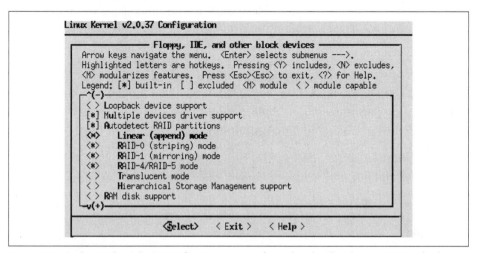

Figure 3-4. Under 2.0 kernels, RAID functions are configured under the Floppy, IDE, and other block devices submenu.

Summary of Kernel Upgrades

In summary, the latest version of the software RAID (multiple devices) driver for Linux is 0.90. However, kernels 2.0 and 2.2 were distributed with an older version (0.36) of the driver. If you are using kernel 2.4 or later, then you already have the latest driver, but you might wish to check the web pages of both Ingo Molnar (*http://people.redhat.com/mingo/raid-patches/*) and Neil Brown (*http://www.cse.unsw.edu.au/~neilb/patches/linux-stable/*) for performance and reliability patches that are waiting to make it into the next kernel revision.

When working with 2.0 and 2.2 kernels, it's essential to upgrade to the 0.90 driver whenever possible. Follow the steps described in this section to download the appropriate patch and apply it to your kernel. If you encounter problems during this process, you might need to try patching different kernel sublevel releases until you find one that patches without errors. Use kernels that do not patch properly at your own risk.

If, for one reason or another, you are working with a 2.0 or 2.2 kernel and cannot upgrade to the 0.90 RAID, than you are in the unfortunate circumstance of having to use the very outdated 0.36 driver. The 0.36 driver is not compatible with the newer 0.90 driver, and you will need to use an older version of the *raidtools* package to manage arrays created for the 0.36 driver. Only four software arrays are supported under version 0.36.

Working with Software RAID

The *raidtools* package, also maintained by Ingo Molnar, provides a set of utilities for creating and managing software arrays. *raidtools* has been the standard software RAID management package for Linux since the inception of the software RAID driver. Over the years, *raidtools* has proven cumbersome to use, mostly because it relies on a configuration file (*/etc/raidtab*) that is difficult to maintain, and partly because its features are limited. In August 2001, Neil Brown released an alternative. His *mdadm* package provides a simple, yet robust way to manage software arrays. *mdadm* is now at version 1.0.1 and has proven quite stable after its first year of development. It has received a positive response on the *Linux-raid* mailing list and will likely become widespread in the future. The rest of this chapter will provide you with examples of building and managing arrays, using the *raidtools* package, as well as *mdadm*.

raidtools

raidtools provides a small, simple command set that allows administrators to create, activate, and stop software arrays. Each array managed by the system is defined in a global configuration file (*/etc/raidtab*) that describes which physical disks are members of each array. */etc/raidtab* also contains metadata about every array, such as its RAID level and failover capabilities. The commands included with the *raidtools* package use the information in */etc/raidtab* to interface with arrays.

There are two notable versions of *raidtools*. Version 0.90 is the most recent implementation, and the only one being maintained. It should be used only in conjunction with the 0.90 driver. An older version (0.42) of *raidtools* is also still available. This version should only be used when working with older systems that still use the 0.36 software RAID driver. Never use *raidtools* with the wrong driver!

Also included with *raidtools* are sample configuration files and documentation (manual pages and cookbooks). Unfortunately, much of the documentation is seriously outdated, sometimes by a factor of years. Adhering to the open source philosophy that "old documentation is better than no documentation," a lot of outdated information is included with the *raidtools* package. It's probably best to double-check a Linux Documentation Project mirror for the most recent information and consult additional reference material and mailing lists in lieu of relying on the documentation in the package.

As of this writing, *raidtools-1.0* has been released in a limited capacity. It can be found in Red Hat 8.0 and will likely become pervasive during the next few months. It fixes several minor bugs and can be used as a replacement for *raidtools-0.90*. Chapter 4 presents more information about *raidtools-1.0* and some new utilities included with it.

raidtools-0.90

Most modern Linux distributions ship with the *raidtools* package. You can install them from your installation media or download them from your vendor. In a Red Hat CD directory, for example, issue the following command:

```
# rpm -ihv ./raidtools-0.90-20.i386.rpm
```

Debian users can use *apt-get* to install the *raidtools*:

```
# apt-get install raidtools2
```

Note that under Debian, *raidtools2*, NOT *raidtools*, provides the 0.90 *raidtools* package. Please be certain you have the proper package installed.

You can also download the source code and compile the package yourself. The most recent version is available at *ftp://ftp.kernel.org/pub/daemons/raid/alpha*. As of this writing, the most recent version is *ftp://ftp.kernel.org/pub/linux/daemons/raid/alpha/ raidtools-19990824-0.90.tar.gz*. You might be aware that a seemingly newer version is available from *http://people.redhat.com/mingo/raidtools/*. There are several known problems with this version (*raidtools-20010914*), including its lack of a key management utility (*raidsetfaulty*). Use this version at your own risk. The *raidtools* package should compile without problems on any recent system, though it does require the *popt* libraries. There are currently no notable configuration options. Download and unpack the archive.

```
# cd /usr/src/raidtools-YYYYMMDD
# ./configure
# make install
```

Compilation will leave you with several executables. Of particular note are *mkraid*, used to create new arrays, and *raidstart*, used to activate arrays that have already been initialized with *mkraid*. Installation will copy binaries to */sbin* and create symbolic links that invoke specific functions for each utility. *raidstop*, for example, is simply a symbolic link that causes *raidstart* to invoke a case switch based on the command line. Manual pages are also installed. Chapter 4 covers each command included with the *raidtools* package in detail.

At the time of this writing, version 1.0 of *raidtools* has just appeared in Red Hat Linux 8.0. Version 1.0 of *raidtools* corrects the issues associated with *raidtools-20010914* and includes some major improvements, such as bug fixes and a couple of new utilities. *lsraid* will allow you to query arrays and member disks. It will even let you generate an */etc/raidtab* file by querying a running array. *raidreconf* allows users to add (or remove) disks to a RAID-0 or RAID-5, usually without data loss. Although these utilities are somewhat new, I'll discuss them throughout this book, since they are particularly useful and will more than likely become widespread.

/etc/raidtab

/etc/raidtab is *raidtools'* primary configuration file. */etc/raidtab* provides a function similar to */etc/fstab*. It provides the kernel with a description of each software RAID, including its RAID level and a list of member disks. All RAID devices must have an entry in */etc/raidtab* to be created or activated using *raidtools*.

Users create */etc/raidtab* by hand, using any text editor. Once */etc/raidtab* is created and contains configuration information about arrays, the *mkraid* command can be used to construct an array based on the parameters defined in */etc/raidtab*. *mkraid* will complain if it cannot find a valid file at */etc/raidtab*. This process is similar to creating the boot configuration file */etc/lilo.conf* and consequently running */sbin/lilo* to rebuild the boot block.

Here is a typical */etc/raidtab* that describes a RAID-0 with two ATA component disks:

```
raiddev                 /dev/md0
raid-level              0
persistent-superblock   1
chunk-size              64

nr-raid-disks           2
nr-spare-disks          0

device                  /dev/hda1
raid-disk               0

device                  /dev/hdb1
raid-disk               1
```

Each array begins with a raiddev entry, followed by a list of array properties and an entry for each array member. A valid entry in */etc/raidtab* must contain at least a defined raid-level, a chunk-size, the total number of raid disks (nr-raid-disks) and two device/raid-disk pairs. chunk-size is a bit counterintuitive because it applies only to arrays that support disk striping (RAID-0, RAID-4, and RAID-5), yet it is required for any array you define in */etc/raidtab*. That's because the utilities in the *raidtools* package (*mkraid*, most notably) check for a chunk-size even if the defined RAID level doesn't support one. So when you work with linear mode or RAID-1, for example, you must provide a chunk-size, even though it's technically only a place-holder.

There are no global options in */etc/raidtab*. Each section, or stanza, applies to the last parsed raiddev entry. Once an array is defined, it may be included as a member disk in a subsequent array section. This allows you to combine multiple arrays into a hybrid array (as in RAID-10, for example).

Chapter 4 provides details about each */etc/raidtab* parameter.

raidtools-0.42

It's unlikely that you will be able to locate a package file for this outdated version of *raidtools*. So, in most cases, you will be stuck compiling the tools yourself. Download version 0.42 of the *raidtools* *(ftp://ftp.kernel.org/pub/linux/daemons/raid/ raidtools-pre3-0.42.tar.gz)* and unpack it.

One important caveat when working with this version is that it requires a patched kernel to compile. By default, the *configure* command assumes that your kernel is in */usr/src/linux*, but you can change that by using the --with-linux parameter.

```
# cd /usr/src/raidtools-0.42
# ./configure --with-linux=/usr/src/linux-2.0.37
# make
# make install
```

Installation will leave you with an older version of *mkraid*, as well as several deprecated utilities that are used to start (*mdrun*), stop (*mdstop*), and manage (*mdcreate*, *ckraid*) arrays. Manual pages are also installed by default.

Debian users can install version 0.42 of *raidtools* using *apt-get*:

```
# apt-get install raidtools
```

The rest of this chapter covers the current version of *raidtools* and the *md* driver. However, if you are working with legacy arrays, then you will have to use the 0.42 version of *raidtools* or *mdadm* to manage them. I strongly recommend that you upgrade old arrays whenever possible.

mdadm

Over the years, many users have become quite frustrated by the problems involved in using *raidtools* and */etc/raidtab* to manage software RAID. On small systems, the problems presented by *raidtools* are tolerable. But on large systems with multiple arrays, each with the potential for dozens of member disks, managing */etc/raidtab* can become daunting. *mdadm* provides a slightly different approach from *raidtools*. The idea behind *mdadm* is that the kernel, as well as administrators, should be able to manage arrays without resorting to a complicated, structured configuration file.

mdadm uses a *Universally Unique ID (UUID)* to identify each array and member disk. A UUID is a 128-bit number that is guaranteed to be reasonably unique on both the local system and across other systems. It is randomly generated, using system hardware and timestamps as part of its seed. *mdadm* uses the UUIDs found in the array superblock to scan member disks, determining which array they belong to and what the array properties are. Many programs use UUIDs to tag devices uniqely. In fact, kernel RAID autodetection uses these UUIDs, too. See the *uuidgen* and *libuuid* manual pages for more information.

mdadm provides all the same functions that *raidtools* provides, in addition to some new features. The only disadvantage of *mdadm* is that it's new. Neil Brown began working on *mdadm* in June of 2001, and it has undergone only a few revisions. *mdadm* can also manage legacy arrays created under the 0.36 *md* driver, which are normally managed with *raidtools-0.42*. In this book. I'll describe how to manage arrays using both *raidtools* and *mdadm*. The final decision is yours to make, but I urge you to at least try *mdadm*.

You can download the most recent *mdadm* tarball from *http://www.cse.unsw.edu.au/ ~neilb/source/mdadm/* and issue *make install* to compile and install *mdadm* and its documentation. In addition to the binary, some manual pages and example files are included.

```
# tar xvf ./mdadm-1.0.0.tgz
# cd mdadm-1.0.0.tgz
# make install
```

Or, you can download and install the package file found in the *rpm* directory under the above URL.

```
# rpm -ihv mdadm-1.0.0.i386.rpm
```

mdadm has five major modes of operation. The first three modes—Create, Assemble, and Build—are used to configure and activate arrays. Manage mode is used to manipulate devices in an active array. Follow or Monitor mode allows administrators to configure event notification and actions for arrays. The remaining options are used for various housekeeping tasks and are not attached to a specific mode of operation, although the *mdadm* documentation calls these options Misc mode. The following list describes the major modes of operation in *mdadm*.

Create mode

Used to create a new array. With Create mode, you have the option to define a new array at the command line or create an array defined in */etc/mdadm.conf*.

Assemble mode

Used to start an array that already exists.

Build mode

Used only for creating or starting legacy arrays (kernel version 0.36). It should never be used with the 0.90 *md* driver.

Manage mode

Used to add and remove disks to a running array. This mode is useful for removing failed disks and adding spare or replacement disks. Manage mode can also be used to mark a member disk as failed. Manage mode replicates the functions of *raidtools* programs such as *raidsetfaulty*, *raidhotremove*, and *raidhotadd*.

Follow (or Monitor) mode

> Used to implement some of *mdadm's* best and unique features. With Follow/
> Monitor mode, you can daemonize *mdadm* and configure it to send email alerts
> to system administrators when arrays encounter errors or fail. You can also use
> Follow mode to arbitrarily execute commands when a disk fails. For example,
> you might want to try removing and reinserting a failed disk in an attempt to
> correct a nonfatal failure without user intervention.
>
> Follow/Monitor mode also allows arrays to share spare disks, a feature that has
> been lacking in Linux software RAID since its inception. That means you need
> to provide only one spare disk for a group of arrays or for all arrays. It also
> means that system administrators don't have to manually intervene to shuffle
> around spare disks when arrays fail. Previously, this functionality was available
> only with hardware RAID. When Follow/Monitor mode is invoked, it polls
> arrays at regular intervals. When a disk failure is detected on an array without a
> spare disk, *mdadm* will remove an available spare disk from another array and
> insert it into the array with the failed disk.

The remaining options, which fall under the Misc mode, are used for tasks that
include stopping arrays, marking arrays as read-only or read/write, and clearing the
RAID superblock from a disk.

/etc/mdadm.conf

/etc/mdadm.conf is the primary configuration file in *mdadm*. Unlike */etc/raidtab*,
mdadm does not rely on */etc/mdadm.conf* to create or manage arrays. Rather, *mdadm.
conf* is simply an extra way of keeping track of software RAIDs. Using a configuration file with *mdadm* is useful, but not required. Having a configuration file means
that you can quickly manage arrays without spending extra time figuring out what
the array properties are and where disks belong. Unlike the configuration file for
raidtools, *mdadm.conf* is concise and simply lists disks and arrays. The configuration
file usually contains two types of lines, each starting with either the DEVICE or ARRAY
keyword. Whitespace separates the keyword from the configuration information.
DEVICE lines specify a list of devices that are potential member disks. ARRAY lines specify device entries for arrays, as well as identifier information. This information can
include lists of one or more UUIDs, *md* device minor numbers, or member devices.

A simple *mdadm.conf* file might look like this:

```
DEVICE     /dev/sda1 /dev/sdb1 /dev/sdc1 /dev/sdd1
ARRAY      /dev/md0 devices=/dev/sda1,/dev/sdb1
ARRAY      /dev/md1 devices=/dev/sdc1,/dev/sdd1
```

In general, it's best to set up an */etc/mdadm.conf* file after you have created an array.
You should update the file when new arrays are created. Without an *mdadm.conf*
file, you'd need to specify more detailed information about an array on the command line in order to activate it. That means you'd have to remember which devices
belonged to which arrays. That could be a hassle on systems with a lot of disks.

mdadm even provides an easy way to generate `ARRAY` lines. The output is a single long line, but I have broken it here to fit the page:

```
# mdadm --detail --scan
ARRAY /dev/md0 level=raid0 num-devices=2                    \
          UUID=410a299e:4cdd535e:169d3df4:48b7144a
```

If there were multiple arrays running on the system, *mdadm* would generate an array line for each one. Thus, after you're done building arrays, you could redirect the output of *mdadm --detail --scan* to */etc/mdadm.conf*. Just make sure you manually create a `DEVICE` entry as well. Chapter 4 contains a complete reference for *mdadm.conf*.

The RAID Superblock

Starting with version 0.36 of the *md* driver (kernel version 2.0.35), each disk in an array includes a superblock that describes array properties and stores them on each member disk. The superblock consists of a 4K block of data written to member disks when the array is initialized for the first time. The RAID superblock contains metadata about the array, including its RAID level and member disks. The superblock also contains the UUID I mentioned earlier. It might be helpful to think of the superblock as an on-disk representation of an array's entry in */etc/raidtab*. However, keep in mind that the superblock is part of the *md* driver and is not dependent on userspace utilities. The superblock also allows the kernel to automatically start arrays when the system boots.

The superblock is written near the end of each member disk or partition, at the start of the last 64K block. That means that although the superblock is only 4K long, the overhead for an *md* member disk is at least 64K. In cases in which there isn't a round number of 64K blocks, you can lose up to 128K worth of disk space for the superblock. So, if there isn't an even number of 64K blocks on the disk, the superblock is at an offset that is 64K less than the last odd-sized block. On member disks that are the same size, the superblock will reside at the same location for each disk. If member disks have varying sizes (in linear mode, for example) then the superblock won't be at a uniform location.

New arrays should always be created with an *md* superblock. That means setting the `persistent-superblock` parameter to 1 when working with */etc/raidtab* and *raidtools*. *mdadm* automatically enables the *md* superblock by default. Both *mdadm* and *raidtools* also provide a way to disable the superblock. This is necessary for backward compatibility with *md* driver versions prior to 0.36.

Examining Arrays Using /proc/mdstat

The best way to find out if there are already software arrays connected to your system is to use the */proc* filesystem. */proc* is an interface to important kernel data structures. You can get valuable information about the state of a running Linux system by looking at special files in */proc*. These special files act as a window into the running kernel. The *proc* filesystem is essential for monitoring the health of any software array.

Once the RAID patches are applied to a kernel and the system is booted using the new kernel, the pseudofile */proc/mdstat* will provide information about the current state of RAID devices and the *md* driver. Once arrays are configured and activated, information about their status will also be displayed. Initially, */proc/mdstat* merely reports the available RAID levels:

```
$ cat /proc/mdstat
Personalities : [linear] [raid0] [raid1] [raid5]
read_ahead not set
unused devices: <none>
```

This */proc/mdstat* indicates that support for linear mode RAID devices, as well as RAID-0, RAID-1, and RAID-4/5, is compiled into the running kernel. There are currently no active arrays. When there are active arrays, information about each one is reported by */proc/mdstat*. In this example, there is an active RAID-1 with two member disks (*/dev/sdb1* and */dev/sdc1*) and one spare disk (*/dev/sdd1*):

```
# cat /proc/mdstat
Personalities : [linear] [raid0] [raid1] [raid5]
read_ahead 1024 sectors
md0 : active raid1 sdd1[2] sdc1[1] sdb1[0]
      17920384 blocks [2/2] [UU]

unused devices: <none>
```

/proc/mdstat is a read-only file that is used only to examine arrays and the RAID subsystem. Chapter 4 contains a detailed discussion of */proc/mdstat* and other related parts of the */proc* filesystem. The rest of this chapter provides more examples of how to use */proc/mdstat* to make sure you are creating arrays properly.

Existing Arrays

If you have inherited a system that already uses software RAID, you need to decide whether you're going to continue maintaining that array or retire it and migrate the data to a new array (hardware or software). The rest of this chapter focuses on constructing new software arrays. If you plan to keep maintaining an array that already exists, read Chapters 4 and 7.

If you want to scrap an existing RAID, this section offers some advice that will help you dismantle the array. It's vital to keep in mind that reconfiguring an array or reusing its member disks in new arrays means that existing data will be lost. So it's very important to back up any data before proceeding.

In certain cases, it's possible to remove a member disk without losing data on an array. For example, removing an unused spare disk from a RAID-1 or RAID-5 will not cause data loss, although it might reduce fault tolerance.

If you plan to scrap all your existing arrays and use hardware RAID, skip straight to Chapter 5; the preparatory steps in this section do not apply to that situation.

Finally, if you are experimenting with various RAID levels and plan to reuse partitions that you have already included in another array, you might need to take some additional steps before building the new array. Remember that reusing these partitions means that the data on them will be destroyed, along with your array. Furthermore, you will not be able create a new array using partitions that are members of an array that is already running. So to reuse disks, you'll first have to stop any active arrays of which they are members.

Stopping an array

The *raidstop* command can be used to deactivate a running array created or started using *raidtools*:

```
# raidstop /dev/md0
```

Here's how to stop an array using *mdadm*:

```
# mdadm -S /dev/md0
```

If an array contains a mounted filesystem, both *raidstop* and *mdadm* will return an error. Filesystems should be unmounted using the *umount* command before they are stopped.

Once an array is stopped, its resources (member disks and *md* device special files) can be reclaimed and used in new arrays. If you attempt to use a member disk that is already part of a running array, *mkraid* and *mdadm* will generate errors on the command line, warning that the device is already part of an array. The *md* driver will also generate errors using *syslog*. Likewise, if you attempt to create an array using a device special file that is already in use, *mkraid* and *mdadm* will generate device busy errors, and the *md* driver will record them using *syslog*.

Reusing member disks

 Some of the techniques used in this section can result in data loss or corruption if they are used improperly, or even if you make a simple typo at the command line. Please be extremely cautious when attempting them.

Whenever you attempt to create new array using *mdadm* or *mkraid*, you will be warned about using member disks that already have a RAID superblock on them, even if they're not part of an array that's currently in use. So if you have a dormant disk in your system and it used to be part of an array, but hasn't been used for some time, there will still be a RAID superblock on it.

mdadm will warn you if potential member disks already contain RAID superblocks, and you will have to assert that you want to create the array:

```
# mdadm -C -n2 -l0 /dev/md3 /dev/sd{d,e}1
mdadm: /dev/sde1 appear to be part of a raid array:
    level=1 disks=2 ctime=Wed Mar 20 23:17:38 2002
Continue creating array? y
mdadm: array /dev/md3 started.
```

mkraid also generates a warning when you try to include disks that already have a RAID superblock in a new array, but its safeguards are slightly more obtuse. In the following example, I've created a simple */etc/raidtab* that defines an array including member disks that I know were part of an array that's no longer active:

```
# mkraid /dev/md1
handling MD device /dev/md1
analyzing super-block
disk 0: /dev/sdb1, 17920476kB, raid superblock at 17920384kB
/dev/sdb1 appears to be already part of a raid array -- use -f to force the
destruction of the old superblock
mkraid: aborted.
(In addition to the above messages, see the syslog and /proc/mdstat as well for
potential clues.)
```

Because the loss of data is such a drastic error, even using *mkraid --force* will return a warning. Using *mkraid --really-force* is the only way to successfully reuse partitions that already contain data and array superblocks. Even after the second warning, a countdown allowing five additional seconds to cancel the order is displayed.

```
# mkraid --really-force /dev/md1
DESTROYING the contents of /dev/md0 in 5 seconds, Ctrl-C if unsure!
handling MD device /dev/md0
analyzing super-block
disk 0: /dev/sdb1, 17920476kB, raid superblock at 17920384kB
disk 1: /dev/sdc1, 17920476kB, raid superblock at 17920384kB
disk 2: /dev/sdd1, 17920476kB, raid superblock at 17920384kB
```

Unfortunately, the extra checks that *mdadm* and, to a greater degree, *mkraid*, perform can become tedious when you're experimenting with various array configurations—especially when you're forced to wait five seconds each time you reuse disks.

The *dd* command is useful for erasing the RAID superblock from previously used partitions. To erase the RAID superblock, you will need to know where it's located.

```
disk 0: /dev/sdb1, 17920476kB, raid superblock at 17920384kB
disk 1: /dev/sdc1, 17920476kB, raid superblock at 17920384kB
disk 2: /dev/sdd1, 17920476kB, raid superblock at 17920384kB
```

The previous output is generated by *mkraid* when a new array is constructed. In this case, the superblock was written to each disk at block 17920384. The *md* driver uses a 4 KB block size. Don't worry about recording the location of the RAID superblock, because each time an array changes status, this information is reported via *syslogd*. That means the superblock location is recorded each time an array is started, stopped, or encounters an error. Look for a *syslog* entry similar to this one (kern. info):

```
Apr 25 11:54:59 jaded kernel: md: sdd1 [events: 00000001]<6>(write) sdd1's sb /
    offset: 17920384
Apr 25 11:54:59 jaded kernel: md: sdc1 [events: 00000001]<6>(write) sdc1's sb /
    offset: 17920384
Apr 25 11:54:59 jaded kernel: md: sdb1 [events: 00000001]<6>(write) sdb1's sb /
    offset: 17920384
```

Use *dd* to zero the superblock of each member disk you wish to reuse:

```
# dd if=/dev/zero of=/dev/sdb1 bs=1k seek=17920384 count=4
```

 Be extremely careful when using *dd* to erase RAID superblocks or to modify any information on hard disks. If you accidentally specify the wrong device or make a mistake on the command line, you could destroy all data on the disk. When working with *dd*, *if=* specifies the input file to use. Data from the input file is written to the output file, specified by *of=*. In this example, we take input from */dev/zero* (a character special file that generates zeros) and write it to */dev/sdb1*, which means zeros are written to the output file. *bs=1k* specifies a block size of 1 KB. That means 1 KB worth of zeros is read from */dev/zero* and then written to */dev/sdb1* at a time. *seek=* specifies how many blocks to advance (also using the 1 KB block size) in the output file. Finally, *count=4* tells *dd* to write only 4 blocks' worth of data to the output file.

dd performs a seek to block 17920384 of */dev/sdb1* (using a 1 KB block size) and then writes null bytes (*/dev/zero*) into each location for the next four blocks.

Repeat this process for each old member disk that you wish to reuse. If you're experimenting, it might be useful to create a shell script to help automate this process.

mdadm also provides a mechanism, *--zero-superblock*, that allows you to removethe RAID superblock from disks that were part of an array. *mdadm* allows you to remove the superblock from more than one disk at a time:

```
# mdadm --zero-superblock /dev/sd{b,c}1
```

Now when you create a new array, you will not be prompted for additional confirmation before the new array is created. It might seem that going through these steps is more complicated and time-consuming than simply confirming the additional warning messages produced by *mkraid* and *mdadm*. This is undeniably true for *mdadm*, but remember that *mkraid* forces you to wait an additional five seconds before creating the array. Also, there are other times when it is desirable to remove unwanted RAID superblocks. For example, it's a good idea to remove the RAID superblock from any disk that's no longer part of an array. After all, you don't want the kernel to inadvertently start an array you are no longer using or consider a disk that should no longer be part of any array, especially when that might mean vital arrays cannot be built because their disks are already in use.

Creating an Array

Now that the kernel supports RAID and you have the required utilities, it's time to partition disks and create arrays. At this point, all disks that you plan to include in an array should be connected to the system. Remember that each array can contain a maximum of MD_SB_DISK, as defined by the kernel. By default, that maximum is 27, but since arrays can also act as member disks, this limit is avoidable. In addition, a maximum of 256 software RAID devices are available for use.

Partitioning with fdisk

You don't need to partition disks before using them in an array, but partitioning does provide a couple of advantages. First, partitioning is necessary if you want the kernel to automatically start arrays, because the *md* driver uses the partition type to identify member disks. Second, *md* devices don't support partitioning directly, but in some cases, having a filesystem that spans an entire array is undesirable. Using software RAID for system partitions means that smaller partitions are necessary. After all, you don't want */var* or */boot* to span a whole array.

If you have a lot of disks, then you might not want to go through the trouble of partitioning each disk—a process that can take a lot of time if you have more than a few drives. In that case, you can simply use a whole, unpartitioned disk as an array member (*/dev/sda*, for example). This means that you won't be able to autostart arrays, however, so you'll have to include commands to start *md* devices in your system initialization scripts.

The rest of this chapter assumes that disk-sized partitions are used, but unless you want to subpartition or need to automatically start arrays, you can skip the rest of this section. Replace the use of partitioned disks found in the examples throughout the rest of this chapter with unpartitioned devices. Where I use */dev/sdb1* to denote a single disk-sized partition as an array member disk, you could simply use */dev/sdb*.

The site *http://cgi.cse.unsw.edu.au/~neilb/patches/linux/* contains patches that enable you to subpartition software arrays. The web page is indexed by kernel revision and patch name.

Use any standard partitioning utility to partition disks connected to your system. Since *fdisk* is generally available on all Linux systems, I'll discuss it here, but you can use whichever utility you prefer. The partitioning utility you choose doesn't need any special features, but to take advantage of automatic RAID activation at boot time, you need a partitioning utility that allows you to set a partition to the type *Linux Raid Auto* (or hexadecimal code 0xFD). Download the latest version of your partitioning software to ensure that you can take advantage of this feature. This process marks a drive for autodetection and allows the kernel to automatically start arrays at boot time, which means that administrators don't need to modify startup scripts each time they add an array.

Some GUI partitioning utilities might not allow you to set a drive to this nonstandard type. If, for some reason, you are unable to make these changes using GUI partitioning software, I recommend downloading the current version of *fdisk* and following the examples below. The latest version of *fdisk* will support the *Linux Raid Auto* partition type. (Older versions may not have this option.) You must create partitions on each drive that you plan to use in your array. If you don't want the kernel to automatically start arrays, you can use an unpartitioned block device instead, such as */dev/sda* or */dev/hda*, instead of */dev/sda1* or */dev/hda1*.

Partitioning for autodetection

The example that follows creates a single partition (*/dev/sdb1*) on the second SCSI drive (*/dev/sdb*) and marks it as an automatically detectable RAID partition:

```
# fdisk /dev/sdb
Command (m for help): n
Command action
   e   extended
   p   primary partition (1-4)
p
Partition number (1-4): 1
First cylinder (1-1116, default 1): 1
Last cylinder or +size or +sizeM or +sizeK (1-1116, default 1116): 1116
```

Change the drive type of */dev/sdb1* to *Linux Raid Auto* (0xFD) so it can be detected automatically at boot time:

```
Command (m for help): t
Partition number (1-4): 1
Hex code (type L to list codes): fd
Changed system type of partition 1 to fd (Linux raid autodetect)
```

When the partitions that are part of an array are all set to *Linux Raid Auto*, the kernel will automatically start that array when the system boots. Autodetection works only with MS-DOS style partition tables. So if you're using Sun, Amiga, or another architecture that has its own partition type, you will have to start arrays manually or use system initialization scripts. The kernel starts arrays before *rc* scripts run. So if you need to defer array startup until after you have performed other functions, then it's important to not set the type to *Linux Raid Auto*.

Partitioning without autodetection

If you don't want to use autodetection, but still plan to partition your disks, set partitions to type *Linux* (0x83). This is the default partition type, but to be certain the proper type is assigned, set the type manually:

```
# fdisk /dev/sdb
Command (m for help): t
Partition number (1-4): 1
Hex code (type L to list codes): 83
Changed system type of partition 1 to 83 (Linux)
```

Write the new partition table to the disk and exit *fdisk*.

```
Command (m for help): w
The partition table has been altered!

Calling ioctl() to re-read partition table.
Syncing disks.
```

You should follow the process shown here to create partitions on each disk you plan to use in an array. If you create a new partition on a disk that is in use (that is, a disk that contains a mounted partition), *fdisk* will complain. You must then restart your system before using the new partition. In the following example, */dev/sda* contains mounted partitions, but */dev/sda13* is currently set to type *Linux* (0x83) instead of *Linux Raid Auto* (0xFD):

```
# fdisk /dev/sda13
Command (m for help): t
Partition number (1-13): 13
Hex code (type L to list codes): fd
Changed system type of partition 13 to fd (Linux raid autodetect)

Command (m for help): w
The partition table has been altered!

Calling ioctl() to re-read partition table.
Re-read table failed with error 16: Device or resource busy.
Reboot your system to ensure the partition table is updated.
```

Once partitions are created, you can use *fdisk* to compare each of the new partitions. Make certain that they meet your specifications and that partitions for arrays are the same size when necessary:

```
# fdisk -l

Disk /dev/sda: 255 heads, 63 sectors, 553 cylinders
Units = cylinders of 16065 * 512 bytes
   Device Boot    Start     End    Blocks   Id  System
/dev/sda1   *         1      16    128488+  83  Linux
/dev/sda2            17      33    136552+  82  Linux swap
/dev/sda3            34      84    409657+  83  Linux
/dev/sda4            85     553   3767242+   5  Extended
/dev/sda5            85     276   1542208+  83  Linux
```

Important Rules for Partitioning

Here are some points to remember when you are partitioning.

- If you don't require autodetection and plan to use whole disks as array members, you don't need to partition member disks individually.

- Set partitions to type *Linux Raid Auto* (0xFD) if you want the kernel to automatically start arrays at boot time. Otherwise, leave them as *Linux* (0x83).

- RAID-1 and RAID-4/5 arrays should contain member disks that have partitions of the same size. If these arrays contain partitions of differing sizes, the larger partitions will be truncated to reflect the size of the smallest partition.

- RAID-0 and linear mode arrays can contain partitions that have varying sizes without losing any disk space. Remember that when the smaller disks that belong to a RAID-0 become full, only the remaining disks are striped. So you might see variable performance on a RAID-0 with member disks of differing sizes as the array fills up.

- Using matched drives is strongly recommended when working with any nonlinear mode array. Please see the "Matched Drives" section in Chapter 2 for further details.

```
/dev/sda6              277        407   1052226  83  Linux
/dev/sda7              408        553   1172713+ 83  Linux

Disk /dev/sdb: 255 heads, 63 sectors, 1116 cylinders
Units = cylinders of 16065 * 512 bytes
   Device Boot     Start       End    Blocks  Id  System
/dev/sdb1               1      1116   8964238+ fd  Linux raid autodetect

Disk /dev/sdc: 255 heads, 63 sectors, 1116 cylinders
Units = cylinders of 16065 * 512 bytes
   Device Boot     Start       End    Blocks  Id  System
/dev/sdc1               1      1116   8964238+ fd  Linux raid autodetect

Disk /dev/sdd: 255 heads, 63 sectors, 1116 cylinders
Units = cylinders of 16065 * 512 bytes
   Device Boot     Start       End    Blocks  Id  System
```

In addition to the system drive, two partitions are defined in the preceding listing. There is a partition on each of the second and third SCSI drives: */dev/sdb1* and */dev/sdc1*. A fourth drive with no partitions defined resides at */dev/sdd*.

Linear (Append) Mode

Linear mode requires a minimum of two disks, but does not require that member disks be the same size or type. Since the system writes to each disk until it is full, the speed and size of individual disks is largely irrelevant, in terms of aggregate RAID performance.

The following is a very simple linear array using *etc/raidtab*:

```
# A linear array with two member disks

raiddev                 /dev/md0
 raid-level             linear
 chunk-size             64
 persistent-superblock  1
 nr-raid-disks          2

 device                 /dev/sdb1
 raid-disk              0

 device                 /dev/sdc1
 raid-disk              1
```

raiddev begins the definition of a new array, */dev/md0* in this case. All entries that follow apply to the previously defined array, until another raiddev entry is parsed. raid-level, as the name implies, sets the array type for the current array.

As I mentioned earlier, chunk-size would normally define the number of kilobytes to write to each member disk for arrays that support disk striping. However, when working with linear mode arrays, the chunk-size defines the *rounding factor*. Each component disk is sized so that it is a multiple of the rounding factor. Because of the way the RAID superblock is placed on each array member, rounding factors of less than 64 KB are effectively equal to 64 KB.

The chunk-size, regardless of what type of array is used, must be defined as any power of two. In fact, for the rest of this chapter, we'll create arrays with a 64 KB chunk-size. You might notice some errors in the system boot messages and your log files, which warn about using a chunk-size with linear mode (or RAID-1). These warnings arise from the inconsistencies between the kernel RAID driver and the requirements of *raidtools* for parsing */etc/raidtab*. These warnings can be safely ignored.

persistent-superblock takes a Boolean value and controls whether a RAID super-block is written to member disks. The persistent-superblock should always be enabled when creating new arrays, but can be disabled for backward compatibility.

nr-raid-disks indicates that there are two disks in the array */dev/md0*. Later in the file, each disk is defined by identifying its device name and its order in the array, using the device/raid-disk pair. To use more than two disks, you need only add additional device and raid-disk entries and increment the nr-raid-disks value.

Once */etc/raidtab* is created, the *mkraid* program is used to build and activate the array:

```
# mkraid /dev/md0
handling MD device /dev/md0
analyzing super-block
disk 0: /dev/sdb1, 17920476kB, raid superblock at 17920384kB
disk 1: /dev/sdc1, 17920476kB, raid superblock at 17920384kB
```

The array was created successfully.

If you use *mdadm*, you don't need a configuration file. The array we showed previously can be created with the following command:

```
# mdadm -Cv -llinear -n2 /dev/md0 /dev/sd{b,c}1
mdadm: array /dev/md0 started.
```

The options are simple.

-C, --create
> Create a new array.

-v, --verbose
> Be more verbose.

-l, --raid-level
> Select the RAID level: linear, 0, 1, 4, or 5.

-n, --raid-disks
> Set the number of member disks in the array.

In addition to the options, *mdadm* takes a RAID device and a list of member partitions as its parameters. Note that the member disks are specified using standard shell expansions. The disk letters encapsulated in braces are expanded into */dev/sdb1* and */dev/sdc1* when *mdadm* is run. Consult the manual pages for your shell as needed; I use *bash*.

Increasing the number of member disks using *-n* or *--raid-devices* allows you to specify additional disks to be included in the array. List more disks on the command line individually, or as part of the glob (*/dev/sd{b,c,d}1*, for example). You could also use the long form of the command to accomplish the same task.

```
# mdadm --create --verbose --level=linear --raid-devices=2 \
/dev/md0 /dev/sdb1 /dev/sdc1
```

I'll use the short form of the command through the rest of this chapter. Chapter 4 contains a complete reference to all of the options in *mdadm*.

Both *mkraid* and *mdadm* automatically activate newly created arrays. Information about the array and its member disks is now available via the */proc/mdstat* pseudo-file.

```
# cat /proc/mdstat
Personalities : [linear] [raid0] [raid1] [raid5]
read_ahead 1024 sectors
md0 : active linear sdc1[1] sdb1[0]
      35840768 blocks 64k rounding

unused devices: <none>
```

Next, create a filesystem on the new array. In this example, and throughout the rest of this chapter, I'll use the ext2 filesystem. If you want to use another filesystem, then simply substitute that command in place of *mke2fs*. Chapter 6 covers some newer filesystems available for Linux.

```
# mke2fs /dev/md0
mke2fs 1.27 (8-Mar-2002)
Filesystem label=
OS type: Linux
Block size=4096 (log=2)
Fragment size=4096 (log=2)
4480448 inodes, 8960192 blocks
448009 blocks (5.00%) reserved for the super user
First data block=0
274 block groups
32768 blocks per group, 32768 fragments per group
16352 inodes per group
Superblock backups stored on blocks:
     32768, 98304, 163840, 229376, 294912, 819200, 884736, 1605632, 2654208, /
     4096000, 7962624

Writing inode tables: done
Writing superblocks and filesystem accounting information: done
```

The preceding commands (*mkraid* or *mdadm*, and *mke2fs*) need to be executed only once. Each time the system boots, mount the array like any normal hard disk partition:

```
# mount /dev/md0 /mnt/raid/linear
# df -h /mnt/raid/linear
Filesystem        Size  Used Avail Use% Mounted on
/dev/md0           34G   20k   31G   1% /mnt/raid/linear
```

You can modify your *rc* scripts to mount the array after it has been activated by using *raidstart* or *mdadm*. If you are using RAID autodetection, then an entry for the array can also be added to */etc/fstab* so it will be mounted automatically when the system restarts.

```
/dev/md0      /mnt/raid/linear    ext2    defaults    1 2
```

Now, when the system restarts, the array (containing an ext2 filesystem) is mounted at */mnt/raid/linear* and is usable like any normal filesystem. You can install software, store music, video, and image files, or create a database.

Be warned that some distributions (Red Hat, for one) halt system initialization if an */etc/fstab* entry could not be properly checked and mounted. So if the kernel doesn't automatically start your array, an entry in */etc/fstab* might be preventing the system from booting successfully. It's a good idea to place commands that will manually start arrays in your initialization scripts before filesystems are checked and mounted, even if you're already successfully using autodetection. This will provide additional stability and, at worst, display some innocuous warnings on the console.

Linear mode is also good for reusing old ATA disks that vary in speed and size because the variations between these disks will have minimal impact on the overall performance of the array. The following example shows four ATA drives as members of a linear array:

```
# A linear array with four ATA member disks

raiddev                     /dev/md0
 raid-level                 linear
 chunk-size                 64
 persistent-superblock      1
 nr-raid-disks              4

 device                     /dev/hda1
 raid-disk                  0

 device                     /dev/hdb1
 raid-disk                  1

 device                     /dev/hdc1
 raid-disk                  2

 device                     /dev/hdd1
 raid-disk                  3
```

Use *mdadm* to create an identical array:

```
# mdadm -Cv -llinear -n4 /dev/md0 /dev/hd{a,b,c,d}1
```

RAID-0 (Striping)

You can create a stripe with *raidtools* by making a few simple changes to the */etc/ raidtab* file used earlier for the linear mode array:

```
# A striped array with two member disks

raiddev                     /dev/md0
raid-level                  0
 chunk-size                 64
 persistent-superblock      1
 nr-raid-disks              2

 device                     /dev/sdb1
 raid-disk                  0

 device                     /dev/sdc1
 raid-disk                  1
```

Since you've changed the array type to striped (0), the chunk-size now has an impact on array performance. Since the chunk-size defines the amount of data that gets written to the member disk during each write, choosing a chunk-size that approximates the average write size (average file size) is desirable. Remember that unless you first erase the RAID superblocks from previously used disks, *mdadm* will prompt you for confirmation.

Run *mkraid* to create and activate the RAID-0:

```
# mkraid /dev/md0
handling MD device /dev/md0
analyzing super-block
disk 0: /dev/sdb1, 17920476kB, raid superblock at 17920384kB
disk 1: /dev/sdc1, 17920476kB, raid superblock at 17920384kB
```

Alternatively, use *mdadm* to create a two-disk stripe with a 64 KB chunk-size on */dev/md0*, using disk partitions */dev/sdb1* and */dev/sdc1*:

```
# mdadm -Cv -l0 -c64 -n2 /dev/md0 /dev/sd{b,c}1
mdadm: array /dev/md0 started.
```

/proc/mdstat now reports that the new RAID-0 array has been created and is online:

```
# cat /proc/mdstat
Personalities : [linear] [raid0] [raid1] [raid5]
read_ahead 1024 sectors
md0 : active raid0 sdc1[1] sdb1[0]
      35840768 blocks 64k chunks
```

You can now use *mke2fs* to create a filesystem:

```
unused devices: <none>
```

Separating disks in a RAID-0 onto different controllers will help improve your overall array performance. You can arrange device/raid-disk entries in your */etc/raidtab* file contrary to the physical layout of disks and controllers. In this example, I have four disks connected to a two-channel SCSI controller. */dev/sda* and */dev/sdb* are on channel A, and */dev/sdc* and */dev/sdd* are on channel B. Notice how I alternate the device entries in this example */etc/raidtab* file:

```
raiddev                 /dev/md0
 raid-level             0
 chunk-size             64
 persistent-superblock  1
 nr-raid-disks          4

 device                 /dev/sda1
 raid-disk              0

 device                 /dev/sdc1
 raid-disk              1

 device                 /dev/sdb1
 raid-disk              2

 device                 /dev/sdd1
 raid-disk              3
```

When using *mdadm*, simply alternate devices on the command line to achieve the same effect:

```
# mdadm -Cv -l0 -n4 -c64 /dev/md0 /dev/sd{a,c,b,d}1
```

You can follow this methodology for any number of controllers. Remember that Linux will logically arrange disks in detection order, beginning with */dev/sda*.

RAID-1 (Mirroring)

Setting up a mirror is slightly different from using linear mode or RAID-0. We already know that mirroring replicates data across all member disks. This allows a RAID-1 to continue functioning even if a disk fails. The simplest RAID-1 configuration must contain at least two member disks. In this example, */dev/sdb1* and */dev/sdc1* are member disks of the RAID-1 at */dev/md0*:

```
# A RAID-1 with two member disks

raiddev                 /dev/md0
 raid-level             1
 nr-raid-disks          2
 chunk-size             64

 device                 /dev/sdb1
 raid-disk              0

 device                 /dev/sdc1
 raid-disk              1
```

chunk-size has no effect on RAID-1 because no disk striping is involved. But chunk-size is still required as a placeholder. Note also that the persistent-superblock isn't needed for RAID-1. Use *mkraid* to create this array:

```
# mkraid /dev/md0
handling MD device /dev/md0
analyzing super-block
disk 0: /dev/sdb1, 17920476kB, raid superblock at 17920384kB
disk 1: /dev/sdc1, 17920476kB, raid superblock at 17920384kB
```

Or, using *mdadm*:

```
# mdadm -Cv -l1 -n2 /dev/md0 /dev/sd{b,c}1
mdadm: array /dev/md0 started.
```

Whenever a new mirror is created, resynchronization occurs:

```
# cat /proc/mdstat
Personalities : [linear] [raid0] [raid1] [raid5]
read_ahead 1024 sectors
md0 : active raid1 sdc1[1] sdb1[0]
      17920384 blocks [2/2] [UU]
      [=======>.............]  resync = 40.2% (7212864/17920384)
finish=6.4min speed=27652K/sec
unused devices: <none>
```

Now */proc/mdstat* reports information about the array and also includes information about the resynchronization process. Resynchronization takes place whenever a new array that supports data redundancy is initialized for the first time. The resynchronization process ensures that all disks in a mirror contain exactly the same data.

The resynchronization is about 40 percent done and should be completed in less than six and a half minutes. You can begin creating a filesystem on the array even before resynchronization completes, but you probably shouldn't put the array into production until it finishes.

Once the initial synchronization is complete, the progress bar no longer appears in */proc/mdstat*:

```
# cat /proc/mdstat
Personalities : [linear] [raid0] [raid1] [raid5]
read_ahead 1024 sectors
md0 : active raid1 sdc1[1] sdb1[0]
      17920384 blocks [2/2] [UU]

unused devices: <none>
```

When a disk does fail, it's useful to be able to automatically promote another disk into the array to replace the failed disk. When using *raidtools*, the nr-spare-disks and spare-disk parameters are used to define additional fault tolerance features. nr-spare-disks defines the number of extra, unused disks that the array can use to replace failed disks. It's also important to note that the sequence of spare disks begins with zero and is not an offset of the nr-raid-disks variable. The spare-disk parameter is combined with the device parameter to define disks that will be inserted into the array when a member disk fails. In this example, we still have a two-disk mirror consisting of */dev/sdb1* and */dev/sdc1*. But this time, a spare disk (*/dev/sdd1*) is also specified.

```
# A RAID-1 with 2 member disks and 1 spare disk

raiddev            /dev/md0
 raid-level        1
 chunk-size        64
 nr-raid-disks     2
 nr-spare-disks    1

 device            /dev/sdb1
 raid-disk         0

 device            /dev/sdc1
 raid-disk         1

 device            /dev/sdd1
 spare-disk        0
```

Create an array using this *etc/raidtab* file with *mkraid*:

```
# mkraid /dev/md0
handling MD device /dev/md0
analyzing super-block
disk 0: /dev/sdb1, 1614501kB, raid superblock at 1614400kB
disk 1: /dev/sdc1, 1614501kB, raid superblock at 1614400kB
disk 2: /dev/sdd1, 1614501kB, raid superblock at 1614400kB
```

If you are using *mdadm*, the *-x* flag defines the number of spare disks. Member disks are parsed from left to right on the command line. Thus, the first two disks listed in this example (*/dev/sdb1* and */dev/sdc1*) become the active RAID members, and the last disk (*/dev/sdd1*) becomes the spare disk.

```
# mdadm -Cv -l1 -n2 -x1 /dev/md0 /dev/sd{b,c,d}1
mdadm: array /dev/md0 started.
```

If a disk in this array failed, the kernel would remove the failed drive (either */dev/sdb1* or */dev/sdc1*) from */dev/md0*, insert */dev/sdd1* into the array and start reconstruction. In this case */dev/sdc1* has failed, as indicated by (F) in the following listing. The *md* driver has automatically inserted spare disk */dev/sdd1* and begun recovery.

```
# cat /proc/mdstat
Personalities : [linear] [raid0] [raid1] [raid5]
read_ahead 1024 sectors
md0 : active raid1 sdd1[2] sdb1[1](F) sdb1[0]
      17920384 blocks [2/1] [U_]
      [====>...............]  recovery = 20.1% (3606592/17920384)
finish=7.7min speed=30656K/sec
unused devices: <none>
```

RAID-1 is certainly not limited to arrays with only two member disks and one spare disk. The following example describes a four-disk mirror with two dedicated spare disks.

```
raiddev                 /dev/md0
 raid-level             1
 nr-raid-disks          4
 nr-spare-disks         2
 chunk-size             64

 device                 /dev/sdb1
 raid-disk              0

 device                 /dev/sdc1
 raid-disk              1

 device                 /dev/sdd1
 raid-disk              2

 device                 /dev/sde1
 raid-disk              3

 device                 /dev/sdf1
```

```
spare-disk          0

device              /dev/sdg1
spare-disk          1
```

In this example, data is mirrored onto each raid-disk, so there are four copies of the data, while the remaining two disks (*/dev/sdf1* and */dev/sdg1*) are spares that will be inserted automatically as members in the event of a disk failure.

mdadm users can replicate this setup with the following command:

```
# mdadm -Cv -l1 -n4 -x2 /dev/md0 /dev/sd{b,c,d,e,f,g}1
```

Failed disks and spare disks can also be manually removed from and inserted into arrays as well. See the "Managing Disk Failures" section in Chapter 7 for more information on how to manage disk failures.

While this array can withstand multiple disk failures, it has a write overhead equal to its number of member disks. So each block of data is written to disk four times, making this arrangement very reliable, but extremely slow for write operations. Distributing member disks across multiple controllers or I/O channels will help alleviate the write performance bottleneck. In contrast to the write performance hit, read performance is potentially fast because data can be read in parallel from all four members. A solution like this might be ideal for applications that are mission-critical and read-intensive, but that are generally read-only. Video-on-demand is a good example of such a situation.

RAID-4 (Dedicated Parity)

Since RAID-4 requires that a single drive be dedicated for storing parity information, a minimum of three drives are needed to make RAID-4 useful. Using less than three drives would offer no increase in storage capacity over RAID-1.

A two-drive RAID-4 system would not offer better performance or fault tolerance when compared with RAID-1 or RAID-0. Therefore, in situations in which only two drives are available, RAID-0 or RAID-1 should be used. Furthermore, RAID-5 offers much better performance when compared with RAID-4; almost everyone should choose the former.

The following is a sample RAID-4 configuration using */etc/raidtab*:

```
# RAID-4 with three member disks

raiddev                  /dev/md0
 raid-level              4
 chunk-size              64
 persistent-superblock   1
 nr-raid-disks           3

 device                  /dev/sdb1
 raid-disk               0
```

```
device              /dev/sdc1
raid-disk           1

device              /dev/sdd2
raid-disk           2
```

Use *mkraid* to construct this array:

```
# mkraid /dev/md0
handling MD device /dev/md0
analyzing super-block
disk 0: /dev/sdb1, 17920476kB, raid superblock at 17920384kB
disk 1: /dev/sdc1, 17920476kB, raid superblock at 17920384kB
disk 2: /dev/sdd1, 17920476kB, raid superblock at 17920384kB
```

Or *mdadm*:

```
# mdadm -Cv -l4 -c64 -n3 /dev/md0 /dev/sd{b,c,d}1
mdadm: array /dev/md0 started.
```

When this array is initialized, the last member disk listed in */etc/raidtab*, or on the command line using *mdadm*, becomes the parity disk—*/dev/sdd1*, in this case. RAID-4 also supports spare disks.

Like other arrays with redundancy, */proc/mdstat* will indicate that the initial resynchronization phase is underway. Parity RAID resynchronization ensures that all stripes contain the correct parity block.

```
# cat /proc/mdstat
Personalities : [linear] [raid0] [raid1] [raid5]
read_ahead 1024 sectors
md0 : active raid5 sdd1[2] sdc1[1] sdb1[0]
      35840768 blocks level 4, 64k chunk, algorithm 0 [3/3] [UUU]
      [========>...........]  resync = 40.2% (7206268/17920384) finish=8.1min
speed=21892K/sec
unused devices: <none>
```

As with RAID-1, you don't have to wait until the initial resynchronization is complete before you create a filesystem. But remember that until the process is finished, you won't have data redundancy. Notice that this time, the resynchronization is slower than with the RAID-1 we created earlier. That's because parity information must be generated for each stripe. Also, RAID-4 has a write bottleneck caused by its dedicated parity disk. You will also notice that resynchronization for a RAID-4 requires a lot more CPU overhead. Examine the processes *raid5d* and *raid5syncd*, which handle the resynchronization, using *top* or another processes-monitoring program. On my test system, these processes use about 60 percent of the CPU during the resynchronization. That compares to about 2 percent for a RAID-1 initial synchronization.

RAID-5 (Distributed Parity)

RAID-5, for the same reasons as RAID-4, requires a minimum of three disks to be more useful than a RAID-0 or RAID-1 array. Configuration is nearly identical to other levels, except for the addition of the parity-algorithm variable. parity-algorithm is used to select the algorithm that generates and checks the checksum information used to provide fault tolerance. A simple */etc/raidtab* for RAID-5 is shown here:

```
# RAID-5 with three member disks

raiddev                 /dev/md0
 raid-level             5
 chunk-size             64
 persistent-superblock  1
 parity-algorithm       left-symmetric
 nr-raid-disks          3

 device                 /dev/sdb1
 raid-disk              0

 device                 /dev/sdc1
 raid-disk              1

 device                 /dev/sdd1
 raid-disk              2
```

The left-symmetric algorithm will yield the best disk performance for a RAID-5, although this value can be changed to one of the other algorithms (right-symmetric, left-asymmetric, or right-asymmetric). While left-symmetric is the best choice, it is not the default for *raidtools*, so be certain to explicitly specify it in */etc/raidtab*. If you forget to include a parity-algorithm, then the array will default to left-asymmetric.

Execute *mkraid* to create this array:

```
# mkraid /dev/md0
handling MD device /dev/md0
analyzing super-block
disk 0: /dev/sdb1, 17920476kB, raid superblock at 17920384kB
disk 1: /dev/sdc1, 17920476kB, raid superblock at 17920384kB
disk 2: /dev/sdd1, 17920476kB, raid superblock at 17920384kB
```

Create the same RAID-5 using *mdadm*:

```
# mdadm -Cv -l5 -c64 -n3 -pls /dev/md0 /dev/sd{b,c,d}1
mdadm: array /dev/md0 started.
```

mdadm defaults to the left-symmetric algorithm, so you can safely omit the *-p* option from the command line.

After you issue *mkraid* or *mdadm* to create the array, */proc/mdstat* will report information about the array, which, as in RAID-1 and RAID-4, must also undergo an initial resynchronization:

```
# cat /proc/mdstat
Personalities : [linear] [raid0] [raid1] [raid5]
read_ahead 1024 sectors
md0 : active raid5 sdd1[2] sdc1[1] sdb1[0]
      35840768 blocks level 5, 64k chunk, algorithm 2 [3/3] [UUU]
      [========>............] resync = 40.2% (7219776/17920384)
finish=6.0min speed=29329K/sec
unused devices: <none>
```

RAID-5 provides a cost-effective balance of performance and redundancy. You can add more disks, using device/raid-disk, or spare disks, using device/spare-disk, to create large, fault-tolerant storage. The following example is for a five-disk RAID-5, with one spare disk. Notice once again how I've ordered the disks so they alternate between I/O channels.

```
# A 5-disk RAID-5 with one spare disk.

raiddev                 /dev/md0
raid-level              5
chunk-size              64
persistent-superblock   1
nr-raid-disks           5
nr-spare-disks          1

 device                 /dev/sdb1
 raid-disk              0

 device                 /dev/sdf1
 raid-disk              1

 device                 /dev/sdc1
 raid-disk              2

 device                 /dev/sdg1
 raid-disk              3

 device                 /dev/sdd1
 raid-disk              4

# The spare disk.
 device                 /dev/sdh1
 spare-disk             0
```

Or, create the same array using *mdadm*:

```
# mdadm -C -l5 -c64 -n5 -x1 /dev/md0 /dev/sd{b,f,c,g,d,h}1
```

Hybrid Arrays

One of the most important features of software RAID is its ability to use existing arrays as member disks. This property allows you to not only create extremely large arrays, but to combine different RAID levels to achieve different degrees of performance and redundancy. The major benefit of using hybrid arrays is their ability to withstand multiple disk failures.

As I mentioned in Chapter 2, it's advisable to spread member disks across multiple I/O channels whenever possible. This not only increases array performance but, in the case of a mirror, also helps prevent array failure if an I/O channel becomes unavailable because of a disk controller failure or faulty cabling. For example, imagine that */dev/sda* and */dev/sdb* are member disks of */dev/md0*, a RAID-1, and that they are connected to the same controller A. If controller A fails, then all of */dev/md0* becomes unavailable.

Now imagine that each disk is connected to its own controller. For instance, suppose */dev/sda* is connected to controller A and */dev/sdb* is connected to controller B. In this case, either controller A or B can fail without crashing */dev/md0* (see Figure 3-5), because the other controller's disk is still operational.

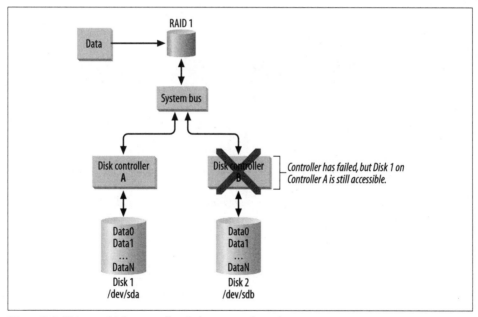

Figure 3-5. Using multiple controllers help prevent downtime.

Dispersing disks among multiple controllers is equally important when working with hybrid arrays. For example, take the case of a RAID-10 (mirrors combined into a stripe). Assume that we have two mirrors that each contain two member disks. */dev/md0* contains */dev/sda* and */dev/sdb*, and */dev/md1* contains */dev/sdc* and */dev/sdd*. If we placed both */dev/sda* and */dev/sdb* on controller A and the remaining disks on controller B, a failure of either controller would crash */dev/md2*, our RAID-0 (Figure 3-6). Since a RAID-0 cannot withstand any disk failures, the entire RAID-10 would also become unavailable.

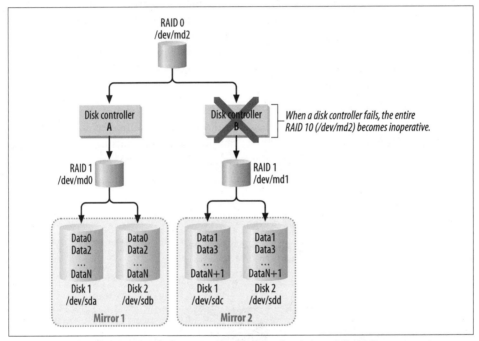

Figure 3-6. If disks are not arranged intelligently, a controller failure will crash a RAID-10.

But what if we arranged our mirrors so that */dev/sda* and */dev/sdc* were on controller A and */dev/sdb* and */dev/sdd* were on controller B? (See Figure 3-7.) In this case, the failure of a single controller would only place our mirrors into degraded mode, leaving */dev/md2* operational.

Remember, you don't have to rearrange hardware to facilitate this arrangement. Just create an */etc/raidtab* or *mdadm* command that reflects the physical layout of your hardware.

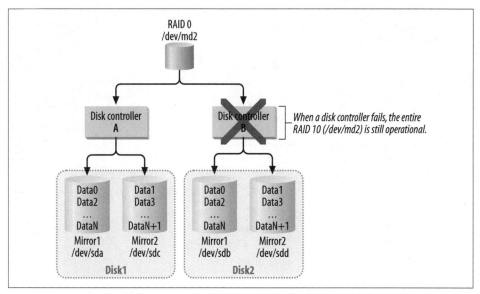

Figure 3-7. Distributing disks means you can survive controller loss.

RAID-10 (striped mirror)

Since */etc/raidtab* is parsed in order, it is essential to define arrays from the bottom up. That is, arrays that are also component disks should appear before the array that contains them. For example, a simple */etc/raidtab* that defines a RAID-10 (two mirrors combined into a stripe) might look like this:

```
A RAID-10: Two 2-disk mirrors are combined into a RAID-0

# The first mirror

raiddev                        /dev/md0
 raid-level                    1
 chunk-size                    64
 nr-raid-disks                 2

 device                        /dev/sdb1
 raid-disk                     0

 device                        /dev/sdc1
 raid-disk                     1

# The second mirror

raiddev                        /dev/md1
```

```
raid-level                      1
chunk-size                      64
nr-raid-disks                   2

device                          /dev/sdd1
raid-disk                       0

device                          /dev/sde1
raid-disk                       1

# The mirrors (/dev/md0 and /dev/md1 are
# combined into a RAID-0.

raiddev                         /dev/md2
 raid-level                     0
 chunk-size                     64
 persistent-superblock          1
 nr-raid-disks                  2

 device                         /dev/md0
 raid-disk                      0

 device                         /dev/md1
 raid-disk                      1
```

Given the preceding file, run *mkraid* on both of the mirrors (*/dev/md0* and */dev/md1*) and finally on the stripe (*/dev/md2*). The same feat can be accomplished with the following *mdadm* commands:

```
# mdadm -C -n2 -l1 /dev/md0 /dev/sd{b,c}1
# mdadm -C -n2 -l1 /dev/md1 /dev/sd{d,e}1
# mdadm -C -n2 -l0 -c64 /dev/md2 /dev/md{0,1}
```

After each RAID-1 is initialized using *mkraid* or *mdadm*, it will commence resynchronization. */proc/mdstat* should report two-disk mirrors at */dev/md0* and */dev/md1* and a RAID-0 at */dev/md2*, which consists of */dev/md0* and */dev/md1*.

```
# cat /proc/mdstat
Personalities : [raid0] [raid1]
read_ahead 1024 sectors
md2 : active raid0 md1[1] md0[0]
      35840640 blocks 64k chunks

md1 : active raid1 sde1[1] sdd1[0]
      17920384 blocks [2/2] [UU]

md0 : active raid1 sdc1[1] sdb1[0]
      17920384 blocks [2/2] [UU]

unused devices: <none>
```

Once all three arrays are activated, simply build a filesystem on the stripe—*/dev/md2*, in this case—and then mount */dev/md2*.

```
mke2fs /dev/md2
mount /dev/md2 /mnt/array
```

You could also add a spare disk to each of the mirroring arrays to make the solution more robust. And you can combine more than two mirrors into a RAID-0:

```
A RAID-10: Three 2-disk mirrors are combined into a RAID-0

# Each mirror has its own spare disk

raiddev                 /dev/md0
  raid-level            1
  chunk-size            64
  nr-raid-disks         2
  nr-spare-disks        1

  device                /dev/sdb1
  raid-disk             0

  device                /dev/sdc1
  raid-disk             1

  device                /dev/sdd1
  spare-disk            0

# Mirror #2

raiddev                 /dev/md1
  raid-level            1
  chunk-size            64
  nr-raid-disks         2
  nr-spare-disks        1

  device                /dev/sde1
  raid-disk             0

  device                /dev/sdf1
  raid-disk             1

  device                /dev/sdg1
  raid-disk             0

# Mirror #3

raiddev                 /dev/md2
  raid-level            1
  chunk-size            64
  nr-raid-disks         2
  nr-spare-disks        1

  device                /dev/sdh1
```

```
raid-disk                    0

device                       /dev/sdi1
raid-disk                    1

device                       /dev/sdj1
raid-disk                    0

# Mirrors /dev/md0, /dev/md1 and /dev/md2 are
# combined into a RAID-0, /dev/md3.

raiddev                      /dev/md3
  raid-level                 0
  chunk-size                 64
  persistent-superblock      1
  nr-raid-disks              3

  device                     /dev/md0
  raid-disk                  0

  device                     /dev/md1
  raid-disk                  1

  device                     /dev/md2
  raid-disk                  2
```

Given the preceding file, run *mkraid* on each component RAID-1 and finally on */dev/ md3*, the RAID-0. Or, with *mdadm*:

```
# mdadm -C -n2 -l1 -x1 /dev/md0 /dev/sd{b,c,d}1
# mdadm -C -n2 -l1 -x1 /dev/md1 /dev/sd{e,f,g}1
# mdadm -C -n2 -l1 -x1 /dev/md1 /dev/sd{h,i,j}1
# mdadm -C -n3 -l0 -c64 /dev/md2 /dev/md{0,1,2}
```

Clearly, it's a waste of resources to provide a separate spare disk to each component array. Unfortunately, the *md* driver does not directly support the sharing of spare disks. However, *mdadm* does let you share spare disks virtually. (See Chapters 4 and 7.)

While RAID-10 is both fast and reliable, the wasted disk space can make it undesirable. Half of all disk space on a RAID-10 is unusable.

RAID-50 (striped parity)

Since the disk requirements for RAID-10 are so high, you might find it more economical to combine RAID-5 into a RAID-0, a hybrid configuration called RAID-50. This hybrid array offers good read and write performance and can survive multiple disk failures, in the same manner that RAID-10 can. RAID-50 uses only one disk's worth of space for each RAID-5 component array, making it more cost-effective. The following */etc/raidtab* file defines two RAID-5 arrays, each consisting of three disks at */dev/md0* and */dev/md1*. Those arrays are combined in a RAID-0 at */dev/md2*.

```
# First RAID-5

raiddev                      /dev/md0
 raid-level                  5
 chunk-size                  64
 persistent-superblock       1
 nr-raid-disks               3
 parity-algorithm            left-symmetric

 device                      /dev/sdb1
 raid-disk                   0

 device                      /dev/sdc1
 raid-disk                   1

 device                      /dev/sdd1
 raid-disk                   2

# Second RAID-5

raiddev                      /dev/md1
 raid-level                  5
 chunk-size                  64
 persistent-superblock       1
 nr-raid-disks               3
 parity-algorithm            left-symmetric

 device                      /dev/sde1
 raid-disk                   0

 device                      /dev/sdf1
 raid-disk                   1

 device                      /dev/sdg1
 raid-disk                   3

# The two RAID-5's are combined into a single
# RAID-0.

raiddev                      /dev/md2
 raid-level                  0
 chunk-size                  64
 persistent-superblock       1
 nr-raid-disks               2

 device                      /dev/md0
 raid-disk                   0

 device                      /dev/md1
 raid-disk                   1
```

Use the following commands to create the same RAID-50 using *mdadm*:

```
# mdadm -C -n3 -l5 -c64 -pls /dev/md0 /dev/sd{b,c,d}1
# mdadm -C -n3 -l5 -c64 -pls /dev/md1 /dev/sd{e,f,g}1
# mdadm -C -n3 -l0 -c64 /dev/md2 /dev/md{0,1}
```

Since each RAID-5 must undergo its initial synchronization, the CPU will be heavily utilized when you create a RAID-50. If the system is performing other tasks, then you might want to wait until each initial synchronization has completed before creating a filesystem on */dev/md2* and carrying out any other administrative tasks. It might also be worthwhile to initialize each RAID-5 individually, waiting for its initial synchronization to complete before creating the second one.

Finishing Touches

If you use *mdadm* to create arrays, then you should probably take a minute to create an */etc/mdadm.conf* file before you move on. First, create the file */etc/mdadm.conf*, using any editor and a DEVICE line that lists all RAID member disks. On my system, for example, I create the file with the following line:

```
DEVICE    /dev/sd*
```

This means that *mdadm* will examine all the *sd* device files on my system (*/dev/sdb1* through */dev/sdh1*) when looking for member disks. Next, you should execute *mdadm* with the *--detail* and *--scan* options to generate array lines and redirect the output so that it is appended to */etc/mdadm.conf*.

```
# mdadm --detail --scan >> /etc/mdadm.conf
```

You should be left with an *mdadm.conf* file that contains the DEVICE line you created, plus an ARRAY line for each active RAID.

```
# cat /etc/mdadm.conf
DEVICE    /dev/sd{b,c,d,e,f,g,h}1
ARRAY /dev/md1 level=raid0 num-devices=5          \
    UUID=66b78871:dc09da58:60f57124:978e5dbf
ARRAY /dev/md0 level=raid1 num-devices=2          \
    UUID=b047f5a4:b6f459e0:fb04a323:46a1a012
```

Arrays that are not active will not be scanned by *mdadm*. Remember that you aren't obligated to create an *mdadm.conf* file, but it will make managing arrays using *mdadm* much easier. Now you can start both arrays with a simple command:

```
# mdadm -As
mdadm: /dev/md1 has been started with 5 drives.
mdadm: /dev/md0 has been started with 2 drives.
```

Without the configuration file, you would need to know at least which disks were members. And you would need to execute a command such as the following for each array, every time you wanted to activate it:

```
# mdadm -A /dev/md1 /dev/sdc1 /dev/sdg1 /dev/sdd1   \
    /dev/sdh1 /dev/sde1
```

If you're using *raidtools*, start arrays with the *raidstart* command:

```
# raidstart /dev/md1
```

Or, start all arrays listed in */etc/raidtab*:

```
# raidstart -a
```

As I mentioned earlier in this chapter, you can stop an active array by using either *raidstop* or *mdadm -S*. Don't forget to unmount filesystems first.

```
# raidstop /dev/md0
# mdadm -S /dev/md1
```

Irrespective of which management tools you decided to use, you can now add entries for your arrays to */etc/fstab*, provided that you are using kernel RAID autodetection. Otherwise, you will need to add entries to your system startup scripts to activate arrays using *mdadm* or *raidstart*.

The Next Step

Even if you spend large amounts of time planning and architecting your array, making a mistake is nearly inevitable. I think the best advice I can give for building these systems is: *don't worry if it doesn't work perfectly the first time around*. Trying out multiple solutions and then deciding which one best suits your needs is much more worthwhile than sitting at a whiteboard for three weeks, trying to plan in advance. Hopefully, this chapter has given you the information you need to get started in building a software RAID solution.

Choosing an appropriate RAID level is only the first step. You might need to trade some of the dollars you had planned to spend on storage capacity for a hardware controller. Chapter 5 offers advice on how to make that decision. But software RAID might help you to prototype the right system without spending much money. The next chapter offers reference material on the *md* driver, *raidtools*, and *mdadm*, which will help supplement the material in this chapter. Chapter 4 also contains more */etc/raidtab* and *mdadm* examples that can help make your configurations more robust by using spare disks and hybrid arrays.

CHAPTER 4

Software RAID Reference

This chapter contains reference information about kernel RAID parameters and management tools, including the *raidtools* package and the newer *mdadm*. It also contains many example configurations and an in-depth guide to software RAID and the */proc* filesystem.

Much of the material in this chapter is an amalgamation of my own experimentation with software RAID, combined with material from manual pages, the Linux kernel source code, and the various versions of the Software-RAID HOWTO and supporting documents. Linas Vepstas wrote the original version of "The Software-RAID HOWTO," which was extremely useful to me when I built my first software RAID. A replacement document, written from the ground up, was released by Jakob Oestergaard in January 2000.

The HOWTO documents, quick-starts, and examples that are distributed with the *raidtools* package and with many versions of Linux often contain erroneous or missing information simply because they are out of date. While I am quick to complain about some existing documentation, I am grateful to all the unpaid volunteers who have, over the years, contributed to various parts of the RAID documentation, the kernel driver documentation, and the *Linux-raid* mailing list, especially Jakob Oestergard, Linas Vepstas, Neil Brown, and Ingo Molnar.

Kernel Options

When you are configuring the kernel, the software RAID kernel features are all found under the *Multiple devices driver support (RAID and LVM)* subsection, regardless of the configuration method you use. Feel free to compile each level into the kernel statically or as a module.

```
[*] Multiple devices driver support (RAID and LVM)
<*>   RAID support
<M>     Linear (append) mode
<*>     RAID-0 (striping) mode
```

```
<M>   RAID-1 (mirroring) mode
<*>   RAID-4/RAID-5 mode
<M>   Multipath I/O support
```

With older versions of the kernel, it was necessary to enable support for *Development and/or Incomplete Code/Drivers*. But with version 2.4, you no longer need to enable that option because the RAID code is stable and included as part of the standard kernel.

Here is a list of kernel options for software RAID.

Multiple devices driver support (CONFIG_MD)

CONFIG_MD enables support for representing multiple physical block devices as a single logical device. CONFIG_MD must be enabled before RAID options will appear during kernel configuration. CONFIG_MD is also needed for LVM support.

RAID support (CONFIG_BLK_DEV_MD)

CONFIG_BLK_DEV_MD activates the base RAID driver, which contains code that is shared among all software RAID levels. Individual RAID levels must be selected after CONFIG_BLK_DEV_MD is enabled. RAID levels will not appear during kernel configuration unless this option is selected first.

Linear (append) mode (CONFIG_MD_LINEAR)

CONFIG_MD_LINEAR allows multiple drives to be concatenated end-to-end so that when a single member disk becomes full, data will be written to the next disk until all disks are full.

RAID-0 (striping) mode (CONFIG_MD_RAID0)

CONFIG_MD_RAID0 enables support for RAID-0 (striping), which allows multiple disks to be arranged so they are evenly filled, one chunk at a time. If disks of differing sizes are used, data is evenly distributed across all disks until one disk becomes full. The data then continues to be evenly distributed across remaining disks, although you won't experience the same level of performance. Thus, if three 4 GB drives and a single 6 GB drive are used, data is evenly distributed across all disks until the 4 GB drives (16 GB of data) are full. At that point, data is written only to the remaining 6 GB disk.

RAID-1 (mirroring) mode (CONFIG_MD_RAID1)

CONFIG_MD_RAID1 activates support for disk mirroring. Each disk in a RAID-1 contains exactly the same data. There is an additional write operation for each disk, making write performance with RAID-1 slower than with other RAID levels. (Note that write performance is a function of the number of member disks.) However, read performance is improved because requests are distributed across each disk in the mirror. If disks used in a RAID-1 are not the same size, each disk is truncated to the size of the smallest disk.

RAID-4/RAID-5 mode (CONFIG_MD_RAID5)

CONFIG_MD_RAID5 enables RAID-4/RAID-5 mode and activates support for either of these parity RAID levels. The choice between the two is made in an */etc/*

raidtab configuration file or on the command line with *mdadm*, and not in the kernel configuration itself. While RAID-4 stores parity information on a single disk, RAID-5 provides redundancy by spreading parity information across each member disk. That means RAID-5 performs better than RAID-4 because operations are distributed across all disks, instead of all but one disk. Like RAID-1, devices used in a RAID-4 or RAID-5 are truncated to the size of the smallest disk.

Multipath I/O support (CONFIG_MD_MULTIPATH)

CONFIG_MD_MULTIPATH enables support for multipath, which allows Linux to address a single disk using multiple controller paths. Disks that support multipath operation are connected to more than one I/O channel. If one controller or channel becomes unavailable, the operating system is still able to communicate with the disk. Multipath is very new feature and is not covered in this book.

Deprecated Kernel Options

The following options are no longer shown in the configuration options for current kernel revisions. These features were originally experimental, but are now a standard part of the RAID subsystem. If you are using a kernel newer than 2.2.X, the options are enabled transparently as part of multiple devices support (CONFIG_BLK_DEV_MD). When using older kernels, you must explicitly enable these features if you require them.

Autodetect support (CONFIG_AUTODETECT_RAID)

CONFIG_AUTODETECT_RAID enables support for RAID autodetection during boot time. Traditionally, users have to execute commands from their *init* scripts in order to manually activate RAID devices. Autodetection allows the kernel to scan block devices for information about the arrays they belong to, and consequently to activate the devices while the system boots. This saves administrators from having to run the *raidstart* command in the system's startup files or at the command line. For RAID devices to be successfully autodetected, you must use *fdisk* or an equivalent partitioning program to set them to partition type *Linux Raid Auto* (0xFD). Some programs might simply list *Linux RAID* as the partition type. Please refer to the "Partitioning with fdisk" section of Chapter 3 for more information on this.

Boot support (CONFIG_MD_BOOT)

CONFIG_MD_BOOT is available with the RAID patches for older kernels and is standard in 2.4 and higher. Boot support allows arrays to be used at boot time, meaning that Linux can boot from a software RAID-1. That means a disk failure won't result in an unavailable system after a reboot. In addition to enabling this kernel parameter, you need to pass special flags to the boot loader. You can find details on using LILO to boot an array in Chapter 7.

md Block Special Files

The block special files */dev/md[0-255]* provide access to software RAID devices. The *md* driver uses a major number of 9. On most systems, all of these files are created when the system is installed. If an *md* block special file is missing, you will get an error like: `error opening /dev/md31: No such file or directory` from *mdadm* or *raidtools*. You can create the file yourself using the *mknod* command. The following example creates the block special file used to access */dev/md31* with a umask of 0660:

```
# mknod -m 0660 /dev/md31 b 9 31
# chown root.disk /dev/md31
```

I specified b for block special file, 9 for the *md* major number, and 31 for the minor number. In general, the minor number and the number for the device name are the same. I also made certain that user and group ownership was set to root and disk, respectively. Repeat these commands for any device file you need to create manually.

Some distributions also come with the *MAKEDEV* program, usually found in */dev*, although sometimes it is found as a symbolic link to */sbin/MAKEDEV*. *MAKEDEV* can be used to create all the special files for any character or block device. It's more user-friendly than *mknod*, but *MAKEDEV* might not be available on all systems.

The following example uses *MAKEDEV* to create all the block special *md* files:

```
# /dev/MAKEDEV -v md
create md0                    b   9   0 root:disk 660
create md1                    b   9   1 root:disk 660
[...]
create md30                   b   9  30 root:disk 660
create md31                   b   9  31 root:disk 660
```

MAKEDEV will overwrite old device nodes. If you are working on a system on which the major or minor device numbers for your *md* devices have been altered, please be careful.

/proc and Software RAID

The */proc* filesystem is a virtual filesystem that provides information about the system and the running kernel. Files located in */proc* provide vital information about memory, devices, and processes. Here is also where you look for current information on active RAID devices. Virtual files under */proc* provide information in real time. By default, the kernel is configured to support the */proc* filesystem. However, to be certain that your kernel supports */proc*, look for its entry in the File systems subsection of the kernel configuration:

```
File systems --->
  ...
  [*] /proc file system support
  ...
```

Files located in *proc* are usually displayed using the *cat* command, but you can use any program in which you can view a text file. Most of the files in *proc* merely provide information (they are read-only), but some actually offer the means to manipulate the way a running kernel operates. In that case, administrators usually write new values to a file using the *echo* command.

/proc/mdstat

/proc/mdstat provides a way to examine the state of the *md* driver, including information about active software arrays. When no arrays are running, displaying */proc/mdstat* simply shows which RAID levels the kernel supports.

```
# cat /proc/mdstat
Personalities : [linear] [raid0] [raid1] [raid5]
read_ahead not set
unused devices: <none>
```

In this example, there are no active arrays, but this kernel supports linear, RAID-0, RAID-1, and RAID-4/5. The read_ahead value is not currently set, because no arrays are active. read_ahead defines the number of sectors the kernel should cache during sequential reads. Finally, unused devices is also empty, because there are no devices in the *md* subsystem that are not currently in use by an array.

If arrays are defined, */proc/mdstat* provides detailed information about them, as shown in the following code:

```
# cat /proc/mdstat
Personalities : [linear] [raid0] [raid1] [raid5]
read_ahead 1024 sectors
md2 : active raid1 sde1[1] sdd1[0]
      17920384 blocks [2/2] [UU]

md1 : active raid0 sdc1[1] sdb1[0]
      35840768 blocks 64k chunks
```

First, note that read_ahead is now set to 1024 sectors. That means that during sequential reads, the kernel will attempt to cache a maximum of 1024 sectors worth of data, or about 512 K (1024 sectors, with approximately 512 bytes per sector). The default value of 1024 sectors is a hard limit set by the *md* driver. Next, each array is listed, with the most recently activated array first. In this case, */dev/md2*, a RAID-1, is listed first because it was activated most recently. Let's examine */dev/md2* one line at a time to get a better understanding of the information reported:

```
md2 : active raid1 sde1[1] sdd1[0]
```

The first line is fairly straightforward. The array */dev/md2* is an active RAID-1 containing two member disks: */dev/sde1* and */dev/sdd1*. The numbers in square brackets ([ ]) following each member disk indicate the index number of that member disk. The information corresponds to either a raid-disk entry in */etc/raidtab* or to the order in which member disks were listed on the command line using *mdadm*. Here, */dev/sdd1* is the first raid-disk and */dev/sde1* is the second.

```
17920384 blocks [2/2] [UU]
```

This line shows information about the state of the array and its size. This array contains 17920384 blocks. Blocks reported in */proc/mdstat* are always 1 KB in size. The next data element [2/2] shows that there are two disks in the array and that both are active. The final field [UU] shows that both disks are error-free and operating normally. If a disk had failed, these fields would indicate that disks were missing from the array and which disks had failed. For example:

```
17920384 blocks [2/1] [_U]
```

Notice that there are two member disks, but only one disk is currently operational ([2/1]). The next field ([_U]) uses the underscore to indicate that the first disk has failed.

Depending on what type of array is defined, slightly different information is available through */proc/mdstat*.

```
md1 : active raid0 sdc1[1] sdb1[0]
      35840768 blocks 64k chunks
```

This example describes a RAID-0 at */dev/md1*. The first line provides the same information that the RAID-1 example provides, but the second line omits information about the status of member disks and instead includes information about the chunk-size. Since RAID-0 does not support redundancy, there's no need to provide information about how many member disks are online versus how many have failed. The failure of a single disk in a RAID-0 means that the entire array is failed. chunk-size, which isn't a factor when working with RAID-1, is a requirement for RAID-0. So chunk-size information, instead of failure information, is provided for RAID-0 arrays.

RAID-4 and RAID-5 arrays show a combination of the information provided for RAID-0 or RAID-1 arrays:

```
md1 : active raid5 sde1[3] sdd1[2] sdc1[1] sdb1[0]
      53761152 blocks level 5, 64k chunk, algorithm 2 [4/4] [UUUU]
```

Here, a RAID-5 array defined at */dev/md1* contains four member disks. The second line provides information about the chunk size and health of the array (four out of four disks are operational). In addition, the output shows the parity algorithm used, which is algorithm 2 in this case, corresponding to the left-symmetric algorithm. The numeric value reported here comes from a case switch found in the kernel RAID-5 code in the file */usr/src/linux/drivers/block/raid5.c*. Each of the usable algorithms is defined there by name.

You might be wondering why the second line contains redundant information about which RAID level is in use. Let's look at a RAID-4 example to clarify.

```
md1 : active raid5 sde1[3] sdd1[2] sdc1[1] sdb1[0]
        53761152 blocks level 4, 64k chunk, algorithm 0 [4/4] [UUUU]
```

Notice that raid5 is listed as the array type on the first line, but level 4 is listed on the second line. That's because RAID-4 uses the RAID-5 driver. So when working with these RAID levels, be certain to examine the second line of *md* device output to make certain that the proper RAID level is reported. Finally, while parity algorithm 0 (left asymmetric) is listed, the parity algorithm has no effect on RAID-4. The entry is simply a placeholder and can be safely ignored.

Failed disks

When a disk fails, its status is reflected in */proc/mdstat*.

```
md1 : active raid1 sdc1[1] sdb1[0](F)
        17920384 blocks [2/1] [_U]
```

The first line lists disks in backward order, from most recently added to first added. In this example, the (F) marker indicates that */dev/sdb1* has failed. Note on the following line that there are two disks in the array, but only one of them is active. The next element shows that the first disk (*/dev/sdb1*) is inactive and the second (*/dev/sdc1*) is in use. So a U denotes a working disk, and an _ denotes a failed disk. The output is a bit counterintuitive because the order of disks shown in the first line is the opposite of the order of U or _ elements in the second line. Furthermore, the order in both lines can change as disks are added or removed.

Resynchronization and reconstruction

/proc/mdstat also provides real-time information about array reconstruction and resynchronization. The following mirroring array is nearly halfway done with its initial synchronization.

```
md1 : active raid1 sdc1[1] sdb1[0]
        17920384 blocks [2/2] [UU]
        [=========>..........]  resync = 46.7% (8383640/17920384)
    finish=5.4min speed=29003K/sec
```

In this example, the process is 46.7 percent complete (also indicated by the progress bar). The first number in parentheses indicates how many blocks are ready, out of the total number of blocks (the second number). The resynchronization is expected to take another 5.4 minutes, at the rate of roughly 29 MB (29003K) per second.

Recovery looks nearly identical, except that the failed disk and the newly inserted disk are both displayed.

```
md1 : active raid1 sdd1[2] sdc1[1] sdb1[0](F)
        17920384 blocks [2/1] [_U]
        [=>..................]  recovery =  6.1% (1096408/17920384)
    finish=8.6min speed=32318K/sec
```

Note that on the third line, the process is called recovery. Remember from Chapter 3 that recovery occurs when a new disk is inserted into an array after a disk fails. Resynchronization, on the other hand, happens when a new array is created or when disks aren't synchronized.

Although three disks are listed on the first output line, only two disks appear as array members on the second line. That's because, when this array was built, only two member disks were defined. So the number of member disks will always remain constant. Each failed disk, like active member disks and spare disks, has its own disk index. When a disk in the array fails, it is removed from the raid-disk index and added to the failed-disk index, and that's why the array disk count remains at two.

Once the recovery is complete, remove the old failed disk using *raidhotremove* or *mdadm -r*, and the */proc/mdstat* entry will return to normal.

```
md1 : active raid1 sdd1[0] sdc1[1]
      17920384 blocks [2/2] [UU]
```

If the spare disk also fails during recovery, the *md* driver will halt the reconstruction process and report both failures in */proc/mdstat*, unless additional spare disks are available. In that case, the *md* driver will insert the next available spare disk and restart the recovery process.

```
md0 : active raid5 sdh1[4](F) sdg1[3] sdd1[2] sdf1[1](F) sdb1[0]
      53761152 blocks level 5, 64k chunk, algorithm 2 [4/3] [U_UU]
            resync=DELAYED
unused devices: <none>
```

/proc/sys/dev/raid

The */proc/sys* directory provides interfaces for manipulating tunable kernel parameters. These parameters, which affect various aspects of the kernel, can be fine-tuned while the system is running. For more general information about */proc/sys*, consult the file in the */usr/src/linux/Documentation/sysctl* directory of your kernel source code, as well as */usr/src/linux/Documenation/filesystems/proc.txt*.

Two files in the */proc/sys/dev/raid* subdirectory provide a way to tune the speed at which array resynchronization (and reconstruction) takes place. speed_limit_min and speed_limit_max define the minimum and maximum speeds at which resynchronization occur. The latter is especially useful on slower, or heavily utilized, systems, where you might find that the resynchronization process slows down the system too much. In that case, you could change the maximum speed—in effect, throttling the resynchronization process to a more suitable level. The *md* driver does provide its own I/O thottling and will attempt to perform recovery nonintrusively, but using speed_limit_min and speed_limit_max can provide a quick fix if something goes haywire.

You'll need to experiment with your system to see the maximum speed it can handle. Adjusting the minimum speed affects the low-end limit for resynchronization. It might be a good idea to simulate a drive failure and play with these values so that you aren't surprised when a real disk failure happens.

 You can simulate a disk failure by using the *raidsetfaulty* or *mdadm --fail* commands, which are described later in this chapter. You can also simulate a disk failure by disconnecting the cable connected to a drive or by removing a drive from a hot-swap enclosure. Remember, as I warned in the section "Hot-swap" in Chapter 2, that you should not disconnect hardware while the system is powered on, unless you have equipment that supports this operation. When simulating a disk failure, the *md* driver will not register that a disk has failed until an I/O operation is performed. That means you might have to access or create a file on the array before the *md* driver reports the failure. Running the *sync* command to flush filesystem buffers from memory to disk might also be required.

The default limits (100 KB and 100,000 KB, respectively) can be changed by echoing new values into the pseudofiles:

```
# echo "5000" > /proc/sys/dev/raid/speed_limit_min
# echo "50000" > /proc/sys/dev/raid/speed_limit_max
```

This changes the low and high limits to 5 MB and 50 MB, respectively. You can add the above commands to your system initialization scripts if you want to change the default values of speed_limit_min and speed_limit_max automatically each time the system boots. Most distributions now provide the configuration file */etc/sysctl.conf* to preserve changes to */proc/sys* across reboots. For instance, you can alter resynchronization speeds by adding the following lines to */etc/sysctl.conf*:

```
dev.raid.speed_limit_min = 5000
dev.raid.speed_limit_max = 50000
```

Consult the manual pages for *sysctl* and *sysctl.conf* for further details.

raidtools

raidtools is the traditional package used to manage software arrays. Although the newer *mdadm* is more feature-rich, *raidtools* is in wider use throughout the software RAID community. While it's a bit more complex to manage arrays using *raidtools*, the package has proved reliable for many years. *raidtools* has remained at version 0. 90 for several years, but the prerelease for version 1.0 of raidtools became available during the course of this writing, although it has not been officially released yet. The new version has some new utilities, including a tool that allows users to generate */etc/*

raidtab files by querying an active array, which is very useful if you've accidentally deleted your */etc/raidtab* file. The additions to version 1.0 are covered in this section, but keep in mind that I used a narrowly released beta version during my testing, and that some functionality might have changed since then.

Version 1.0 fixes several known bugs in the 0.90 release of *raidtools*. *raidtools-20010914* (version 0.90.0), in addition to having some minor bugs, was released without a vital utility, *raidsetfaulty*.This utility is used to manually induce a disk failure and had been included with previous releases. Instead, *raidtools-20010914* shipped with a new program named *raidhotgenerateerror*, whose name makes it look like a replacement for *raidsetfaulty*. Unfortunately, *raidhotgenerateerror* does not perform the same function as *raidsetfaulty* and should not be used as a replacement. *raidhotgenerateerror* is merely a utility for testing error handling in the *md* driver. This has caused some confusion among Linux RAID users. Because of these inconsistencies, I advise against using *raidtools-20010914*. Instead, download and use the previous release *raidtools-19990824* from *ftp.kernel.org/pub/daemons/raid/alpha*. If you are working with a version of *raidtools* that came installed with your distribution, check to see if you have */sbin/raidsetfaulty* on your system. If it doesn't exist, then it's likely that you are working with a repackaged version of *raidtools-20010914*. In that case, I recommend installing the previous version from source, or using a newer version if one is available and tested. The beta version of *raidtools-1.0* corrects many of the problems with the *raidtools-20010914* release and also contains *raidsetfaulty*. It likely that *raidtools-1.0* will be in wide release by the time this book is in print.

The /etc/raidtab File

The current *raidtools* package requires a configuration file, which, by default, is named */etc/raidtab*. The */etc/raidtab* file contains a stanza about each software array connected to the system. (A stanza is a collection of keywords and variables that describe a single array.) The configuration is parsed from top to bottom so that previously defined arrays may be used in subsequent stanzas. This is useful when creating hybrid arrays like RAID-10, but it also means that the order of the stanzas in */etc/raidtab* is extremely important. Each stanza begins with a `raiddev` directive and continues with other directives from the following list.

`raiddev` *mddevice*

> The `raiddev` parameter begins the configuration of an array. All subsequent directives are assumed to refer to the most recent `raiddev` directive. `raiddev` takes the full path to the device block special file as its argument (for example, `raiddev` */dev/md2*). A unique `raiddev` directive is required for each array.

`raid-level` *level*

> `raid-level` specifies the mode of the current array. This parameter takes an alphanumeric value (see Table 4-1) that corresponds to kernel RAID levels.

Table 4-1. raid-level parameters

raidtab entry	Description
linear	Linear concatenation
0	Striping
1	Mirroring
4	Single parity drive
5	Distributed parity
multipath	Multipath I/O

> Each `raid-level` directive defined in */etc/raidtab* corresponds to the previously defined raiddev entry. In addition, support for the RAID level you have selected using `raid-level` must be compiled into your kernel, or be available as a loadable module, before the array can be started.

`nr-raid-disks` *integer*

> The `nr-raid-disks` directive defines the number of active member disks in the current array. This number does not include any spare disks that might be used in an array that supports failover. (Use the `nr-spare-disks` parameter to indicate the number of spare disks in the current array.) `nr-raid-disks` takes an integer value greater than zero and is required once for each array that is defined using the raiddev parameter. Subsequently, a number of device and `raid-disk` entries equal to the number defined with `nr-raid-disks` is required to specify the block special file and disk order for each member disk.

`nr-spare-disks` *integer*

> Spare disks provide a mechanism for hot failover in the event of a drive failure. `nr-spare-disks` takes an integer value greater than zero and equal to the number of available spares. As with `nr-raid-disks`, spares must be specified later by using the device and `spare-disk` parameter. Spare disks are optional for arrays that support failover (mirroring, RAID-4, and RAID-5). RAID-0 and linear mode do not support the use of spare disks, so `nr-spare-disks` is never used with these RAID levels. Spares need to be defined in */etc/raidtab* if you want automatic failover. You can manually replace a failed disk using *raidhotremove* and *raidhotadd*, but that requires user intervention.

`persistent-superblock` *boolean*

> The `persistent-superblock` directive determines whether an array contains a RAID superblock. The RAID superblock allocates a small area for metadata at the end of each member disk. This metadata allows the kernel to identify disk

order and membership even in the event that a drive has moved to a different controller. It is essential for autodetection. persistent-superblock should be enabled for any newly created array.

This parameter should be set to zero only when you need to provide backward compatibility with versions of the *md* driver that did not support a RAID superblock (version 0.35 and earlier). Set persistent-superblock to zero when a legacy array is being used with the new *md* driver.

parity-algorithm *algorithm_name*

The parity-algorithm directive specifies the algorithm used to generate parity blocks. Note that this directive is used only with RAID-5. Parity is used to reconstruct data during a drive failure. There are four choices available, and they determine how parity is distributed throughout the array (Figure 4-1). *Left-symmetric*, *right-symmetric*, *left-asymmetric*, and *right-asymmetric* are all valid choices, but *left-symmetric* is recommended because it yields the best overall performance.

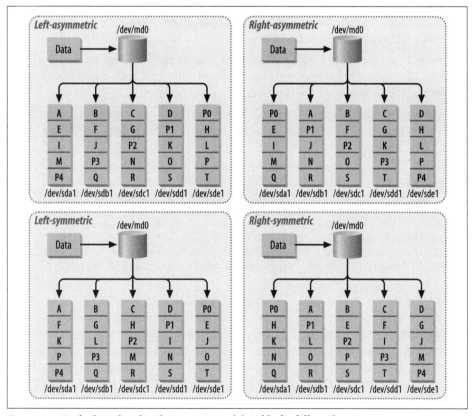

Figure 4-1. Each algorithm distributes parity and data blocks differently.

You can specify the parity-algorithm by name in */etc/raidtab* or use its numerical equivalent (see Table 4-2). If you fail to specify a parity-algorithm in */etc/raidtab*, the *md* driver will default to *left-asymmetric*, which is not an optimal choice. So be certain to select *left-symmetric* explicitly.

Table 4-2. Parity algorithms

Name	Numeric value
left-asymmetric (default)	0
right-asymmetric	1
left-symmetric (best choice)	2
right-symmetric	3

chunk-size *size*

> chunk-size specifies the size of the array stripe in kilobytes. Values may range from 4 to 4096 kilobytes and must be powers of two. A bigger chunk-size will work well for large, sequential operations, but a smaller chunk-size will yield better performance for smaller, random operations. Most users should choose a chunk-size of about 64 KB.
>
> With linear mode, the chunk-size specifies the rounding factor for the array. The rounding factor helps evenly group I/O operations. It's similar to the chunk-size, except it does not spread I/O across multiple disks.
>
> chunk-size has no effect on RAID-1, but to satisfy error checking in *raidtools*, you must specify a valid chunk-size for any RAID-1 defined in */etc/raidtab*.

> The chunk-size is written into the RAID superblock during array initialization. If you determine that you need to adjust the chunk-size after your array is up and running, you will need to rebuild the array using *mkraid* or *mdadm*. Be advised that your data will be lost if you need to change the chunk-size for an array that has already been brought online. It is possible to adjust the chunk-size of an existing array using *raidreconf*, but all the caveats regarding *raidreconf* still apply. See the "raidreconf" reference entry later in this chapter.

device *devpath*

> The device directive specifies the block special device of an individual array member. The full path to the block device should be used. The total number of device entries must equal the sum of the numbers defined by nr-raid-disks and nr-spare-disks. In an array with four nr-raid-disks and one nr-spare-disk, a total of five device entries are required. Each device entry must be paired with either a raid-disk or a spare-disk index entry.

raid-disk *index*

> raid-disk takes an integer value that indicates the sequence number of a member disk. The value of the raid-disk directive should increase sequentially for each new device entry. After a new array is defined using raiddev, the index number for all device entries is reset. That is to say, each array has a separate list of member disks starting at zero.

spare-disk *index*

> The spare-disk directive also takes an integer value beginning with zero. This parameter indicates the order of spare disks in an array. In the event of a disk failure, available spare disks will be brought online in the order in which they are indexed in */etc/raidtab*.

parity-disk *index*

> parity-disk specifies an out-of-sequence member disk as the parity drive in a RAID-4 array. Normally, the last member disk is used for parity. However, the parity-disk directive allows administrators to flag any member disk as a parity drive. This directive is accompanied by both a device entry and a raid-disk entry.

failed-disk *index*

> The failed-disk parameter lets you flag one or more member disks as failed during array initialization. Flagging a device as failed can be useful for testing data redundancy without having to force a drive failure through a less gentle method. Flagging a device as failed also allows you to evaluate the performance of parity algorithms. Finally, the parameter can be used to create an array with a missing disk, which is a useful trick to use as part of migrating an existing system disk to software RAID. (See "Converting to Software RAID" in Chapter 7 for more details.) failed-disk takes an integer value beginning with zero. Much like the parity-disk directive, failed-disk should be accompanied by device and raid-disk entries.

raidtools Commands

The following referemce section describes the commands in the *raidtools* package. The fundamental command is *mkraid* command, which is responsible for creating a RAID device.

lsraid

```
lsraid [mode] [options] -a mddevice
lsraid [mode] [options] -d memberdevice
```

lsraid is included with release 1.0 of *raidtools*. It allows users to examine arrays and generate */etc/raidtab* files by querying active arrays. *lsraid* is useful for checking devices, diagnosing problems, and recovering lost configuration files. *lsraid* was written by Joel Becker at Oracle Corporation.

Options

-A

> Specifies array mode. Displays information about an array. When combined with the *-a* option, array mode will query an active array. When combined with the *-d* option, array mode will read the RAID superblock from a member disk instead of querying the array.

-D

> Denotes disk mode. Displays information about member disks. When used with the *-a* option, disk mode returns information about each array member. When combined with *-d*, disk mode returns information about the specified member disks.

-R

> Specifies raidtab mode. Queries an array or member disk and generates an */etc/raidtab* file based on the RAID superblock it finds.

-a device

> Selects an active *md* device to query. If the *md* device is inactive, *lsraid* indicates the device major and minor numbers and specifies that the array is offline.

-d device

> Selects which block device (member disk) to query. *lsraid* reads the RAID superblock from the member disk.

-f

> When combined with *-A*, displays only member disks that have failed.

-g

> When combined with *-A*, displays only member disks that are working.

-s

> When combined with *-A*, displays only spare disks in an array.

-l

> When combined with *-D*, displays the superblock from any member disk that may not be consistent with the rest of the array.

-h, --help

> Displays configuration flags and exits.

-V, --version

> Displays the command version and exits.

Example usage

The following displays information about an *md* device:

```
# lsraid -A -a /dev/md0
[dev   9,   0] /dev/md0                                      \
    226805E6.2D643610.E36B8421.BBD29055 online
[dev   8,  17] /dev/sdb1                                     \
    226805E6.2D643610.E36B8421.BBD29055 good
[dev   8,  33] /dev/sdc1                                     \
    226805E6.2D643610.E36B8421.BBD29055 good
[dev   8,  49] /dev/sdd1                                     \
    226805E6.2D643610.E36B8421.BBD29055 good
```

The following lists information about the array of which */dev/sdb1* is a member:

```
# lsraid -A -d /dev/sdb1
[dev   9,   0] /dev/md0                                    \
    226805E6.2D643610.E36B8421.BBD29055 online
[dev   8,  17] /dev/sdb1                                   \
    226805E6.2D643610.E36B8421.BBD29055 good
[dev   8,  33] /dev/sdc1                                   \
    226805E6.2D643610.E36B8421.BBD29055 good
[dev   8,  49] /dev/sdd1                                   \
    226805E6.2D643610.E36B8421.BBD29055 good
```

The following uses multiple instances of *-a* or *-d* to query more than one device at a time:

```
# lsraid -A -a /dev/md0 -a /dev/md1
[dev   9,   0] /dev/md0                                    \
    226805E6.2D643610.E36B8421.BBD29055 online
[dev   8,  17] /dev/sdb1                                   \
    226805E6.2D643610.E36B8421.BBD29055 good
[dev   8,  33] /dev/sdc1                                   \
    226805E6.2D643610.E36B8421.BBD29055 good
[dev   8,  49] /dev/sdd1                                   \
    226805E6.2D643610.E36B8421.BBD29055 good

[dev   9,   1] /dev/md1                                    \
    F12F6203.49568B65.232305F6.08909BDA online
[dev   8,  97] /dev/sdg1                                   \
    F12F6203.49568B65.232305F6.08909BDA good
[dev   8, 113] /dev/sdh1                                   \
    F12F6203.49568B65.232305F6.08909BDA good
```

lsraid with the -R option is especially useful for generating an */etc/raidtab* file that might have been lost because of file corruption or user error:

```
# lsraid -R -a /dev/md0
# This raidtab was generated by lsraid version 0.3.0.
# It was created from a query on the following devices:
#     /dev/md0

# md device [dev 9, 0] /dev/md0 queried online
raiddev /dev/md0
        raid-level            0
        nr-raid-disks         3
        nr-spare-disks        0
        persistent-superblock 1
        chunk-size            64

        device                /dev/sdb1
        raid-disk             0
        device                /dev/sdc1
        raid-disk             1
        device                /dev/sdd1
        raid-disk             2
```

The previous example works only with an online array. If the array is offline, you can combine the -R and -d options to generate an */etc/raidtab* based on the RAID superblocks found on individual disks. *lsraid* will attempt to collate member disks so you can use multiple instances of *-d* to query all potential member disks, letting *lsraid* sort out the mess for you.

```
# lsraid -R -d /dev/sdb1 -d /dev/sdc1 -d /dev/sdd1 -d /dev/sde1 -d /dev/sdf1 -d /dev
    /sdg1 -d /dev/sdh1
lsraid: Device "/dev/sde1" does not have a valid raid superblock
lsraid: Device "/dev/sdf1" does not have a valid raid superblock
# This raidtab was generated by lsraid version 0.3.0.
# It was created from a query on the following devices:
#       /dev/sdb1
#       /dev/sdc1
#       /dev/sdd1
#       /dev/sde1
#       /dev/sdf1
#       /dev/sdg1
#       /dev/sdh1

# md device [dev 9, 0] /dev/md0 queried online
raiddev /dev/md0
    raid-level              0
    nr-raid-disks           3
    nr-spare-disks          0
    persistent-superblock   1
    chunk-size              64

    device                  /dev/sdb1
    raid-disk               0
    device                  /dev/sdc1
    raid-disk               1
    device                  /dev/sdd1
    raid-disk               2

# md device [dev 9, 1] /dev/md1 queried online
raiddev /dev/md1
    raid-level              1
    nr-raid-disks           2
    nr-spare-disks          0
    persistent-superblock   1
    chunk-size              64

    device                  /dev/sdg1
    raid-disk               0
    device                  /dev/sdh1
    raid-disk               1
```

Redirect the output of *lsraid -R* to create or append an */etc/raidtab* file.

mkraid

mkraid [options] mddevice

mkraid (make raid) creates a RAID device from a set of block devices. All previous data on the block devices will be lost, so be careful to back up any data on drives that you are planning to include in an array. *mkraid* must be used to create arrays before filesystems are built and requires an */etc/raidtab* file for successful execution. See the "Example Usage" section below for details on the usage of *mkraid*.

Options

-c, --configfile filename
Specifies the use of a configuration file other than the default */etc/raidtab*.

-f, --force, --really-force, -R
Forces the initialization, even if data or filesystems are detected on any of the block devices to be included in the array. This is a fail-safe to prevent uninitiated users from accidentally destroying their data. The *--really- force* or *-R* flag is undocumented in the command help and manual pages. When the *-f* or *--force* flags are used, *mkraid* will display an additional warning and request that the command be retyped with the *--really-force* flag.

-h, --help
Displays some helpful information about the command.

-u, --upgrade
Upgrades an old RAID to the current version of the kernel's RAID subsystem. This option brings arrays with a RAID superblock up to the current *md* driver version. It does not convert older arrays without superblocks. It is advisable to back up data before attempting this operation.

-V, --version
Displays the command's version.

Example usage

The following creates an array at */dev/md0*, as described in */etc/raidtab*:

```
# mkraid /dev/md0
```

Using alternate configuration files is extremely useful if you are experimenting with many different types of arrays. That way, you can keep copies of array configurations that have been successful, copying and combining them into */etc/raidtab* when you're ready to go into production. The force flag is also useful when experimenting. The following creates, by force, the array */dev/md1* specified in the alternate configuration file */home/derek/myraidtab*:

```
# mkraid --really-force -c /home/derek/myraidtab /dev/md1
```

The following upgrades an array to the kernel's current version:

```
# raidstop /dev/md0
# mkraid -u /dev/md0
```

raidhotadd

raidhotadd *mdevice memberdevice*

raidhotadd inserts a new disk into a running array. After a failed drive has been removed using *raidhotadd*, you can use this command to add a replacement drive.

When a new drive is introduced into an active array, reconstruction commences. Therefore, it's a wise idea to add a new drive when you are certain that the recovery process will not impact users. There may, of course, be times when waiting is not an option. You can also fine-tune the speed at which recovery occurs in order to minimize the impact on the system. Refer to the "*/proc/sys/dev/raid*" section, earlier in this chapter, for details on how to throttle the recovery process.

Options

raidhotadd has no command-line options. It takes an *md* device and a member disk as its only arguments.

Example usage

The following adds */dev/sdc1* to the array */dev/md0*:

```
# raidhotadd /dev/md0 /dev/sdc1
```

raidhotgenerateerror

raidhotgenerateerror *mddevice memberdevice*

raidhotgenerateerror should not be used to administer arrays. I mention it here only because it has caused some confusion among Linux RAID users, as described near the beginning of the "raidtools" section.

raidhotremove

raidhotremove *mddevice memberdevice*

raidhotremove removes a failed disk or a spare disk from an array. This is useful, in combination with *raidhotadd*, for replacing a failed disk with a new, working disk. You could also use *raidhotremove* to remove a spare disk from an array so that it can be used in another array, which is helpful when only one spare disk is available on a system with multiple arrays. In that case, you could use *raidhotremove* to pull the spare disk from a fully functional array and insert it into an array to make up for a failed disk.

There might be some instances when a disk is generating errors at the bus level, but hasn't been marked as failed by the *md* driver. In that case, first use *raidsetfaulty* to fail the drive manually, then use *raidhotremove* to pull it out of the array.

Options

raidhotremove has no command-line options. It takes an *md* device and a member disk as its only arguments.

Example usage

The following removes */dev/sdc1* from the array */dev/md0*:

```
# raidhotremove /dev/md0 /dev/sdc1
```

 raidhotremove and *raidhotadd* are merely software interfaces to the Linux kernel. They operate independently of any hardware connected to the system. Using these commands does not mean you can safely disconnect and reconnect drives from a powered-on system. Doing this with hardware that does not support hot-swap could result in a complete, unrecoverable system failure. For more information on hot-swap, consult the "Hot-swap" and "Single Connector Attachment (SCA)" sections in Chapter 2 and the "Managing Disk Failures" section in Chapter 7.

raidreconf

```
raidreconf [options] -m mddevice
```

raidreconf can reconfigure certain properties of a RAID-0 or RAID-5 without data loss.

First, it can be used to resize an existing array. Normally, if you wanted to add or remove a disk from an array, you would need to back up your data, create a new array, and then restore the data. *raidreconf* circumvents the backup and restore steps by inserting or removing a device and reorganizing the data so that it spans the remaining disks.

raidreconf can also be used to import or export data to or from an array. That means you can take a single block device and use *raidreconf* to transfer data block-by-block onto an already existing software RAID. You can also export data from an existing array onto a single block device, provided the target device has enough space. *raidreconf* can also convert between RAID-0 and RAID-5. Finally, *raidreconf* can alter the chunk-size of an array.

raidreconf does not support linear mode, RAID-1, or RAID-4 and should never be used with these RAID levels.

raidreconf was originally written by Jakob OEstergaard (he is also its current maintainer), but some critical bug fixes were implemented by Danny Cox. *raidreconf* is included with *raidtools-1.0* and is also available from *http://unthought.net/raidreconf/*.

Be advised that *raidreconf* is still very much beta software, even though it looks like it could be widely distributed with *raidtools* in the near future. I strongly recommend checking its web site and version history for a list of known bugs. Take note of the following warning from *http://unthought.net/raidreconf/*:

> Status is, that we do not currently know of any critical bugs in the software, it has already been used for both conversion and re-sizing of various arrays. However: it is very likely that there are serious bugs that will destroy your data, possibly even on disks not related directly to the array you are re-configuring.

raidreconf is also quite slow and requires that arrays be taken offline before any operations can be performed, which means your data won't be accessible for long periods of time. On my test system, for example, it took about three hours to add a disk to an existing five-disk

RAID-0 (using 18 GB drives). The time it takes to perform operations is directly related to the size in blocks of the original array. For example, converting an existing two-disk RAID-0 to a six-disk RAID-5 took only 53 minutes on the same system, also using 18 GB drives. Despite all these caveats, *raidreconf* is still useful, simply because no alternative is available. Just be certain to make a backup before using it on an array with data (as you should always do when using beta software on critical data).

Options

-o raidtab
> Specifies the *raidtab* file that contains the entry for the current (about to be reconfigured) array.

-n raidtab
> Indicates the *raidtab* file that contains the entry for the new (post-reconfigured) array.

-m mdevice, --mddev mddevice
> Specifies the array to reconfigure (for example, */dev/md0*).

-i device, --import device
> Imports data from a single block device into a new array.

-e device, --export device
> Exports data from an existing array to a single block device.

-h, --help
> Displays some helpful information about the command.

-V, --version
> Displays the command's version.

Example usage

The following example imports data from */dev/sda8* to a new array, */dev/md0*, as defined in */etc/raidtab*.

```
# raidreconf -i /dev/sda8 -n /etc/raidtab -m /dev/md0
```

Since */dev/sda8* and */dev/md0* differ in size, the filesystem that is already on */dev/sda8* will need to be resized once it is copied to */dev/md0*. Since it's an ext2 filesystem, we can use *resize2fs* to change the size of the filesystem to fill the new array. But first, we have to *fsck* the filesystem.

```
# e2fsck -fy /dev/md0
# resize2fs /dev/md0
```

To resize an array, simply make a copy of your */etc/raidtab* file and edit the stanza for the array you want to resize to include a new disk, or to remove an existing one. Then use *raidreconf*. Remember that if you remove a disk, you need to be certain that the resulting array is large enough to store the data that's already on it. Whether you add a disk or remove one, you will need to resize the filesystem, using *resize2fs* or the appropriate utility for the filesystem you have chosen. If you add a disk, you should resize the filesystem after you run *raidreconf*. Shrink the filesystem before running *raidreconf* if you are removing a disk. In the next example, the array */dev/md0*, defined in */etc/raidtab*, will be converted to the array defined in */root/raidtab.new*:

```
# raidreconf -o /etc/raidtab -n /root/raidtab.new -m /dev/md0
```

Once the conversion is completed, manually *fsck* the new array to ensure that everything was successful.

```
# e2fsck -f /dev/md0
```

If *e2fsck* (or another filesystem check program) returns no errors, *raidreconf* was a success. Errors mean that something went wrong and that you will need to restore from backups. Using *e2fsck* to repair any problems that are detected is likely to be a fruitless effort.

You can also change the raid-level in the new *raidtab* file to convert between RAID-0 and RAID-5. *raidreconf* also ships with a HOWTO written by Danny Cox.

raidsetfaulty

raidsetfaulty *mddevice memberdevice*

Use *raidsetfaulty* to mark a member disk as failed. For example, if you suspect there are problems with a disk, but the *md* driver hasn't yet kicked it out of the array, you can use *raidsetfaulty* to fail the disk manually. Once a disk is failed, you can use *raidhotremove* to pull it out of the array.

Options

raidsetfaulty has no command-line options. It takes an *md* device and a member disk as its only arguments.

Example usage

The following marks */dev/sdd1*, a member of */dev/md0*, as failed:

```
# raidsetfaulty /dev/md0 /dev/sdd1
```

Once *raidsetfaulty* is executed, */proc/mdstat* will show that the disk has failed. If a spare disk is available, recovery will automatically begin:

```
# cat /proc/mdstat
Personalities : [linear] [raid0] [raid1] [raid5] [multipath]
read_ahead 1024 sectors
md0 : active raid1 sdb1[2] sdd1[0](F) sdf1[1]
      17920384 blocks [2/1] [_U]
      [>....................]  recovery =  4.2% (764480/17920384)
finish=10.4min speed=27302K/sec
unused devices: <none>
```

raidstart

raidstart *[options] mddevice*

Although the modern kernel can now automatically detect and initialize RAID devices, it might be necessary to manually start a device. Maybe the array was not properly initialized when the system booted, or perhaps you are simply experimenting with various types of arrays. The command is also useful for restarting arrays in the unlikely event that they have crashed.

Options

-a, --all
> Applies the command to all RAID devices found in */etc/raidtab*. You will not need to specify an `mddevice`.

-c, --configfile filename
> Uses a configuration file other than the default */etc/raidtab*.

-h, --help
> Displays some helpful information about the command.

-V, --version
> Displays the command's version.

Example usage

The following starts all arrays described in */etc/raidtab*:

> `# raidstart -a`

The following starts all arrays defined in */home/derek/example-raid0*:

> `# raidstart -a -c /home/derek/example-raid0`

The following starts only the array */dev/md2*, as described in */etc/raidtab*:

> `# raidstart /dev/md2`

The following starts */dev/md2*, as defined in */home/derek/example-raid0*:

> `# raidstart -c /home/derek/example-raid0 /dev/md2`

raidstart can also be included in system initialization scripts. This is quite useful in cases in which you don't want the kernel to automatically detect and activate software arrays. Perhaps you would like to defer array startup until after some other scripts have run, or maybe you are not using MS-DOS partitions and simply can't autostart. Simply add the *raidstart* command to the appropriate system initialization files. Many distributions, in fact, provide an initialization script that automatically parses */etc/raidtab* and activates arrays that it finds there. */etc/rc.d/rc.sysinit* on Red Hat performs this function, for example.

I want to point out that many users report that *raidstart* is unreliable, especially in cases when the first component drive listed in */etc/raidtab* has failed or when major or minor numbers for component disks have changed. For that reason, using kernel autodetection, or even *mdadm*, are recommended alternatives.

raidstop

`raidstop [options] mddevice`

raidstop is the counterpart of *raidstart* and is useful for the same reasons. Since member disks can be allocated to only one array at a time, arrays must be deactivated by using *raidstop* before their member disks can become available to use in new arrays.

Options

-a, --all

Applies command to all devices found in */etc/raidtab*. You will not need to specify an mddevice.

-c, --configfile filename

Specifies the use of a configuration file other than the default */etc/raidtab*.

-h, --help

Displays configuration flags and exits.

-V, --version

Displays the command version and exit.

Example usage

The following stops all devices found in */etc/raidtab*:

    # raidstop -a

The following stops all arrays defined in */home/derek/example-raid0*:

    # raidstop -a -c /home/derek/example-raid0

The following stops */dev/md2*, as defined in */home/derek/example-raid0*:

    # raidstart -c /home/derek/example-raid0 /dev/md2

The following stops only the array */dev/md2*, as described in */etc/raidtab*:

    # raidstart /dev/md2

mdadm

mdadm provides a convenient, single-command interface for managing software arrays under Linux. While *mdadm* is fully functional without the use of a configuration file, it does support a configuration file, */etc/mdadm.conf*, which is more concise and straightforward than */etc/raidtab*. With *mdadm*, the configuration file is created after arrays, as a way to preserve information for arrays and member disks, so that they can be reactivated later. *mdadm* can be used as a total replacement for *raidtools*.

mdadm

    mdadm [mode] mddevice [options] memberdevices

mdadm has several modes of operation: Create, Build, Assemble, and Monitor. Each of these modes has its own command-line switch. In addition to these modes, there are many management features that operate independently. These standalone features are grouped into Manage or Miscellaneous mode. Most *mdadm* options have a long and a short form, although a few options have only a long form, to safeguard against using them accidentally. You can use whichever form you prefer.

General options for mdadm

-h, --help
> Displays general help for *mdadm*. The *--help* option can also be combined with other options to display topic-specific help (for example, *mdadm --create -help*).

-V, --version
> Displays the *mdadm* version.

-v, --verbose
> Increases verbosity. This option can be combined with other options to increase the amount of information that *mdadm* displays.

Create and Build modes

```
mdadm --create mddevice [options] memberdevices
mdadm --build mddevice [options] memberdevices
```

The Create and Build modes are similar in that they are both used to create new arrays. However, Build mode is used only for backward compatibility, to create legacy arrays without a RAID superblock. Never use Build mode to create a new array.

Options

-C, --create
> Creates a new array.

-B, --build
> Creates an old-style array without a RAID superblock.

-c, --chunk=
> Sets the array chunk-size in kilobytes. The chunk-size is a power of two between 4 and 4096. For example, *-c128* or *--chunk=128* sets a chunk-size of 128 KB. The default is 64 KB.

--rounding=
> Sets the rounding factor, which linear mode uses to align I/O operations. The rounding factor is similar to chunk-size, with the exception that it does not distribute operations across multiple disks. The default value of 64 KB should be fine for most users. The same rules that apply to chunk-size apply to rounding (for example, *--rounding=8* for 8 KB rounding).

-l, --level=
> Specifies the RAID level: linear, RAID-0, RAID-1, RAID-4, or RAID-5. For Build mode, only linear and RAID-0 are supported. For example, type *-l5* or *--level=5* for RAID-5.

-p, --parity=, --layout=
> Sets the parity algorithm for RAID-5. The parity algorithmoptions are *left-asymmetric*, *right-asymmetric*, *left-symmetric*, or *right-symmetric*. The best choice is *left-symmetric* (which is also the default). Choices may also be abbreviated as *la*, *ra*, *ls*, and *rs*. Examples include *-pls*, *--parity=left-symmetric*, or *--layout=left-symmetric*.

-n, --raid-disks=

Defines the number of member disks in an array. This is equivalent to `nr-raid-disks` when working with */etc/raidtab* and *raidtools*. Like `nr-raid-disks`, it does not include spare disks. For example, type *-n5* or *--raid-disks=5* for five member disks.

-x, --spare-disks=

Defines the number of spare disks in an array (equivalent to `nr-spare-disks` in */etc/ raidtab*). For example, enter *-x1* or *--spare-disks=1* for a single spare disk.

-z, --size=

Manually sets the size in kilobytes of member disks in a RAID-1, RAID-4, or RAID-5. By default, the size is automatically computed by *mdadm*. The *--size* must be a multiple of the *--chunk-size* and must leave at least 128 KB at the end of each device for the RAID superblock. This is useful when working with disks of varying sizes. It's also useful if the sizes of your disks are incorrectly calculated. For example, with a chunk size of 64 KB, *-z16000* or *--size=16000* sets the size of each component disk to 1 GB (64 KB * 16,000).

-f, --force

Normally when a RAID-5 is created, *mdadm* builds the array with a missing disk and then inserts the remaining disk into the array. This induces recovery, instead of the slower resynchronization process. The *--force* option causes *mdadm* to create an array the traditional way, using resynchronization instead of recovery to initialize the array.

--run

Starts the array even if *mdadm* detects problems. Using *--run* will prevent *mdadm* from requiring confirmation for potentially dangerous operations. For example, if *mdadm* detects an existing filesystem or RAID superblock on a member disk, *--run* will nonetheless force the array online, possibly destroying data.

--readonly

Starts the new array as read-only.

Example usage

All *--create* and *--build* operations must contain at least *--raid-disks* and *--level* options. The following creates a RAID-0 at */dev/md0* with a chunk-size of 128 KB and two member disks.

```
# mdadm --create /dev/md0 --level=0 --chunk=128 --raid-disks=2 /dev/sda1 /dev/sdb1
```

The following commands use the short form of *mdadm* to create a four-disk RAID-0 at */dev/ md1*. We don't need to specify the chunk-size because the default chunk-size of 64 K is what we want.

```
# mdadm -C /dev/md1 -l0 -n4 /dev/sda1 /dev/sdb1 /dev/sdc1 /dev/sdd1
```

The list of component disks can be abbreviated using standard shell expansions. Consult the manual pages for the particular shell you use to be sure you are using the proper semantics. I use the Bourne-again shell (*bash*).

```
# mdadm -C /dev/md1 -l0 -n4 /dev/sd[a-d]1
# mdadm -C /dev/md1 -l0 -n4 -c64 /dev/sd{a,b,c,d}1
```

The three previous examples are equivalent. The list of devices is expanded from left to right, so */dev/sda1* becomes the first member disk in the array and */dev/sdd1* becomes the last.

Linear mode uses a rounding factor instead of a chunk-size. This command creates a linear mode array with two disks and a rounding factor of 128 KB:

```
# mdadm -C /dev/md0 -llinear -n2 --rounding=128 /dev/hd{a,b}1
```

RAID-1 does not require a chunk-size:

```
# mdadm -C /dev/md0 -l1 -n2 /dev/sd{a,b}1
```

RAID-5 can take both both a chunk-size and a parity algorithm. The following example creates a five-disk RAID-5 at /dev/md0, using a chunk-size of 128 KB and the *left-symmetric* algorithm:

```
# mdadm -C /dev/md0 -l5 -c128 -pls -n5 /dev/sd[a-e]1
```

By default, RAID-5 will automatically choose the *left-symmetric* parity algorithm, and all levels that use striping default to a 64 KB chunk-size. So you don't need to specify either option on the command line if the defaults meet your needs.

Use the *-x* option to specify spare disks for arrays that support redundancy. In this example, a RAID-1 is created at /dev/md0 with /dev/sda1 and /dev/sdb1 as its member disks. /dev/sde1 is a spare disk. The last disk listed on the command line becomes the spare disk.

```
# mdadm -C /dev/md0 -l1 -n2 -x1 /dev/sd{a,b,e}1
```

RAID-5 can also use spare disks. Normally, the last disk listed on the command line becomes a spare disk (or the last two disks, if you specified *-x2*, and so on). However, because of the way that *mdadm* creates a RAID-5, this isn't always the case. I mentioned in earlier chapters that resynchronization occurs when an array is initialized and that recovery occurs when an array rebuilds after being in degraded mode. Under RAID-5, recovery is faster than resynchronization, so *mdadm* attempts to force recovery mode to synchronize disks, rather than using the slower resynchronization process.

To facilitate this, *mdadm* creates an array with N-1 member disks and X+1 spare disks, as specified by the --raid-disks (*-n*) and --spare-disks (*-x*) options. The kernel then initiates recovery when it notices the array is degraded and inserts one of the spare disks into the array. In the following example, a five-disk RAID-5 with one spare disk is created at /dev/ md0. /dev/sdf1 becomes the spare disk because *mdadm* assembles the array using the first four disks and then inserts the last (/dev/sdf1) of the two spare disks. This induces recovery, and /dev/sde1 becomes the only remaining spare disk.

```
# mdadm -C /dev/md0 -l5 -n5 -x1 /dev/sd{a,b,c,d,e,f}1
```

To force *mdadm* to initialize a RAID-5 using resynchronization instead of recovery, while honoring the device order at it appears on the command line, use the *--force* or *-f* option:

```
# mdadm -C /dev/md0 -f -l5 -n5 -x1 /dev/sd{a,b,c,d,e,f}1
```

mdadm can also create hybrid arrays:

```
# mdadm -C /dev/md0 -l1 -n2 -x1 /dev/sd{a,b,c}1
# mdadm -C /dev/md1 -l1 -n2 -x1 /dev/sd{d,e,f}1
# mdadm -C /dev/md2 -l0 -c64 -n2 /dev/md{0,1}
```

This example creates two mirroring arrays, each with a spare disk (/dev/md0 and /dev/md1). The third command combines both of these arrays into a RAID-0 with a chunk-size of 64 KB.

Assemble mode

`mdadm --assemble mddevice [options] memberdevices`

Assemble mode activates an array that has already been created using *--create* or *--build*. It might be helpful to think of Assemble mode as being similar to the *raidstart* command.

Options

-A, --assemble
> Assembles (starts) an existing array.

-u, --uuid=
> Specifies the UUID of an array to assemble. Disks are scanned for a RAID superblock containing the UUID and combined into an array.

-m, --super-minor=
> Uses the minor number to identify which member disks belong to an array. All software arrays have a major number of 9. By default, each array has a minor number that corresponds to the number of its device special name. Thus, */dev/md1* has a minor number of 1, and */dev/md22* has a minor number of 22.

-s, --scan
> Scans the configuration file */etc/mdadm.conf* for information that could be used to assemble the array listed on the command line. This is useful for assembling arrays without having to remember their UUIDs, minor numbers, or component devices. See the "*/etc/mdadm.conf*" section, later in this chapter, for more information.

-c, --config=
> Specifies an alternate location for */etc/mdadm.conf*. See the "*/etc/mdadm.conf*" section, later in this chapter, for more information.

-R, --run
> Starts an array when possible, even if some of its member disks are missing or unavailable. This is useful for starting a RAID-1, RAID-4, or RAID-5 in degraded mode.

-f, --force
> Starts an array even if the RAID superblocks found on member disks are inconsistent.

Example usage

Assemble the array named */dev/md1* from all disks whose names begin with */dev/sd* and that bear the specified UUID:

```
# mdadm --assemble /dev/md1 --uuid=0bd9fe83:702b6f5e:ab4d0e06:7dd7dbf4 /dev/sd*
```

You can examine the first partition of SCSI disks A through Z for the array with UUID 0bd9fe83:702b6f5e:ab4d0e06:7dd7dbf4 and start it on */dev/md1*:

```
# mdadm -A /dev/md1 -u0bd9fe83:702b6f5e:ab4d0e06:7dd7dbf4 /dev/sd[a-z]1
```

Search SCSI disks A through Z for member disks with the minor number 1 and combine them into */dev/md1*:

```
# mdadm -A /dev/md1 --super-minor=1 /dev/sd[a-z]1
```

The following command looks in */etc/mdadm.conf* for a list of devices to scan for the minor number 1 and the UUID `0bd9fe83:702b6f5e:ab4d0e06:7dd7dbf4`. When both a UUID and a minor number are specified, both items must match the member disk for the disk to be considered an array component.

```
# mdadm -A /dev/md1 -m1 -u0bd9fe83:702b6f5e:ab4d0e06:7dd7dbf4
```

Combine the *--scan* option with the *-A* assemble option to activate an *md* device, using an array entry found in */etc/mdadm.conf*:

```
# mdadm -A --scan /dev/md0
```

Start all arrays that have entries in */etc/mdadm.conf*:

```
# mdadm -As
```

Refer to the "*/etc/mdadm.conf*" section, later in this chapter, for further information on how to create a configuration file and use it with assemble mode.

Monitor mode

```
mdadm --monitor mddevice [options]
```

Monitor, or Follow, mode allows administrators to configure email notification, set up event handling, and share spare disks between arrays.

Options

-F, --follow, --monitor
> Enables Follow mode for the specified array(s). *mdadm* will not exit when Follow mode is invoked. Instead, it polls arrays and monitors for critical events. Run *mdadm* in the background as necessary.

-m, --mail=
> Sets the email address to notify when a failure event occurs. Example: *-mderek* or *--mail=derek*.

-p, --program=, --alert=
> Executes the specified program when an event occurs. You can create homegrown scripts to help *mdadm* monitor and manage arrays. Examples of these options include *-pmymdmonitor.sh* or *--program=/usr/local/sbin/mymdmonitor.pl*.

-d, --delay=
> Changes the number of seconds to wait between polling arrays (for example, *-d30* or *--delay=30* for thirty seconds). The default is one minute.

-s, --scan
> When used in Monitor mode, consults */etc/mdadm.conf* for a `MAILADDR` line that indicates where to email results, and for a `PROGRAM` line that indicates what program to run, instead of taking those pieces of information from the command line.

Example usage

When monitor mode is invoked, *mdadm* will not exit, so it's a good idea to run it in the background and redirect its output to a file that you can examine. The following example polls */dev/md1* every sixty seconds (the default) and sends critical event notifications to *root*:

```
# nohup mdadm --monitor /dev/md1 --mail=root &
```

If an *md* device is not specified on the command line, *mdadm* will monitor all devices listed in */etc/mdadm.conf*. The next example monitors all arrays listed in the configuration and sends notifications to *derek@azurance.com*.

```
# nohup mdadm --monitor --mail=derek@azurance.com &
```

It's useful to invoke *mdadm* in monitor mode when the system boots. You can do this by creating an *rc* script for it at specific runlevels or adding it to */etc/rc.local* where available. Chapter 7 covers practical usage of *mdadm --monitor*.

mdadm reports the following events via email:

Fail mddevice
> A member disk that was part of *mddevice* has failed and was marked as faulty.

FailSpare mddevice spare-disk
> The *spare-disk* that was added to *mddevice* failed before reconstruction completed.

In addition to *Fail* and *FailSpare*, *mdadm* reports the following events to the program specified on the command line using *--program=* or in */etc/mdadm.conf*.

DeviceDisappeared mddevice
> An array that was active during the last poll is no longer active.

NewArray mddevice
> An array that was inactive during the last poll is now active.

RebuildStarted mddevice
> The array has begun reconstruction.

Rebuild[20,40,60,80] mddevice
> The percentage complete for an array that is undergoing resynchronization or reconstruction. The status is reported at 20, 40, 60, and 80 percent.

SpareActive mddevice spare-disk
> A spare disk that was inserted to replace a failed disk has been activated, meaning that the rebuild process has completed.

MoveSpare mddevice mddevice
> A spare disk has been moved from one array to another.

Event names and device information is passed to the receiving program as command-line options. So if you decide to develop your own monitoring utilities, parsing the command line passed to your script or program will provide you with the event, the *md* device name, and in some cases, the name of a spare disk or additional *md* device. To get an idea of how the events work, I suggest using *echo* as the program to execute:

```
# nohup mdadm --monitor --program=/bin/echo &
```

The previous example creates the file *nohup.out* in the current directory or in your home directory. Because we have set *echo* as the event program to execute, *mdadm* will print any event information to *nohup.out*.

The next example imports an email address and event program from */etc/mdadm.conf* and polls all arrays listed in the configuration file every thirty seconds:

```
# nohup mdadm --monitor --scan --delay=30 &
```

Manage and Miscellaneous modes

```
mdadm [options] mddevice memberdevices
mdadm mddevice [options] memberdevices
mdadm [options] memberdevices
mdadm [options]
```

The remaining options fall into the loosely defined categories of Manage and Miscellaneous modes. For the most part, these options work individually, but some of them can be combined to provide additional functionality. Many of these options are used on arrays, while some of them are used directly on member disks. See the "Example usage" section that follows for some common tasks.

Options

-Q, --query
> Queries an array or member disk to determine array properties, member disk properties, or both in cases when an array is also a member disk (in a hybrid array, for example). *--query* displays very brief information: array size, RAID level, and status. For member disks, it displays the disk sequence instead of the array size.

-D, --detail
> Prints verbose details about an active array.

-E, --examine
> Prints the contents of the *md* superblock from a member disk. This is usually a single device, but in the case of hybrids, it can also be an array.

-b, --brief
> When combined with either *--detail* or *-examine*, generates a configuration file entry for an array. When combined with *--detail*, an active array is queried and used to generate the configuration entry. When combined with *--examine*, the RAID superblock is read from a member disk and used to generate the configuration entry. In general, it's best to use the *--detail* form when possible because on-disk superblocks could occasionally contain incorrect information.

-s, --scan
> When combined with *--detail* or *--examine*, provides results similar to *--brief*. The difference in this case is that *--scan* queries multiple arrays or member disks and generates */etc/mdadm.conf* entries for each array it discovers. *mdadm --detail --scan* looks for active arrays in */proc/mdstat* and generates configuration file entries for each array. *mdadm --examine --scan* looks for a list of potential member disks in */etc/mdadm.conf*,

reads the RAID superblock from each disk, and then generates a configuration line for each unique array. See the "*/etc/mdadm.conf*" section, later in this chapter, for more information.

-S, --stop

Stops a running array. Equivalent to the *raidtools* command *raidstop*.

-a, --add

Adds a disk to an inactive array or hot-adds a disk to an active array. This option works like the *raidtools* command *raidhotadd*.

-r, --remove

Removes a member disk from an active array. This option works like the *raidtools* command *raidhotremove*.

-f, --fail, --set-faulty

Marks a member disk in an active array as failed. This option works like the *raidtools* command *raidsetfauly*.

-R, --run

Starts an inactive array. When *mdadm* assembles arrays that are missing component disks, it will mark the arrays as inactive, even if they can function with disks missing (for example, a RAID-1, RAID-4, or RAID-5 that is in degraded mode). The *--run* option will start an inactive array that has already been assembled. *--run* works as a standalone option, but it can also be combined with *--assemble* to automatically start a degraded array.

-o, --readonly

Marks an array as read-only.

-w, --readwrite

Marks an array as read/write.

--zero-superblock

Erases the RAID superblock from the specified device.

Example usage

The query option outputs brief information about an array or member disk. For example:

```
# mdadm --query /dev/md0:
/dev/md0: 34.18GiB raid5 3 devices, 1 spare. Use mdadm --detail for more detail.
/dev/md0: No md super block found, not an md component.
```

When used on member disks, *--query* will output disk sequence information. The following example uses the short form of the command:

```
# mdadm -Q /dev/sdc1
/dev/sdc1: is not an md array
/dev/sdc1: device 2 in 3 device active raid5 md0.  Use mdadm --examine for more
    detail.
```

When an array is also a member disk, as in the case of a hybrid array, *--query* displays information about both of its roles:

```
# mdadm -Q /dev/md1
/dev/md1: 17.09GiB raid1 2 devices, 0 spares. Use mdadm --detail for more detail.
/dev/md1: device 1 in 2 device active raid0 md2.  Use mdadm --examine for more
    detail.
```

The output of *mdadm --detail* displays information about an active array. There is some overlap between this information and the data found in */proc/mdstat*, but *mdadm* provides some additional information. In the following example, we have a four-disk RAID-5:

```
# mdadm --detail /dev/md0
/dev/md0:
            Version : 00.90.00
      Creation Time : Wed Mar 13 06:52:41 2002
         Raid Level : raid5
         Array Size : 53761152 (51.27 GiB 55.05 GB)
        Device Size : 17920384 (17.09 GiB 18.35 GB)
       Raid Devices : 4
      Total Devices : 4
    Preferred Minor : 0
         Persistance : Superblock is persistant

        Update Time : Wed Mar 13 06:52:41 2002
              State : dirty, no-errors
     Active Devices : 4
    Working Devices : 4
     Failed Devices : 0
      Spare Devices : 0

             Layout : left-symmetric
         Chunk Size : 64K

    Number   Major   Minor   RaidDisk   State
        0       8      17        0      active sync   /dev/sdb1
        1       8      33        1      active sync   /dev/sdc1
        2       8      49        2      active sync   /dev/sdd1
        3       8      65        3      active sync   /dev/sde1
               UUID : 3d793b9a:c1712878:1113a282:465e2c8f
```

The first section of the listing displays general information about the array, including the version of the *md* driver that created it, the creation date and time, the RAID level, the total size, and the total number of disks.

The second section displays information about the current state of the array. Update Time reflects the last time that the array changed status. This includes disk failures, as well as normal operations such as array activation. State reflects the health of the array; in this case, the array is operating within normal parameters, as indicated by no-errors. The dirty state might be a bit confusing, since it implies that there is a problem. Dirty simply means that there are array stripes that haven't yet been committed to disk by the kernel. When an array is stopped, dirty stripes are written and the array becomes clean. Both dirty and clean indicate normal operation.

Next, a list of Active Devices, Working Devices, Failed Devices, and Spare Devices is displayed. Active Devices reflects the number of functioning (non-failed) array members, but does not include spare disks. Working Devices is the total number of non-failed disks in the array (Active Devices + Spare Devices). Failed Devices and Spare Devices display the number of each of those types, respectively.

The next section displays properties that are specific to the RAID level. Layout reports the parity algorithm in use, followed by the Chunk Size in kilobytes. Because both of these options are specific to various RAID levels, they will not appear in all output of *mdadm -D*. In this example, both settings are displayed because RAID-5 is in use. A mirroring array would display neither because it does not support striping and does not use parity, while a RAID-0 would display only Chunk Size.

The last section displays a list of all array member disks, including their major and minor numbers, their positions in the array, current states, and block special files. Finally, the UUID of the array, if available, is displayed.

The *-E* or *--examine* option is used to display information about a member disk, as opposed to information about the array.

```
# mdadm --examine /dev/sdb1
/dev/sdb1:
              Magic : a92b4efc
            Version : 00.90.00
               UUID : 3d793b9a:c1712878:1113a282:465e2c8f
      Creation Time : Wed Mar 13 06:52:41 2002
         Raid Level : raid5
        Device Size : 17920384 (17.09 GiB 18.35 GB)
        Raid Devices : 4
       Total Devices : 4
     Preferred Minor : 0

        Update Time : Wed Mar 13 06:52:41 2002
              State : dirty, no-errors
      Active Devices : 4
     Working Devices : 4
      Failed Devices : 0
       Spare Devices : 0
           Checksum : 79b87088 - correct
             Events : 0.1

             Layout : left-symmetric
         Chunk Size : 64K

      Number  Major  Minor  RaidDisk  State
 this    0      8     17       0      active sync   /dev/sdb1
    0    0      8     17       0      active sync   /dev/sdb1
    1    1      8     33       1      active sync   /dev/sdc1
    2    2      8     49       2      active sync   /dev/sdd1
    3    3      8     65       3      active sync   /dev/sde1
```

The above output is from a member disk (*/dev/sdb1*) from the array used in the previous *--detail* example. The *-E* or *--examine* option reads the *md* superblock from an array member and displays the information found there. The *--detail* option, in contrast, looks at the array as a whole. *--examine* is used to query individual member disks. However, since you can combine arrays into larger arrays (such as RAID-10), the member disk that is displayed by the *--examine* option could actually be an array in its own right, instead of an individual disk. While much of the information provide by *--detail* and *--examine* overlaps, you can see that there are some pieces of information that are unique to each option.

Magic shows the magic number* used by the kernel RAID subsystem to mark the beginning of a RAID superblock. This hexadecimal number (a92b4efc) is a constant defined in the Linux kernel. Every *md* superblock stores Checksum information about itself. When *mdadm* examines a component disk, it computes the Checksum for the superblock and compares it to the value already stored there. In this case, that computation matched the value found on the disk. If there had been a discrepancy, it would have been noted here. Immediately following is the event counter, which displays the number of Events in the array's history.

Combine the *--brief* option with *--detail* to generate array entries suitable for */etc/mdadm.conf*. For instance, the following command generates an entry for */dev/md0*. You might find it convenient to redirect the output to */etc/mdadm.conf/*.

```
# mdadm --detail --brief /dev/md0
ARRAY /dev/md0 level=raid5 num-devices=4 UUID=41d0ebc5:befadd9f:cfab6144:dfa13287
```

Stop the array at */dev/md0*:

```
# mdadm --stop /dev/md0
```

Stop the arrays at */dev/md0*, */dev/md1*, and */dev/md2* using the short form of *--stop*:

```
# mdadm -S /dev/md0 /dev/md1 /dev/md2
```

Run an array that was partially assembled, but not activated, because a missing disk would have started it in degraded mode:

```
# mdadm --run /dev/md0
```

Mark */dev/md0* as *--readonly* using the short form:

```
# mdadm -o /dev/md0.
```

Mark */dev/md0* as *--readwrite* using the short form:

```
# mdadm -w /dev/md0.
```

Erase the RAID superblock from */dev/sda1*. This option has no short form.

```
# mdadm --zero-superblock /dev/sda1
```

The *--zero-superblock* option also works on multiple disks:

```
# mdadm --zero-superblock /dev/sd{a,b,c,d,e,f}1
```

/etc/mdadm.conf

Although *mdadm* does not rely on a configuration file, using one will make array management much easier. */etc/mdadm.conf* contains four types of lines that provide information to *mdadm*. DEVICE lines tell *mdadm* which block devices are member disks of an array, and ARRAY helps *mdadm* identify arrays that have already been created. MAILADDR and PROGRAM lines provide information about where to send email alerts and what program to execute when *mdadm* is monitoring arrays.

---

* Magic numbers have a few different definitions in computer programming. In this case, the magic number is used to let programs like *raidtools* or *mdadm* know that a particular disk block marks the beginning of the RAID superblock. The number itself, in this case, is arbitrary and simply acts as a marker. See the magic number entry in the jargon file 4.3.1 for more information: *http://www.tuxedo.org/jargon/html/entry/magic-number.html*.

DEVICE lines

DEVICE entries have the following format:

```
DEVICE      device1 device2 ... deviceN
```

DEVICE lines can contain a complete list of individual block devices or use shell expansions to shorten the list and make managing the configuration file less tedious. In the following example, the first two ATA disks and all SCSI devices are considered potential array components:

```
DEVICE      /dev/hda /dev/hdb /dev/sd*
```

The wildcard in the previous example can also be confined to the first partition only:

```
DEVICE      /dev/sd*1
```

You might not want to scan every SCSI device, since cycling through SCSI device special files that don't point to real disks is a waste of time. In the following example, the first two partitions of the first four SCSI disks are considered member disks:

```
DEVICE      /dev/sd[abcd][12]
```

You can also specify multiple wildcard entries on a single line. The next example includes the first partition of the first four IDE disks and the first partition of the first eight SCSI disks:

```
DEVICE      /dev/hd[abcd]1 /dev/sd[a-h]1
```

Or, give each entry its own line:

```
DEVICE      /dev/hdb1
# /dev/sdb1 /dev/sdc1 and /dev/sdd1
DEVICE      /dev/sd[bcd]1
# /dev/sdk1 /dev/sdk2 /dev/sdl1 /dev/sdl2 /dev/sdm1
# and/dev/sdm2
DEVICE      /dev/sd[klm][12]
```

DEVICE lines can be shortened using the abbreviation DEV. For example:

```
DEV /dev/hd[abcd]1
```

ARRAY lines

ARRAY lines are bit different from DEVICE lines, in that they have two fields, an *md* device name, and a list of identification information:

```
ARRAY  mddevice idtype=info idtype=info ... idtype=info
```

Valid identifier types are as follows:

uuid=

A 128-bit hexadecimal number that matches the UUID stored in the RAID superblock. A separator may appear after every 4 bits, but is not necessary. Use *mdadm -D* to determine the UUID of an active array. In this example, the separator appears after every 32 bits: uuid=6055c0b4:c3ec7631:c069b1fc:695acc70.

super-minor=

The array's minor number, as stored in the RAID superblock (for example, `super-minor=0`). The minor number is written to the superblock when the array is created. In general, if an array was created on */dev/md0*, the minor number is 0, and so on. However, if arrays are started on different *md* devices than the ones on which they were originally created, the minor number still remains the same.

devices=

A comma-separated list of devices that make up the array (for example, `devices=/dev/sda, /dev/sdb, /dev/sdc`). Devices listed in a device identifier must also appear on a DEVICE line.

level=

The RAID level of the array (for example, `level=1`). This option is only included for compatibility with the output of *mdadm --examine --scan*.

num-devices=

The total number of devices in an array (for example, `num-devices=6`). This is also used for compatibility with *mdadm --examine --scan*.

spare-group=

The identifier used by *mdadm* when in monitor mode to keep track of moveable spare disks (for example, `spare-group=database`). The value is an arbitrary text mnemonic. *mdadm* will move spare disks, as needed, between arrays that are in the same spare group.

A typical entry using a UUID is:

```
ARRAY  /dev/md0  UUID=ea3cb40f:b0bb05c1:b6525f1c:bf21268e
```

An ARRAY line that uses the minor number:

```
ARRAY  /dev/md0  superminor=0
```

The following uses a device list to provide identification:

```
ARRAY  /dev/md0  devices=/dev/sdb1,/dev/sdc1,/dev/sdd1
```

Identification methods can be combined to place multiple conditions on what is required to activate an array. For example, you can combine a UUID with a RAID level and the number of member disks to further narrow the scope of an ARRAY line:

```
ARRAY  /dev/md0  level=raid5 num-devices=6 UUID=6055c0b4:c3ec7631:c069b1fc:695acc70
```

In the previous example, */dev/md0* is a RAID-5 with six member disks and a UUID of `6055c0b4:c3ec7631:c069b1fc:695acc70`. When *mdadm -As /dev/md0* is executed, all of these conditions must be true, or the array will not be started.

The following example might be appropriate on a system that has a two-member IDE array at */dev/md0* and a six-member SCSI array, with the UUID ea3cb40f: b0bb05c1:b6525f1c:bf21268e at */dev/md1*.

```
ARRAY    /dev/md0   spare-group=home_directories        \
     super-minor=0 devices=/dev/hda1,/dev/hdb1
ARRAY    /dev/md1   spare-group=home_directories        \
UUID=ea3cb40f:b0bb05c1:b6525f1c:bf21268e                \
devices=/dev/sda1,/dev/sdb,/dev/sdc
```

The arrays in the previous example both belong to the spare group home_directories. So *mdadm* will share spare disks between the two arrays as needed. Don't forget that DEVICE lines listing the member disks for each of these arrays also need to be included in your */etc/mdadm.conf* file. For example:

```
DEVICE   /dev/sd[a-z]1 /dev/hda /dev/hd?1
ARRAY    /dev/md0   spare-group=home_directories        \
     super-minor=0 devices=/dev/hda1,/dev/hdb1
ARRAY    /dev/md1   spare-group=home_directories        \
         UUID=ea3cb40f:b0bb05c1:b6525f1c:bf21268e  \
         devices=/dev/sda1,/dev/sdb,/dev/sdc
```

Once you have created */etc/mdadm.conf*, you can easily assemble arrays without providing detailed information on the command line. The following example starts */dev/md0* based on its ARRAY entry in */etc/mdadm.conf*:

```
# mdadm -As /dev/md0
```

MAILADDR lines

/etc/mdadm.conf should have only one MAILADDR line, which should contain a single email address. The address listed will receive email alerts from *mdadm* when it is invoked in monitor mode. For example:

```
MAILADDR      derek@azurance.com
```

If you need to send alerts to more than one user, set up aliases in your mail transport agent. Using a MAILADDR line in */etc/mdadm.conf* is not necessary, but it does mean that you can omit the *--mail* option on the command line when using *mdadm* in Monitor mode.

PROGRAM lines

The PROGRAM line specifies the name of a program or script to execute when an event is detected in monitor mode. This eliminates the need to provide a program name on the command line with *--program* in monitor mode. */etc/mdadm.conf* should have only one PROGRAM line, containing the full pathname to execute. For example:

```
PROGRAM /usr/local/sbin/mymdalert.pl
```

Maintaining /etc/mdadm.conf

You should create */etc/mdadm.conf* after you have built your first array and should update any time you create a new array. Add the DEVICE, MAILADDR, and PROGRAM entries by hand. ARRAY lines, however, can be added automatically by invoking *mdadm*. Combining *-scan* with either the *--detail* or *--examine* options causes *mdadm* to scan */proc/mdstat* and generate an ARRAY line for any array it finds there:

```
# mdadm --detail --scan
ARRAY /dev/md0 level=raid0 num-devices=4 UUID=6055c0b4:c3ec7631:c069b1fc:695acc70
ARRAY /dev/md1 level=raid0 num-devices=2 UUID=930c4aaa:08c1fe3a:5c436830:3f4c5daa
```

The *--detail* option is useful to create ARRAY lines from active arrays. If an array is not currently active, invoke *mdadm* with the *--examine* and *--scan* options to scan all devices in */etc/mdadm.conf* for RAID superblocks and then use the information to organize member disks and create ARRAY lines.

mdadm can also generate an ARRAY entry for one array at a time. To do this, just combine the *--brief* option with *--examine* or *--detail* and specify an *md* device or member disk on the command line:

```
# mdadm --detail --brief /dev/md0
# mdadm --examine --brief /dev/sda1
```

The first command looks at an active array (*/dev/md0*, in this case) and generates an ARRAY entry. The second command queries member disk */dev/sda1* and generates an ARRAY line based on its RAID superblock. Use *--detail* to create an ARRAY line, when possible.

You can also redirect the output of *mdadm* to append the ARRAY lines automatically to */etc/mdadm.conf*:

```
# mdadm --detail --scan >> /etc/mdadm.conf
# mdadm --detail --brief /dev/md0 >> /etc/mdadm.conf
```

But don't forget to edit the file and add DEVICE lines that include all your member disks. You should also add PROGRAM and MAILADDR lines as needed.

## CHAPTER 5

Hardware RAID

Today, nearly every RAID controller manufacturer supports Linux in at least one of its product lines. Furthermore, most of these vendors now provide open source drivers for their cards, although in a few cases, the drivers have been developed by philanthropic programmers. Some vendors have even ported their management applications to Linux, although none of them yet provide source code for these applications. The vendors and products discussed in this section are:

- Mylex AcceleRAID 352 (SCSI)
- Adaptec 2100S (SCSI)
- Promise FastTrak100 (ATA)
- 3ware Escalade 7500 (ATA)
- LSI Logic MegaRAID Elite 1650 (SCSI) and MegaRAID i4 (ATA)

The sections devoted to individual controllers apply generally to other models from the same vendor, since they often share the same firmware and management interfaces. I'll point out any differences of which I'm aware. The introductory sections of this chapter will provide useful information, even if you choose a vendor that I have not covered.

Choosing a RAID Controller

There are quite a number of issues involved in determining which RAID controller to purchase. Chapter 2 covered basic hardware considerations and should help you differentiate between some of the available controllers. Chapter 2 can also help you choose between purchasing a SCSI or ATA controller, which is the first step in selecting a RAID controller.

I would like to point out that although hardware RAID controllers have traditionally been SCSI-only, the demand for inexpensive and consumer-grade solutions has prompted many vendors to include ATA controllers in their product lines. There are even a few companies that specialize solely in ATA RAID controllers. While many vendors now produce ATA controllers, many of them are low-quality and geared toward consumer desktop systems, not servers. One reason for this trend is the increasing omnipresence of ATA RAID on desktop motherboards. This makes it convenient for ATA RAID chipset manufacturers to build RAID cards to supplement their product lines.

However, not all ATA RAID controllers are created equal. There are also some vendors that specialize in high-end controllers that many organizations are now using to create terabyte storage systems at costs much lower than SCSI solutions, and with comparable performance. If you do choose ATA, I urge you to investigate thoroughly the solution you are considering, so that you don't end up with commodity hardware in a server. Some users even purchase ATA RAID controllers only for the extra channels, running Linux software RAID instead of using the controller's RAID capabilities.

Regardless of which disk protocol you choose, RAID controllers share some additional properties that you should consider before your purchase.

Motherboard and System Compatibility

The most important issue to consider when purchasing a RAID controller is its interoperability with the rest of your system. Many controllers are designed specifically to work in server motherboards or with specific motherboard chipsets. Some controllers are even incompatible with certain hard disks and drive firmware. I cannot stress enough the importance of doing your own research before purchasing. When possible, avoid getting technical information of any kind from sales representatives. Instead, check the support section of the vendor's web site for known issues, mine the archives of related discussion lists, and in general, search the Web for user reports about the controller. The Storage Review web site (*http://www.storagereview. com*) is a good place to look for third-party evaluations.

During my evaluation of hardware RAID controllers, I encountered compatibility issues with nearly every card I tested. I used several different motherboards (each with a different BIOS and chipset) and found that each card had problems with at least one of the motherboards, ranging from data corruption to general system failure. In some, but not all cases, upgrading the controller and the motherboard to the most up-to-date firmware resolved the issues. Ironically, the one card that worked with all three motherboards I tested did not work reliably with the disks I was using until I upgraded both the controller and the drive firmware.

Controller Memory

The controller uses memory to cache data during write operations. This process improves overall write performance and helps the system recover from a crash by storing unwritten data in the controller cache and committing the data to disk when the system restarts. The more controller cache you have, the more data the card can buffer before committing the data to disk.

All RAID controllers come with a fixed amount of onboard memory, but it can usually be augmented by purchasing memory expansion kits.

 In some cases, memory expansion kits are available only at the time of purchase. You may not be able to order the kits standalone and install them yourself. While many RAID controllers use standard 72-pin SDRAM DIMMs (Dual Inline Memory Modules), purchasing untested third-party upgrades is likely to void the controller's warranty. Please check with the vendor before upgrading any controller.

Purchasing additional controller memory is a good idea if you typically work with a lot of large files, such as audio, video, or image files. If you have a lot of small files or files of varying sizes, additional cache memory is unlikely to improve performance. In general, additional controller cache memory will improve performance on systems that have a lot of large sequential file I/O. Systems that lean toward random I/O on small files won't see much of a difference. A typical office file server probably doesn't need extra memory. A graphics or video production workstation does.

Battery backed-up cache memory

Many high-end controllers support an optional battery pack that ensures that data in the controller cache memory is preserved during power failures. The amount of memory you have on your controller generally affects how long the cache memory will be preserved when the system loses power. Thus, if you purchase a controller with extra memory, the time that the controller can preserve data in the cache decreases. Cards with less memory can store data in the cache for a longer period because there is less memory to power.

Product specification sheets or pre-sales materials should provide you with a chart showing the length of time that cache memory will be preserved, based on how much memory you have. Some vendors increase the number of batteries based on the amount of memory installed, so that the duration of time when memory is preserved is consistent, regardless of how much memory you purchase. Check the specifications prior to purchase to make sure that the controller and memory combinations meet your needs.

JBOD (Just a Bunch of Disks)

While nearly all controllers support JBOD mode at this point, it's still a good idea to check with your vendor before purchasing. In particular, make sure that Linux will recognize disks that are connected to the controller but are not part of any array. If you don't buy a card that supports JBOD mode, you'll need a separate controller for any non-RAID disks you want to connect to the system. Usually there are a couple of controllers on the motherboard, but it's best to double-check.

Software Considerations

There are also software issues to consider. First, is the controller you are thinking about purchasing supported by Linux? If there is support, is it open source and integrated into the kernel? Or is it available only as a kernel patch or as a binary-only kernel module?

Integrated open source support is obviously the best bet when choosing any piece of hardware for use with Linux, although in some rare cases. a vendor-provided kernel patch might be more desirable.

Be extremely wary of binary-only modules. Forward compatibility is never guaranteed, and support is available only from your vendor, instead of the vast community of open source developers. And you can't fix problems that might arise on your own because you don't have access to the source code.

The availability of user-space tools—that is, tools that are run after the operating system has loaded—is also a consideration. After all, the potential high-availability features of RAID aren't much good if you have to restart your system to run BIOS-level configuration tools to perform essential administrative tasks such as creating a new array, managing failed disks, and adding new spare disks. So, when choosing a controller, look for a vendor that provides open source drivers, preferably integrated into the current stable kernel tree, as well as some user-space management tools.

So far, I have not found any vendor-provided, open source management tools. However, I have been told by at least one vendor that they have plans to open source their command line and GUI management tools, and I think this move will start a trend among other manufacturers. In past years, there have been a few open source projects that provided user-space support for various RAID controllers, but at the time of this writing, they are all unmaintained.

Preparing Controllers and Disks

It's vitally important that all disks used in any hardware array are identical (see the "Matched drives" section in Chapter 2) and that all have the same firmware revision. There are documented cases in which non-uniform firmware revisions have led to data corruption. Furthermore, it's important to use the latest firmware revision for both controllers and disks and, in some cases, even for the BIOS on your motherboard. In general, it's a good idea to upgrade all system components to the most up-to-date firmware before placing any system in production.

Computer equipment, especially disk controllers and hard disks, tends to sit in warehouses for several months before it is shipped to resellers and end users. That usually means that by the time you purchase your equipment, there has been at least one firmware, or controller BIOS, release correcting important bugs that often affect interoperability or performance.

For example, a controller I was working with during the course of this writing wouldn't work consistently using recently purchased SCSI hard disks that were a couple of firmware revisions behind. Hard disks often ship with older firmware, and that doesn't usually affect systems that use standalone disks. However, since hard disk firmware controls environmental factors such as rotation speed and thermal calibration, using disks with varying firmware in an array can be catastrophic. To function optimally, RAID controllers require that all disks be calibrated the same way. Variations in firmware can foil the entire process.

Nearly every vendor provides simple utilities that perform firmware and BIOS upgrades. These utilities are available from vendor web sites and FTP servers. Unfortunately, very few component hardware vendors provide an easy way for Linux users to apply these upgrades without depending on Microsoft products.

 Almost all vendors distribute their upgrades and upgrade utilities in ZIP archives. You will need the *unzip* utility to decompress them. It's also common for some of these vendors to distribute self-extracting ZIP archives with the *.exe* extension. These archives are not self-extracting under Linux, but you can use the *unzip* utility to manually decompress the file's contents.

That's because all of these utilities (with a very small number of exceptions) are designed to run under a DOS-compatible operating system. That means you will need to provide your own bootable DOS disks, onto which you can copy firmware and BIOS upgrades and their associated utilities. The problem is that many Linux, and indeed many Unix, users lack access to Microsoft products. I went through several major headaches when I was trying to upgrade the controllers that I'll be discussing throughout the rest of this chapter, because I simply didn't have a way to create a bootable DOS diskette. Vendors don't provide such diskettes because if they did, they'd have to pay royalties to Microsoft.

One possible solution is that at most places of business, there are systems running Microsoft operating systems. You can easily create a bootable DOS disk on such systems and place the necessary utilities and firmware revisions on them. Unfortunately, I believe that this is illegal.

Fortunately, there are a few workarounds that are relatively hassle-free. Most hard disk manufactures provide drive test utilities that come with bootable disks. You can download one of these bootable floppy disk images from a hard disk vendor's web site, mount the filesystem under another Linux system, and erase the contents of the disk, replacing them with your firmware and BIOS upgrades. Or you can use Free-DOS.

FreeDOS

If you don't have access to a Microsoft operating system to generate a bootable DOS disk and upgrade system hardware, you will find FreeDOS very useful. FreeDOS is a free (GPL) MS-DOS-compatible operating system. You can download a bootable disk image from the FreeDOS web site (*http://www.freedos.org*) and use it to upgrade system hardware with vendor-supplied utilities.

First, download a disk image from *freedos.org*. For each release, a subdirectory named *instdisk* contains bootable disk images for floppy drives of various sizes. For example, *instdisk/1.44* contains bootable images for 1.44 MB floppy disks. Download the file *FD8_144.DSK* from the directory:

```
ftp://ftp.ibiblio.org/pub/micro/pc-stuff/freedos/files/distributions/beta8/
```

Next, use *dd* to write the disk image onto a blank floppy disk:

```
# dd if=/home/derek/FDB8_144.DSK of=/dev/fd0H1440 bs=1k
```

Format another floppy disk and create an MS-DOS filesystem on it:

```
# fdformat /dev/fd0
# mkfs.msdos /dev/fd0
```

Next, mount the newly formatted disk:

```
# mount -t msdos /dev/fd0 /mnt/floppy
```

Copy the firmware upgrades you downloaded from your vendor to the disk. Next, boot the system with the FreeDOS disk inserted. After the system starts, insert the disk with the firmware upgrades and run the vendor-provided utility to update your controllers and disks. You might need to create more than one blank disk in order to store all the firmware files and utilities. Some of them will fill an entire 1.44 MB floppy disk.

General Configuration Issues

While each Linux-compatible RAID controller has vendor-specific drivers and configuration utilities, they all share some common semantics.

Controller Card BIOS

Like motherboards, most RAID controllers (and even many standard disk controllers) have an onboard controller BIOS. The controller BIOS performs many of the same tasks as the BIOS on a motherboard (such as low-level disk maintenance and configuration) and also provides an interface for configuring and managing RAID devices. While some manufacturers also provide user-space tools, you will need to configure the first array using the controller's BIOS if you plan to install an operating system onto an array, and in some cases, even if you plan to install Linux directly to a standalone disk connected to a RAID controller.

If you are interested only in adding a new array to an existing system, and not in adding RAID support to your existing system disks (that is, you plan to keep your existing disk controller), you might be able to utilize user-space tools to configure and initialize arrays. However, not all vendors provide tools to manage controllers using Linux. Please see the specific controller sections later in this chapter for more information, or check with your vendor if you are using a controller that isn't covered in this chapter.

Even if you have user-space tools available, you may wish to use the onboard BIOS to configure arrays. Vendor-provided management tools for Linux are often buggy and incompatible across different Linux distributions and versions (kernels, GUI toolkits, and libraries). Some simply provide WINE-compatible executables. WINE allows you to run Windows programs under Linux. Although WINE is widespread, many programs are unstable when run under it.

Like any standard motherboard BIOS, most controllers follow a fairly standard menu system, with the following conventions:

- Arrow keys and/or TAB move between fields.
- ENTER confirms, enters a submenu, or selects the current field.
- ESC moves to the previous menu or cancels the current dialog.
- PLUS, MINUS, and SPACEBAR change values in the current field.

Some fields might require normal alphanumeric input, and some controllers may adhere to only a subset of these conventions.

System Installation

Normally you need to configure a hardware array using the controller's BIOS before you can install an operating system. However, there are a few exceptions when creating an array first is undesirable.

The first case is when you already have an operating system on a disk that is connected to the controller. This usually happens when you upgrade an existing system by installing a RAID controller. Some controllers support a *pass-through* mode, which means that you can connect an existing system disk to a new controller and boot the system normally, without any additional configuration. However, not all controllers support this pass-through mode. In that case, you first need to configure the existing system disk as a JBOD mode array. I've included cookbook examples for setting up JBOD modes for existing system disks in many of the sections about individual controllers, later in this chapter.

Since many users upgrade from a single disk environment to a RAID-1 configuration, I have also included cookbook examples that will help you migrate from a single disk system to RAID-1, using the controllers that I have evaluated. These procedures are often not documented, even though they represent a common task that many users and system administrators need to perform.

Unfortunately, it's really not possible to move from a single disk system to any RAID level other than JBOD or disk mirroring. Although moving from a single disk to a RAID-0 or RAID-5 might be highly desirable, it is nearly impossible without a backup and recovery step. Unfortunately, some manufacturers imply that these procedures are possible in the way they name their menu items and document the controllers. I'll point out any potential workarounds or migration hazards that I'm aware of in the sections on individual controllers.

If you plan to use arrays only for data drives, you can safely install the operating system onto a single disk and create arrays later. You might need first to create a JBOD mode array that refers to the disk onto which you plan to install the system. When you are ready to create arrays, either reboot the system and use the controller's BIOS or use user-space utilities, if available.

RAID Autoconfiguration

Many RAID controllers come with automatic configuration features. These features are designed to make it easy for users who have no background in RAID to help determine which RAID level best meets their needs. I hope that, having purchased this book, you never need to use these features. Instead, configure your arrays manually, using the material from earlier chapters as a reference.

Autoconfiguration works by asking the user a series of questions that are used to determine performance and redundancy requirements. For example, the controller might prompt the user with the question:

Do you need fault tolerance?

Depending on whether the user answers yes or no, the controller can determine which RAID levels to eliminate from the possible choices. An answer of "no" eliminates RAID-1 and RAID-5, while answering "yes" includes them, but excludes RAID-0 and JBOD. A follow-up question might look like this:

Do you need a spare disk?

Depending on how this question is answered, the controller could determine how to size a potential array, based on the number of disks connected to the system.

Vendors have several different names for the autoconfiguration process, such as Auto Configure, Assisted Configuration, or Configuration Wizard, depending on the controller you purchase. I recommend against using these shortcuts, because they obfuscate the configuration process and build arrays using the lowest common denominator for important array properties. These features also don't take future expansion into account. A system administrator might know that while there are only five disks connected to the controller, one more is arriving next week. Because the controller only makes autoconfiguration suggestions based on hardware that is already connected to the system, it might recommend creating a four-disk RAID-5 with one spare disk. However, the system admistrator will realize that creating a RAID-5 that uses all five disks is a better option. The disk arriving next week can be introduced later and set up as a spare disk.

Write Cache

Controller cache memory operates in one of two modes. Each mode offers trade-offs between performance and reliability.

Write-back caching

When the controller is configured for write-back caching, the controller holds data in the controller's memory until it is full or until the controller is idle and then commits the data to disk. This mode yields the best performance, but it's not as reliable as write-through caching because a system failure could result in the loss of data that is still in the controller's memory, but not flushed to disk.

Having a controller battery is very helpful when using the write-back caching method because a power failure only means that unflushed buffers are stored until the system restarts. Extra controller memory is also important for write-back caching. On heavily used systems with lots of sequential disk I/O, it's a good idea to consider getting a memory upgrade.

Write-through caching

Write-through caching commits data to disk immediately. This method is much slower than write-back caching, but it ensures that all writes are committed to disk and are never lost because a failure occurred while unwritten buffers were waiting in the controller's memory. If you use write-through caching, the amount of memory on your controller is not as important as getting a fast controller and fast disks.

Each array can generally use its own caching method. Thus, it's possible to configure heavily used, less important arrays for write-back caching, and critical, less frequently used system disks for write-through operation.

Don't forget that other system features might help provide the security that write-through caching delivers. Data journaling under XFS or ext3 is one option. Using an uninterruptible power supply (UPS) with automatic system shutdown is always a good idea and might also provide the necessary safeguards required to use write-back caching even in critical situations.

Logical Drives

It should be clear by now that sales sheets and documentation about RAID use many terms interchangeably, although their meaning varies depending on the context. The term *logical drive* is used to mean an array in some software RAID implementations. In the context of a controller, the term logical drive has another meaning. Some controllers let you split a single large array into multiple smaller logical drives. So, while I might create a single RAID-5 that is several hundred gigabytes in size, I can further segment that array by creating logical drives that contain a subset of the total storage space. This is useful when you are working with very large disks, but want to allot a manageable amount of space for system disks. It's also useful if subpartitioning at the operating system level won't work because you need more partitions than are supported by a single disk. Not all controllers implement logical drives.

Using logical drives also helps maximize storage space. Let's say that you have a system with five 18 GB disks. You know already that you need roughly 25 GB to store a MySQL database. It might seem ideal to allocate two disks for a RAID-1 to house the system partitions. That leaves three remaining disks that you could use to create a RAID-5, yielding 36 GB of raw storage space. However, that's not much room for database growth, and neither array has a spare disk. Furthermore, the system partitions on the RAID-1 aren't going to use anywhere near the whole 18 GB allocated to that array. It might make a bit more sense to create a five-disk RAID-5, segmenting it into two logical drives: one drive with a couple of gigabytes for system partitions, and the other with the remaining space for the database. That should leave you with roughly 70 GB of space for the MySQL partition, depending on how you split up the logical disks. You could also create a four-disk RAID-5 with a single spare disk. That would also leave you plenty of room to create an efficient logical drive for system partitions and another logical drive with room for database growth.

 Breaking an array into logical drives does not mean that you can implement different RAID levels on the same set of disks. If you have different performance and redundancy requirements for different filesystems, you need to create separate arrays.

During normal operation, an unsegmented array appears as a logical drive that spans the entire array.

Controller Disk Spin-up

Before a disk can be accessed, it must be spinning at its nominal RPM. This process usually takes only a few seconds and occurs automatically when power is applied to the system. On systems with a lot of SCSI disks, it is useful to defer spin-up until each I/O channel is scanned. This helps underpowered systems with many disks because disks draw additional power during the spin-up process. ATA disks spin up automatically and offer no user control over their startup behavior.

While SCSI controllers can spin up disks, many drives ship with power-on spin-up enabled. That means the disk will spin up as soon as power is applied. If you want to use the controller's deferred spin-up features, you need to enable controller spin-up on individual disks, which is usually accomplished by installing or removing a jumper on each drive. Consult your hard disk manuals for further details.

Mylex

Mylex has two RAID controller product lines, both SCSI-only and both supported directly by the Linux kernel. The entry-level AcceleRAID line currently features a 100 MHz Intel i960 RISC Processor. The high-end eXtremeRAID series boasts a 233 MHz StrongARM SA 110 Processor. Thus, the main difference between the two product lines is the controller's processing power. Within each product line, cards are differentiated by the number of I/O channels present, as well as the amount of cache memory.

Although each card varies slightly in terms of its hardware, they are all managed with the same BIOS and user-space utilities. I evaluated the AcceleRAID 352, a dual-channel controller, but my experiences should apply, regardless of which Mylex card you decide to purchase. For more information about the hardware differences among the available Mylex controllers, consult the Mylex web site at *http://www.mylex.com* or the driver's home page at *http://www.dandelion.com/Linux/DAC960.html*.

The DAC960 Driver

All Mylex cards are supported under the DAC960 driver, written by Leonard Zubkoff. The complete documentation for the driver is included with every kernel (*/usr/src/linux/Documentation/README.DAC960*). The driver documentation contains a complete compatibility list for Mylex RAID controllers. I recommend referring to this list when purchasing any new controller. If your card is not listed there, you may wish to check the DAC960 driver home page at *http://www.dandelion.com/ Linux/DAC960.html*. As long as your controller shares a firmware revision and processor with a controller that is listed as compatible, you will probably have good results in using any new controllers.

Distribution support

Because the DAC960/DAC1100 driver has been in the kernel for such a long time, most distributions now support direct installation to Mylex arrays. I tested installation with Mandrake, Red Hat, and SuSE.

Configuring the kernel

The DAC960/DAC1100 driver is located under the Block Devices submenu (see Figure 5-1) and can be compiled statically or as a loadable kernel module.

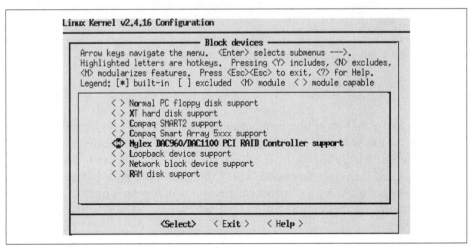

Figure 5-1. Enable the DAC960/DAC1100 driver for Mylex support.

Once you have enabled support for the DAC960/DAC1100 driver, you can rebuild and install the new kernel, using the *make dep* and *make bzImage* commands.

Device special files

The DAC960/DAC1100 uses a *Devfs*-style naming system. All device files are located in the */dev/rd* directory and are named to reflect the controller, logical device, and partition numbers. For example, */dev/rd/c0d0p1* refers to first partition (*p1*) of controller zero's (*c0*) first logical drive (*d0*). In general, */dev/rd/cXdYpZ* refers to controller *X*, logical drive *Y*, and partition *Z*. This naming method is useful because unlike standard SCSI devices, disks do not change names when a disk fails.

Partition limitations

All Mylex arrays and logical drives are limited to seven partitions. This limit can be constraining when you're working with a single large array and also using a standard FHS partitioning scheme.

For example, let's say that you have a 100 GB RAID-5 that you are using for both system and data disks. The seven-partition limit constricts standard filesystem segmentation, because after allocating a separate partition for */boot*, */*, */home*, */usr*, */tmp*, */var*, and *swap*, you've hit the partition limit. You can't even add separate */usr/local* and */opt* partitions when necessary. And the seven-partition limit certainly doesn't leave any room for creating new partitions for databases, network filesystems, or web servers.

In cases such as this, it's useful to simply split a large array into multiple logical drives. You can allocate a couple of small logical drives for system partitions and leave the remaining space on a separate logical drive to partition as needed for larger data filesystems.

Controller Setup

After installing a Mylex RAID controller, you should see a message similar to the following when you power on the system:

```
Scanning Option ROMs...
Mylex AcceleRAID 352 BIOS PLUS V6.01-30 (Nov 14, 2001)
Copyright (c) 2001 IBM Corporation. All rights reserved.
www.mylex.com

   Spinning up drives......
   AcceleRAID 352 Firmware Version 7.00-03
   RAID Adapter Serial #: 10026500327
   PCI Address: F0000000 Bus=2 Dev/Slot=13 Function=0 IRQ=9
   Adapter Memory Size = 64 MB (SDRAM/ECC)
   BIOS Enabled - 8 GB Disk Drive Geometry Selected.
   Press <ALT-M> for BIOS options
   Press <ALT-R> for RAID Configuration options
   No system drives installed
```

If arrays had already been defined, the last line would have displayed the number of arrays (logical drives) in the controller's configuration. The banner also displays the amount of memory installed in the controller, the firmware version, and the card's PCI address, location, and interrupt.

BIOS options

Press ALT-M to enter the BIOS options menu. There are three options, each of which controls the card's ability to boot the system.

BIOS enabled/disabled

The BIOS must be enabled if you wish to boot from disks, arrays, or CD-ROM drives connected to the controller. If you don't want to boot from these devices, you can disable the BIOS and shave a few seconds off the system startup. The remaining options do not apply if this option is disabled.

CD-ROM boot enabled/disabled

If you want to boot from a CD-ROM drive that is connected to your Mylex controller, this option must be enabled. Remember that using a slower device (such as a CD-ROM) on a fast SCSI channel will cause the entire channel to run at the speed of the slowest device. You probably don't want to connect a CD-ROM to an expensive RAID controller. However, this option is quite useful for system installation. Disable it when you're done using the CD-ROM, and don't forget to disconnect the drive.

2 GB/8 GB drive geometry

This option selects how much of an array/disk the BIOS can address. When set to 2 GB, the controller can boot only operating systems found in the first 2 GB of the logical drives that you define. When you use an 8 GB drive geometry, the controller can use the first 8 GB. Set this option before installing an operating system.

EzAssist (RAID configuration)

EzAssist is the primary utility used to configure Mylex controllers and arrays. It is normally invoked when the controller initializes, but can also be installed on a floppy disk and run from an MS-DOS compatible operating system. The latter option is useful when attempts to enter EzAssist at system startup fail. You can download EzAssist from the Mylex web site.

After you press ALT-R to enter the EzAssist RAID configuration menu, the following messages appear on the screen:

```
Checking RAID Configuration Software ...
Loading RAID Configuration Software ...
Starting RAID Configuration Software ...
```

An ASCII animation of the forward slash and backslash characters will appear immediately following the last line. Be aware that on slow systems, it could take some time for the software to start, and the animation will move slowly.

Once the software loads, you will be presented with a list of all Mylex controllers connected to the system. In many cases, you will see a single controller with an entry such as the following:

```
Controller      PCI     PCI    PCI         Firmware
No. Model       Bus     Device Function    Version

0   AcceleRAID 352   2        13       0        7.00-03
```

Navigate the list using the arrow keys and press ENTER when the controller that you wish to administer is highlighted. After rescanning the SCSI bus, if no arrays are currently defined and there are disks connected to the controller, EzAssist will ask if you wish to configure a new array. Otherwise, the following menu options are presented:

- Configure a RAID Drive
- View or Modify Controller Configuration
- Perform Administration On ...
- Rescan for New Devices
- Advanced Options

In order for you to install any operating system on disks connected to a Mylex controller, at least one array must be defined. If you already have an operating system installed, you can create additional arrays using either the EzAssist BIOS utility or the Global Array Manager, once Linux has booted.

Configuring the first array

Before you can install Linux, at least one array must be created. The following instructions explain how to configure an array.

1. Use ALT-R to enter the EzAssist RAID configuration utility.

2. Select your controller.

3. If a dialog pops up, warning that no configuration was detected, answer yes. Otherwise, choose Configure RAID Drive from the main menu.

4. A menu with three configuration methods will appear: Automatic, Assisted, and Custom. Choose Custom and then select Configure a New Disk Array from the menu that appears.

5. The next menu contains a list of all disks connected to the controller, organized by SCSI ID. Select all the disks that you want to include in the new array by highlighting them and pressing the ENTER key. When you are done selecting disks, navigate to and choose Save Array.

6. If there are other unconfigured disks connected to the controller, a dialog will appear, asking if you want to configure logical drives. Choose yes, and then select the array that you just defined from the pop-up dialog that follows.

7. The next screen displays information about your new array. Use the arrow keys to move between fields and make any necessary changes to the array configuration. You can change the RAID level, cache type, and stripe size. In addition, you can alter the array's logical size by moving to the logical size field, using the arrow keys, and typing in the new logical drive size. Changing an array's logical size is useful for splitting a single array into two or more smaller logical drives. As mentioned earlier in this chapter, the DAC960/DAC1100 driver supports only seven disk partitions. So if you need more than that for a large array, you will have to split up the array into more than one logical drive. See the "Partition Limitations" and "Logical Drives" sections, earlier in this chapter.

8. After you have customized your array settings, use the TAB key to activate the menu on the right side of the screen. Then select Add Disk.

9. The array now appears in the dialog window at the bottom of the screen. If you changed the logical size of the array, you have the option to add another logical disk that contains some or all of the remaining space. If you want to add another logical disk, simply tune the array's configuration, as described in step 7, and then repeat step 8. You can also leave the remaining space unallocated and configure it later, but you won't be able to access it until you've assigned it to a logical drive.

10. Choose Apply to commit the array to the controller's memory.

After you select the Apply option, the new configuration is written to the controller's memory, and after a few seconds, you are returned to the main menu. If you created arrays that use redundancy (such as RAID-1 or RAID-5), the initial synchronization process will commence. You can monitor the progress of the rebuild process by selecting Advanced Options and then Background Tasks from EzAssist's main menu. You can now reboot the system and install a new operating system on the array that you just created, or wait until the rebuild process is complete. You may also create additional arrays and fine-tune the controller. See "The DAC960" section, earlier in this chapter.

Configuring an existing disk for standalone JBOD mode

Mylex controllers do not operate in pass-through mode for JBOD. If you are replacing an existing SCSI controller with a Mylex RAID controller and want to access an operating system that was already installed on a single physical disk, you will need to create a logical JBOD drive first.

Before connecting existing disks to the new controller and creating a logical JBOD drive, you should take a few preparatory steps. You can install the Mylex controller along with your existing SCSI controller, or you can wait until you've completed the first six steps and then swap controllers. It's advisable, but not required, to perform steps 1–6 in single-user mode. I also recommend creating a backup copy of /etc/lilo. conf and /etc/fstab before proceeding. It's also a good idea to have a rescue floppy disk or CD-ROM handy.

1. Reconfigure the kernel so that it supports Mylex controllers (see "The DAC960 Driver" section, earlier in this chapter).

2. Copy the new kernel and *System.map* to */boot*.

3. Edit */etc/lilo.conf* and add a new kernel stanza that uses the new kernel. It's essential that this new stanza contain a *root* line that points to the device special file for the new *root* partition. So if your current *root* partition is */dev/sda2*, create a *root* line that reads root=/dev/rd/c0d0p2. In this case, your system disk will be connected to the first channel of the first Mylex controller and appear as logical drive 0. Use a device file that will reflect your new system configuration. In general, you probably want any system disk in JBOD mode to be the first logical drive on the first controller.

4. If */etc/lilo.conf* contains a boot line, remove it. You can add a new boot line after the new controller is installed and the system is brought back online.

5. Execute */sbin/lilo* to rebuild the master boot record.

6. Edit */etc/fstab* to reflect the new Mylex device files. On modern systems that use disk labels, you will likely need to change only the swap entry (which always uses a real device entry instead of a disk label). Thus, if your swap file is located at */dev/sda3*, change it to */dev/rd/c0d0p3* to indicate partition three on the first logical drive of the first controller.

7. At this point, you should power down the system and install the new controller. If the controller is already installed, move your existing disk to the Mylex controller and then power-on the system.

8. Use ALT-R to enter the EzAssist RAID configuration utility.

9. Select the controller that is connected to your existing system disk.

10. If a dialog warning pops up, saying that no configuration was detected, answer yes, and a configuration menu will appear. Otherwise, choose Configure RAID Drive from the main menu.

11. A menu with three configuration methods will appear: Automatic, Assisted, and Custom. Choose Custom, and then select Configure a New Disk Array from the menu that appears.

12. This menu contains a list of all disks connected to the controller, organized by SCSI ID. Select the disk that you want to configure for JBOD mode (see step 3) by highlighting it and pressing the ENTER key. Then navigate to, and select, Save Array.

13. If there are other unconfigured disks connected to the controller, a dialog asking if you want to configure logical drives will appear. Choose yes, and then select the array that you just defined from the pop-up dialog that appears next.

14. The next screen displays information about your new JBOD array. Since only one disk was included in the array, JBOD is the only array type available. You can optionally change the write cache type and stripe size as needed.

15. Use the TAB key to activate the menu on the right side of the screen. Then select Add Disk. The array now appears in the dialog window at the bottom of the screen. Choose Apply to commit the array to the controller's memory.

Once you apply the configuration, a window appears indicating that the new array configuration is being stored in the controller. After a few seconds, you will be returned to the main menu, or to the array creation menu, if there are additional free disks connected to the system. You can now continue to define additional arrays or exit EzAssist and reboot the system.

When the system reboots, your original system disk (now a JBOD mode array) is accessible just like a normal disk, and the operating system boot prompt appears. If the kernel panics, or you encounter unrecoverable problems, simply boot into rescue mode from a floppy disk or CD-ROM and fine-tune */etc/lilo.conf* and */etc/fstab*. Don't forget that if you make changes to */etc/lilo.conf*, you will need to rerun */sbin/lilo* to update the boot sector. If all else fails, you will still be able to re-install your original disk controller and access the system, although you will have to use a rescue disk to restore the original settings to */etc/lilo.conf* and */etc/fstab*.

Converting an existing standalone disk to a mirror

Unfortunately, there is no simple, automatic way to create a new mirror and include a disk with existing data as one of its components. To accomplish the job, start by following the procedures outlined in the previous section. Once the system is working in JBOD with the new Mylex controller, follow these steps:

1. Reboot the system and use ALT-R to enter the EzAssist RAID configuration utility.

2. Select the controller to which your JBOD logical drive is connected.

3. From the main menu, choose Perform Administration On and then select Logical Drive.

4. A pop-up window appears that lists all your logical drives. Choose the drive that you wish to convert to a RAID-1.

5. Now select Advanced Options and Delete Logical Drive. There is a short delay while the RAID configuration is updated.

6. Use the ESC key to return to EzAssist's main menu. Then choose the first option: Configure RAID Drive.

7. A menu with three configuration methods will appear: Automatic, Assisted, and Custom. Choose Custom and then select Configure a New Disk Array from the menu that appears.

8. The next menu contains a list of all disks connected to the controller, organized by SCSI ID. First, select the disk that used to be the JBOD mode disk by highlighting it and pressing the ENTER key.

9. Now select another available disk. This will become the second mirror component. It's important to choose the former JBOD system disk first, since it contains the data. If you want to create a mirror that has more than two member disks, you can select additional disks now.

10. When you're done selecting disks, navigate using the TAB key and select Save Array.

11. If there are other unconfigured disks connected to the controller, a dialog will appear, asking if you want to configure logical drives. Choose yes and then select the array that you just defined from the pop-up dialog that appears next.

12. The next screen displays information about your new array. Since two disks were included in the array, RAID-1 is the default array type. You can optionally change the write cache type and stripe size as needed.

 Depending on how many disks you have selected for inclusion in your new RAID-1, EzAssist will allow you to change the RAID level on the Logical Drive Definition screen. Changing the RAID level to anything other than RAID-1 will be catastrophic and result in total data loss from the previous system.

13. Use the TAB key to activate the menu on the right side of the screen. Then select Add Disk. The array now appears in the dialog window at the bottom of the screen. Choose Apply to commit the array to the controller's memory.

14. After the new configuration is written to the controller, return to the main menu and select Perform Administration On → Physical Device.

15. A list of disks is presented. Select the second disk in the array—that is, the disk that has no preexisting data.

16. Choose Advanced Options from the menu that appears and then select Make Drive Offline.

17. A two-step confirmation appears. Answer yes to both questions. Now the drive is marked offline.

18. Finally, return to the main menu and choose Perform Administration On → Logical Drive.

19. Select the array that contains the member disk that you just marked offline; the disk will appear highlighted and in critical condition.

20. Choose Advanced Options and Rebuild Redundancy Data from the menu that pops up.

21. A confirmation appears. Answer affirmatively. After a short pause, you are returned to the array status menu, and the array is now marked as rebuilding.

You can monitor the progress of the rebuild process by selecting Advanced Options and then Background Tasks from EzAssist's main menu. After the rebuild process has completed, you can reboot your system. System partitions that were on the original JBOD logical drive are now mirrored.

In general, you can delete any JBOD disk and create a new RAID-1 with the former JBOD drive as its first component. The process also works in the other direction. Delete any mirror and then create a JBOD logical drive that contains a former RAID-1 member to return to single disk operation.

Managing Arrays

You can manage arrays using the DAC960/DAC1100 driver's /proc entry, but its functionality is limited. To manage all aspects of your Mylex controller without bringing down the system, you will also need to use the Mylex Global Array Manager.

/proc/rd

The DAC960/DAC1100 driver uses the /proc/rd directory to report information about the status of Mylex controllers and to provide a user interface for performing some online management functions.

/proc/rd/status provides a simple interface for determining the status of all Mylex controllers connected to the system. When all controllers are operating normally, the status file returns OK:

```
$ cat /proc/rd/status
OK
```

If an array is degraded or failed, or a physical disk has failed, */proc/rd/status* reports an alert:

```
$ cat /proc/rd/status
ALERT
```

Detailed status information is provided in controller-specific directories named */proc/rd/cN*, where N is the controller number. Each controller subdirectory contains three files: *current_status*, *initial_status*, and *user_command*. Examine *current_status* using *cat* or a file pager to view the controller state of a controller and its arrays. A lot of information is displayed. The initial output is similar to what is provided by the controller's startup banner and is found in the controller configuration menu under EzAssist:

```
***** DAC960 RAID Driver Version 2.4.11 of 11 October 2001 *****
Copyright 1998-2001 by Leonard N. Zubkoff <lnz@dandelion.com>
Configuring Mylex AcceleRAID 352 PCI RAID Controller
    Firmware Version: 7.00-03, Channels: 2, Memory Size: 64MB
    PCI Bus: 2, Device: 13, Function: 0, I/O Address: Unassigned
    PCI Address: 0xF0000000 mapped at 0xD083F000, IRQ Channel: 9
    Controller Queue Depth: 512, Maximum Blocks per Command: 2048
    Driver Queue Depth: 511, Scatter/Gather Limit: 128 of 257 Segments
```

Next, a list of physical disks is displayed, including an entry for each controller channel. In the interest of brevity, I've included only entries for the first disk and the first controller channel. Normally, each disk and channel is displayed in ascending order, beginning with its SCSI ID.

```
    Physical Devices:
      0:0 Vendor: IBM       Model: DDYS-T18350M      Revision: SA2A
          Wide Synchronous at 160 MB/sec
          Serial Number:          VEY04122
          Disk Status: Online, 35155968 blocks
  [...]

      0:7 Vendor: MYLEX     Model: AcceleRAID 352    Revision: 0700
          Wide Synchronous at 160 MB/sec
          Serial Number:
```

After the physical devices, a list of logical drives (arrays) is displayed. In the following example, there are two arrays. The first (*/dev/rd/c0d0*) is a JBOD logical drive, indicated by RAID-7. The DAC960/DAC1100 driver uses the term RAID-7 to denote JBOD logical drives. The next array (*/dev/c0d1*) is a RAID-0.

```
Logical Drives:
  /dev/rd/c0d0: RAID-7, Online, 35155968 blocks
                Logical Device Initialized, BIOS Geometry: 255/63
                Stripe Size: 64KB, Segment Size: 64KB
                Read Cache Disabled, Write Cache Disabled
  /dev/rd/c0d1: RAID-0, Online, 140623872 blocks
                Logical Device Initialized, BIOS Geometry: 255/63
                Stripe Size: 64KB, Segment Size: 64KB
                Read Cache Disabled, Write Cache Disabled
```

Unfortunately, the components that make up each array are not displayed. To determine which disks are part of each array, you need to either use Mylex-supplied user-space tools or reboot the system and use the EzAssist utility.

Of particular note is the last line of output:

```
No Rebuild or Consistency Check in Progress
```

This line reports whether or not there is a rebuild, consistency check, or initialization in progress. These processes occur when a new, redundant array is brought online for the first time or when a degraded array is being repaired. The percentage of the process that is complete, along with the logical drive number and device special file, are displayed:

```
Foreground Initialization in Progress: Logical Drive 1 (/dev/rd/c0d1) 28% completed
```

/proc/rd/c0/initial_status displays the same information as *current_status*, but it remains a static snapshot of the state of the controller when the system was booted. It does not display any information about array rebuilds or consistency checks.

Finally, *user_command* allows system administrators to perform some administrative tasks on the controller, arrays, and physical disks. To use these commands, simply *echo* them into the *user_command* file:

```
# echo command > /proc/rd/cX/user_command
```

Each controller has its own *user_command* file and can accept the following commands:

flush-cache

Writes all uncommitted data in the controller's memory to disk. You can use this command in conjunction with shutdown scripts (such as those executed by a UPS) to make certain that all buffers have been committed to disk before the system is powered down. For example:

```
echo "flush-cache" > /proc/rd/c0/user_command
```

kill channel:target-id

Marks a physical disk as offline. This is useful for testing hot failover. For example, to kill the disk with SCSI ID 4 on controller 0, use:

```
echo "kill 0:4" > /proc/rd/c0/user_command
```

make-online channel:target-id

> Brings a drive back online after it has failed (and ideally been replaced) or after you have killed it for testing purposes. *make-online* is the opposite of *kill*. For example:
>
> ```
> echo "make-online 0:1" > /proc/rd/c0/user_command
> ```

make-standby channel:target-id

> Marks a drive as a spare. (Standby is yet another term used to mean spare-disk or hot-spare.) This command is useful when an array has already undergone an automatic rebuild. Even though it is no longer in degraded mode, the array has no hot-spare. After the dead disk is replaced, use this command to mark the new disk as the spare disk. For example:
>
> ```
> echo "make-standby 0:1" > /proc/rd/c0/user_command
> ```

rebuild channel:target-id

> Manually initiates a rebuild. If you disabled Automatic Rebuild Management, use this command to start the rebuild manually. The *target-id* always specifies the dead disk that should be synchronized with the remaining working disks. For example, to rebuild the array to which the disk with SCSI ID4 belongs, use:
>
> ```
> echo "rebuild 0:4" > /proc/rd/c0/user_command
> ```

check-consistency logical drive number

> Initiates a consistency check on a logical drive. This process simply verifies that the redundancy information is correct. For example:
>
> ```
> echo "check-consistency 0" > /proc/rd/c0/user_command
> ```

cancel-rebuild

> Cancels all rebuilds that are currently in progress. This command applies to all arrays. For example:
>
> ```
> echo "cancel-rebuild" > /proc/rd/c0/user_command
> ```

cancel-consistency-check

> Cancels all consistency checks that are currently in progress. This applies to all arrays. For example:
>
> ```
> echo "cancel-consistency-check" > /proc/rd/c0/user_command
> ```

Refer to the file */usr/src/linux/Documentation/README.DAC960* for further information about these commands.

The Global Array Manager (GAM)

The Mylex Global Array Manager (GAM) is used to monitor and manage arrays while the system is running. It's included on the CD-ROM packaged with your controller, but I recommend downloading the most recent update from the Mylex web site. Grab the *linux-gam_510.exe* file (it's marked GAM for Linux). Since its location might vary, I haven't included it here, but you can find it by navigating to the Driver/ Support page. Don't forget that the version number might also change slightly. The file is a self-extracting zip archive, so you'll have to use *unzip*, not *gunzip*, to extract the RPM files from it.

```
$ unzip linux-gam_510.exe
Archive:  linux-gam_510.exe
  inflating: sam-client-5.00-10.i386.rpm
  inflating: gam-client-5.00-13.i386.rpm
  inflating: gam-linux-readme_510.txt
  inflating: gam-server-5.00-12.i386.rpm
  inflating: gam-agent-5.00-12.i386.rpm
```

The Global Array Manager is comprised of a client (*gam-client-5.00-13.i386.rpm*) and a server (*gam-server-5.00-12.i386.rpm*) package. The *gam-server* package provides the underlying framework for communicating with the controller, and the *gam-client* package provides the GUI management interface. To install *gam-server* successfully, you must have either *inetd* or *xinetd* installed and running. It's not enough for either program to simply be installed; one of them must be running. That's because the client and server components use TCP/IP to communicate with each other. After installation, a desktop icon is created for KDE and GNOME users. You can also run GAM directly from */opt/gam/bin/gam*. The Global Array Manager is very straightforward to use and is well documented. There's built-in HTML help and an installation guide (*http://www.mylex.com/pub/support/current_raid/Linux-GAM.pdf*). Most of GAM's functions mimic EZAssist.

Adaptec

Adaptec has two RAID controller product lines based on different processors and technologies. This dichotomy stems from Adaptec's history with RAID controllers. In 1999, Adaptec, Inc. acquired Distributed Processing Technology (DPT), a manufacturer of, among other storage products, SCSI RAID controllers. At that time, Linux support for DPT controllers was provided in the form of a GPL kernel patch. Since the acquisition, Adaptec has continued to support Linux in its RAID product line by continuing driver development for controllers based on the original DPT architecture.

After the acquisition, Adaptec began to develop a new product line aimed at OEM controllers. These controllers were featured in server-class systems available from Dell Computer and Hewlett-Packard. Many users will know these controllers as the Poweredge Expandable RAID Controller (PERC). Since the new controllers had a different architecture, a new Linux driver was needed. Eventually, Adaptec released several boxed controllers based on this new architecture. So today, the new driver is used for OEM controllers, as well as some newer boxed products.

 If you have a Dell system with a branded Adaptec controller, you might want to take a look at Matt Domsch's page on the subject: *http://www.domsch.com/linux/*. It's the best resource that I've been able to find for Dell's RAID solutions and Linux.

The controller that you purchase dictates which of the two drivers you need to use. For the DPT-based controllers, use the Adaptec I2O RAID driver (*dpt_i2o*). For OEM and newer controllers, use the AACRAID driver (*aacraid*). I evaluated an Adaptec 2100S, which is a single-channel, SCSI Ultra 160 RAID controller. The 2100S is an I2O card, so throughout the rest of this section, I'll be referring to that driver and its user-space tools. However, the same tools are also available for AAC-RAID controllers.

Linux support for Adaptec RAID controllers is common in many distributions. I tested direct installation to my 2100S controller using Red Hat, SuSE, and Mandrake. The official documentation recommends creating a driver disk by using the included CD-ROM, or by downloading a disk image from the Adaptec web site. However, I have found that out-of-the-box installation works fine, at least with Red Hat, SuSE, and Mandrake. You need to create a driver disk and use a distribution that is officially supported only if you encounter problems and need technical support from Adaptec.

Adaptec I2O RAID Driver

The Adaptec I2O RAID driver currently supports all I2O RAID cards and the DPT SmartRAID V controller. The *dpt_i2o* driver also provides support for some of Adaptec's ATA RAID controllers. Please check the driver's documentation and the Adaptec web site for specific compatibility information. The GPL driver was originally ported to Linux version 2.0.34 and was available as a patch to the kernel. The GPL driver was ported by Karen White (Dell Computer), with help from Mark Salyzyn and Bob Pasteur.

The driver was eventually rewritten from scratch. This new version (2.0) was developed by Deanna Bonds and Mark Salyzyn. Bonds currently maintains the driver for Adaptec. During the development of kernel 2.4, the driver finally made it into the stable kernel tree (2.4.10). That means users no longer have to undergo the arduous process of patching kernels or creating custom driver disks to perform installation.

What Is I2O?

I2O stands for Intelligent Input/Output. I2O is a way to achieve improved system performance by offloading tasks traditionally performed by the CPU onto dedicated I/O processors. I2O also offers a split-driver architecture that allows vendors to create platform-independent hardware drivers, so long as a generic I2O driver for each operating system is available.

Linux contains generic I2O support. In fact, you'll notice an entire subsection of the kernel configuration dedicated to I2O device support. But be certain to use the *dpt_i2o* driver in the SCSI subsection of the kernel configuration, and not the generic I2O driver. The generic driver does not work with Adaptec I2O RAID controllers.

To determine if your card is supported by the *dpt_i2o* driver, look for the Adaptec I2O logo in the card's BIOS banner, or consult the Adaptec web site (*http://www. adaptec.com*) or the *README.dpti* file, located within the kernel source tree in the directory */usr/src/kernel/drivers/scsi*.

Configuring the kernel

Enable Adaptec I2O RAID support (CONFIG_SCSI_DPT_I2O) under the SCSI Low-Level Drivers submenu of the SCSI Support menu. The driver can be compiled statically or as a loadable kernel module (*dpt_i2o*).

```
SCSI support  --->
  ...
  SCSI low-level drivers  --->
    ...
    <*> Adaptec I2O RAID support
    ...
```

Arrays and standalone disks that are connected to Adaptec controllers show up with device entries just like any standard SCSI disk. So the first disk or array connected to the controller gets named */dev/sda* by Linux, the second */dev/sdb*, and so on.

The aacraid Driver

The original *aacraid* driver for Linux was merely a wrapper for the Windows NT driver. This presented both technical and philosophical problems. Eventually, Alan Cox rewrote the *aacraid* driver from the ground up. While some programmers at Adaptec were also working on a new replacement driver, that work was eventually scrapped in favor of Alan's rewrite, partly because his driver had already been integrated into the 2.4 kernel tree. Deanna Bonds is now improving the *aacraid* driver by adding new features, as well as support for new, non-I2O controllers.

Use the *aacraid* driver if you have an OEM or a non-I2O boxed controller. Refer to the file */usr/src/kernel/drivers/scsi/aacraid/README* to determine if your controller is supported by the *aacraid* driver.

Configuring the kernel

The *aacraid* driver is still experimental, so you have to enable support for development drivers before you can see the *aacraid* driver as a configuration option. From the Code Maturity Level Options (the first item in the Linux kernel configuration), choose the option Prompt For Development and/or Incomplete Code/Drivers.

After development support is enabled, look for the Adaptec AACRAID Support (CONFIG_SCSI_AACRAID) option under the SCSI Low-Level Drivers submenu of the SCSI Support menu.

```
SCSI support  --->
  ...
  SCSI low-level drivers  --->
```

```
...
<*> Adaptec AACRAID support (EXPERIMENTAL)
...
```

The driver can be compiled statically or as a loadable kernel module.

Adaptec RAID Setup Utility

The Adaptec RAID Setup Utility is the controller BIOS configuration tool used to create and manage Adaptec arrays. In this section, I'll provide some examples for common tasks using the BIOS Setup Utility, including configuring an array for the first time and converting an existing system to a RAID-1 system. When the card initializes, you'll see a banner that provides information about disks and arrays. Use CTRL-A to enter the utility.

Adaptec controllers also ship with a bootable CD-ROM that contains a more robust GUI configuration tool. You can use that disk, instead of the setup utility, to perform your initial setup.

Configuring the first array

1. Use CTRL-A to enter the Adaptec RAID Setup Utility.

2. After the utility initializes and scans connected disks, press ALT-R to activate the RAID configuration menu.

3. Select Create from the RAID configuration menu. A window that lists the available RAID levels and the default stripe size will appear.

4. Use the TAB or arrow keys to move between each option. Pressing the SPACEBAR selects the RAID level that is currently highlighted. Choose the one that meets your needs.

5. If necessary, navigate to the Stripe Size field and press the ENTER key to bring up a list of available stripe sizes. Use the arrow keys and the ENTER key to select the desired stripe size. The default value is fine for most systems.

6. Navigate to the Okay button and press ENTER to confirm the RAID configuration.

7. The next screen lists available disks. Move up and down the list, using the arrow keys, and then use the ENTER key to select each disk you want to include in the array. A checkmark appears to the left of each disk after it is selected.

 Remember that data on disks included in a new array will be lost. Please back up necessary data before using disks in an array, or use new disks.

8. When you are finished selecting disks, navigate to the Done button, using the TAB key, and press ENTER to create the new array.

9. If you created a RAID-1, a dialog will appear, asking which disk to use as the synchronization source and destination. Since this is a new array and the disks are either new or contain incidental data, just select either option and choose Okay.

10. If any of the disks you included in a new array contain a valid partition table or boot section, the Adaptec RAID Setup Utility will warn you just before the array is created. A dialog for each disk that contains data appears, and you must manually confirm that each disk can be included in the array.

11. After confirming any additional dialogs, you are returned to the Adaptec RAID Setup Utility's main menu. The new array appears in the left column just below the controller's entry. You can use the ENTER key to expand and collapse the array's entry, revealing its member disks.

12. Finally, press ALT-F to bring up the File menu and choose Set System Config. This writes the array configuration into the controller's memory. You may now reboot and begin installing a new Linux operating system. If you created an array with redundancy, the initial resynchronization will begin. You can either wait until it completes or reboot and begin installing an operating system right away. Navigating to the array's entry in the left column will display the percentage complete of the initial resynchronization in the right windowpane.

Configuring an existing disk for JBOD mode

Adaptec RAID controllers support JBOD mode by default. So if you replace an existing SCSI controller with an Adaptec RAID controller, your existing single-disk system will boot normally. You still need to reconfigure and recompile your kernel so it supports either the *dpt_i2o* or the *aacraid* driver. Don't forget to rerun */sbin/lilo*.

I recommend adding support for your Adaptec controller while your disks are still connected to your original SCSI controller. Restart the system and make sure your kernel still works with your original configuration. Next, shut down the system and replace the SCSI controller with your Adaptec RAID controller, connecting your system disks to the RAID controller. Be certain that your system disk is still the first disk after you reconnect to the RAID controller. When you power on the system, Linux should boot normally, provided that the kernel was compiled properly. If you encounter problems, you can revert to your original hardware configuration and troubleshoot.

Converting an existing standalone disk to a mirror

If you want to upgrade an existing system with a single disk to a RAID-1, using an Adaptec RAID controller, you should first compile a new kernel with support for the *dpt_i2o* or *aacraid* driver. Consult the driver sections earlier in this chapter for more information. It's okay to leave the driver for your existing SCSI controller compiled into the kernel. In fact, that will make it easier to revert back to your original config-uration if you encounter any problems. After the driver is enabled, and the new ker-nel is installed, follow these steps:

1. Reconfigure your kernel so that it supports either the *dpt_i2o* driver or the *aacraid* driver, depending on which controller you have.

2. Reboot the system and use CTRL-A to enter the Adaptec RAID Setup Utility.

3. After the utility initializes and scans the connected disks, press ALT-R to activate the RAID configuration menu.

4. Select Create from the RAID configuration menu. A window that lists the avail-able RAID levels and the default stripe size will appear.

5. Use the TAB or arrow keys to move between each option. Pressing the SPACEBAR selects the RAID level that is currently highlighted. Choose RAID-1.

6. Navigate to the Okay button and press ENTER to confirm the RAID configuration.

7. The next screen lists available disks. Use the ENTER key to select your existing sys-tem disk, as well as a second disk to include in the mirror. Move up and down the list using the arrow keys. When a disk is selected, a checkmark appears to its left.

8. When you are finished selecting disks, navigate to the Done button, using the TAB key, and press ENTER to create the new array.

9. A dialog will appear, asking in which direction the initial resynchronization should move. Two choices are presented. Synchronize from the first disk to the second, or synchronize from the second disk to the first. This choice is extremely important. If you make the wrong decision, it will result in a total loss of data. Make certain that data is copied from your existing system disk to the new disk. Generally, this means copying data from disk 0,0,0,0 (the disk with the existing system data) to disk 0,0,1,0 (the second blank hard disk).

10. An additional dialog appears, indicating that there is valid data on at least one of the disks. That's because the first disk, at least, contains a valid partition table and a boot sector. The second disk might also contain some residual but expendable data. After confirming these additional dialogs, you are returned to the Adaptec RAID Setup Utility's main menu. The new array appears in the left column just below the controller's entry. You can use the ENTER key to expand and collapse the array's entry, in order to reveal its member disks.

11. Finally, press ALT-F to bring up the File menu and choose Set System Config. This writes the array configuration into the controller's memory and starts the initial resynchronization. I recommend waiting until the process completes before rebooting the system. Navigating to the array's entry in the left column will display the percentage complete of the initial resynchronization in the right windowpane.

12. Once the resynchronization is complete, you can reboot and begin using your new, redundant Linux system.

The Adaptec Storage Manager

The Adaptec Storage Manager is a user-space application that can monitor and manage Adaptec RAID controllers. It is packaged as an RPM file and included on the CD-ROM that shipped with your controller. You can also download the package file from Adaptec's Linux web site (*http://linux.adaptec.com*). Follow the Linux Downloads link and choose the Storage Manager package for your controller and distribution. Adaptec provides package files for Red Hat and SuSE, and while they are usually a couple of revisions behind each distribution's most recent release, they tend to work even with newer versions of either distribution. You shouldn't have any problem using the RPM files with an unsupported distribution. I tested them with Mandrake and encountered no problems.

The Storage Manager includes a command-line utility for managing arrays and controllers (*raidutil*) and a GUI utility (*dptmgr*) that performs the same functions. It also includes a few daemons that provide event logging and a low-level communication layer for interfacing with the controller.

The Storage Manager RPM (*dptapps*) depends on the driver RPM (*dptdriver*). Since support is now included in the stable kernel, it's undesirable and unnecessary to use the prepackaged RPM kernel and driver that Adaptec provides. Just pass the *--nodeps* option to *rpm* when installing the storage manager:

```
# rpm -ihv --nodeps sm_linux_v314_install.rpm
```

There are a couple of device special files that also need to be created. These would have been created had we chosen the Adaptec installation for *dptdriver*, but because we skipped that step, we have to create them manually. Use *mknod* to create the files manually:

```
# mknod -m644 /dev/dpti0 c 151 0
# mknod -m644 /dev/dpti1 c 151 1
# mknod -m644 /dev/dpti2 c 151 2
# mknod -m644 /dev/dpti3 c 151 3
```

The *-m644* option sets the permissions for each file (rw-r--r--), */dev/dptiN* specifies the filename, and *c* indicates that we are creating a character special file. The device major number is 151, and we need to create minor numbers 0 through 3. That's why we execute the command four times, with slightly different parameters.

Once the files are created, start the DPT engine by executing the startup script that was copied into your *init.d* directory.

```
# /etc/rc.d/init.d/dpt start
```

If everything was successful, you should see several DPT-related processes running:

```
# ps xw | grep dpt
  949 ?        S      0:00 /usr/dpt/dptelog
  967 ?        S      0:00 /usr/dpt/dptcom
  972 ?        S      0:00 /usr/dpt/dpteng
  976 ?        S      0:00 /usr/dpt/dptcom
```

```
977 ?          S      0:00 /usr/dpt/dptcom
978 ?          S      0:00 /usr/dpt/dptscom -DAEMON
984 ?          S      0:00 /usr/dpt/dptelog
985 ?          S      0:00 /usr/dpt/dptelog
```

These processes control event logging and allow the operating system to communicate with the controller. Normally, communication with the controller occurs locally, using a Unix Domain Socket. However, in its default configuration, the *dptapps* package creates a configuration file that exposes the controller to the local Ethernet network when the daemon processes are started. This service is bound to port 2091/tcp by default. You may decide to provide a security mechanism for this port, if you plan to manage your controller from a remote workstation. I recommend disabling the network communication capability to avoid any potential exploitation. Edit the file */usr/dpt/dptmgr.ini* and comment out (use ; to indicate that a line is a comment) or delete the line containing the word TCP in the [Modules] section. This disables remote management via TCP/IP and forces the programs in the *dptapps* package to use Unix Domain Sockets to communicate.

Running */usr/dpt/dptmgr* will invoke the GUI management portion of the Storage Manager. It provides the same functions as the controller BIOS, in addition to some monitoring capabilities. Complete documentation for *dptmgr* is available from the Adaptec web site.

Working with raidutil

raidutil is useful for administering Adaptec controllers at the command line. You can use *raidutil* to create, modify, delete, and manage arrays. Execute *raidutil* with no arguments to get a list of options or read the manual page for details on usage.

After you have installed the *dptapps* package and started the Adaptec daemons, use *raidutil* to ensure that everything is functioning properly. The *-I* switch queries the controller and returns the model and firmware version:

```
# /usr/dpt/raidutil -I
```

Use the *-L* option to view information about the controller's configuration. For example, to list arrays and their components, use the following command:

```
# /usr/dpt/raidutil -L array
```

Promise Technology

Promise Technology, Inc. is one of the oldest manufacturers of ATA RAID controllers. They produce several dual-channel controllers aimed at end users and small businesses (FastTrak), as well as a high-end six-channel controller (SuperTrak).

The low-end controllers are, in essence, software RAID controllers because they rely on the operating system to handle RAID operations and because they store array configuration information on individual component disks. The real value of the controller is in the extra ATA channels. If you purchased a controller that supports a better ATA protocol than your motherboard's built-in ATA controller, you will get improved disk bus performance.

I evaluated the Promise FastTrak 100, a dual-channel Ultra ATA/100 card. The information that I have provided in this section is relevant for any of the FastTrak series RAID controllers. You might also find the Linux ATA RAID HOWTO a useful complement to the material in this section. Download a copy from *http://www.tldp.org/HOWTO/ATA-RAID-HOWTO/index.html* or from any Linux Documentation Project mirror.

Creating an Array

Press CTRL-F to invoke the Promise *FastBuild* utility when the controller's initialization banner appears. Select the Define Array option to create a new array. Use the SPACEBAR to choose between the available options and the arrow keys to navigate between the fields. After choosing a RAID level and stripe size (RAID-0 only), navigate to the bottom section of the screen to select individual disks to be included in the array. The letter Y to the right of a disk indicates that it has been marked for inclusion. When you're finished selecting disks, press CTRL-Y to save the array.

If you created a RAID-1, FastBuild will ask you if you prefer to Create and Build the array (that is, perform an initial resynchronization) or to only Create the array. It's safe to select the Create Only option (answering no to the question that appears), since you are about to install an operating system for the first time. After you finish the installation process, the controller will warn you that an array is not synchronized. At that point, you can use FastBuild to manually build the array, and then continue booting your newly installed Linux operating system.

Next, exit to the main menu by pressing the ESCAPE key. Finally, press the ESCAPE key again to exit the *FastBuild* utility and restart the system.

When the system restarts, the array you just created will be listed in the controller's initialization banner. If you need to make any changes, use CTRL-F to restart the *FastBuild* utility.

Installing Linux onto a Promise Array

Installation on Promise RAID controllers can be problematic for two reasons. First, most Linux installers detect both the arrays defined (logical disks) and the individual ATA disks, and list both as available, valid installation targets during the system configuration. Thus, disks that are members of arrays might also show up in partitioning utilities. It's left up to the user to determine which device is the valid array on which to install the Linux operating system.

When working with Promise controllers, it's important to choose the *ataraid* driver and not the *FastTrak* driver. The *ataraid* driver is open source and was developed by Arjan van de Ven of Red Hat. The *FastTrak* driver is a binary-only driver and is distributed by Promise. Licensing aside, the main difference between the two drivers is that the Promise driver uses the SCSI subsystem to interface with the Linux kernel. That means Promise's binary-only driver needs to perform additional steps to translate commands between SCSI and ATA. Conversely, the open source driver uses ATA directly and is consequently faster and more stable.

 If you are using the SuperTrak controller, the same semantics I describe here will apply, but the SuperTrak controller uses a different driver, also available from Promise. The SuperTrak controllers are also reported to work using Linux's Generic I2O Driver. Your mileage may vary.

When using the *FastTrak* driver, I experienced many system lockups and slow-downs (all non-fatal) while performing normal, low-impact disk operations such as editing files and listing directories. You'll notice many associated entries, as in the following code listing, either in the system logs or printed on the console:

```
FastTrak : Drive Interrupt Time Out.(1)
FastTrak : RESET Channel1 * DEV1(OK)
FastTrak : Drive Interrupt Time Out.(3)
FastTrak : RESET Channel2 * DEV3(OK)
FastTrak : Drive Interrupt Time Out.(3)
FastTrak : RESET Channel2 * DEV3(OK)
```

These messages indicate that I/O commands have timed out before they were completed. The controller must reissue the commands to ensure data integrity. These timeouts can also result in low-level seek and read errors on individual member disks and cause the system to become unstable, requiring a cold reboot. Using the *ataraid* driver eliminates these problems, and it should always be used in lieu of the binary-only *FastTrak* driver.

Unfortunately, most distributions do not currently support direct installation using the *ataraid* driver. That means you'll need to use Promise's *FastTrak* driver disk to install Linux from scratch, and then rebuild the kernel with support for the *ataraid* driver. If you are adding a Promise ATA RAID controller to an existing Linux system, you can simply rebuild the kernel so that it includes the *ataraid* driver and begin using the new controller. The I/O issues associated with the *FastTrak* driver can cause filesystem errors between system reboots. If possible, choose a journaling filesystem such as ext3 or ReiserFS during the installation process. This will save you from some additional headaches if you have to reboot the system a few times before you can upgrade to the *ataraid* driver. Chapter 6 discusses filesystems.

Creating a driver disk

You should download the driver disk appropriate for your distribution from the Promise web site (*http://www.promise.com*). A section of the web site is dedicated to Linux support. Driver disks are provided for Red Hat, SuSE, TurboLinux, and Caldera's OpenLinux. On my Red Hat system, I downloaded the *zip* file for RedHat 7.1/7.2/7.3 (*T-FTS-02-RHD73.zip*). Included in the archive are two additional *zip* files: one file for uniprocessor (*rhup-ftb22.zip*) systems and one file for multiprocessor systems (*rhsmp-ftb22.zip*). Use the following commands to prepare a blank disk and unpack the archive. (Note that this example is for a single-processor Red Hat system.)

```
# mkfs.msdos /dev/fd0
# mount /dev/fd0 /mnt/floppy
# unzip rhup-ftb22.zip -d /mnt/floppy
# sync
# umount /mnt/floppy
```

Installation

Now you can begin system installation. Boot the new system with your installation media and choose the option that lets you specify additional drivers. For Red Hat, that means typing *linux dd* at the boot prompt. When prompted for the driver disk, insert it, and the *FastTrak* driver will load. After a few moments, the installer will execute normally.

During system partitioning, arrays defined on Promise controllers will show up as SCSI disks, a by-product of using the *FastTrak* driver. So if you have one array, it appears as */dev/sda*. A second array would appear as */dev/sdb*, and so on. Detection order is important here. If you have another SCSI controller connected to the system, and it's in a lower- numbered PCI slot, disks connected to that controller could show up as */dev/sda* and shift the lettering of your Promise arrays. Pay careful attention to the size of each disk, so that you are sure to define partitions on the proper disk. Depending on the partitioning method you use, the driver associated with individual disks might also be displayed, clarifying where disks are connected. Arrays defined on Promise controllers should be explicitly marked. For example: `sda: Promise 2+0 Stripe/RAID01.109804 - 38178 MB.`

> The individual disks in your arrays will also show up as standalone ATA disks when using GUI partitioning tools such as Disk Druid. It's very important to create system partitions for installation on the virtual SCSI devices for the array (usually */dev/sda*). Never create partitions on the component disks.

When the time comes to configure your boot loader, be certain to choose LILO. Do not use GRUB with Promise RAID controllers. It's also important to make sure that the master boot record is installed in the proper location: onto the array, not an individual disk. Despite installing Linux onto the proper array partitions, some installation programs still botch the boot loader configuration.

If you're working with a distribution other than Red Hat, download the appropriate zip files to create driver disks for your distribution. I strongly recommend creating a boot disk during the installation process, even if it's a step you normally skip. When the installation is finished, restart the system and use the boot disk you created if you encounter problems. Once the system is online, examine the system logs and system partitions to make certain that you are using the *FastTrak* driver and that software was installed onto the proper devices, as shown here:

```
# grep FastTrak /var/log/messages
Jul 28 17:35:29 bored kernel:PROMISE FastTrak Series Linux Driver Version 1.02.0.22
Jul 28 17:35:29 bored kernel: scsi0 : FastTrak
# df -h
Filesystem          Size  Used Avail Use% Mounted on
/dev/sda2           2.4G  1.7G  696M  71% /
/dev/sda1           197M  9.4M  177M   5% /boot
```

These system logs indicate that the *FastTrak* driver is bound to the first SCSI channel (*scsi0*), and the output of *df -h* shows that the partitions are located on */dev/sda*. If the output of *df -h* reported partitions on an ATA device (*/dev/hda*, for example), or if the Promise initialization messages did not appear in the system logs, something went wrong during the installation and Linux was installed to a standalone ATA disk instead of the array.

Configuring the ataraid Driver

After your system is up and running with the *FastTrak* driver, I recommend converting to the *ataraid* driver for increased stability and performance. If you are only adding a Promise controller to an existing system, start with the steps in this section.

Native support for Promise RAID controllers is located in the *ATA/IDE/MFM/RLL Support* section of the Linux kernel configuration. First enable Development Support because the *ataraid* driver is still experimental. Then enable the following features:

```
<*> ATA/IDE/MFM/RLL support
IDE, ATA and ATAPI Block devices  --->

  <*> Enhanced IDE/MFM/RLL disk/cdrom/tape/floppy support
  ...
  <*>    Include IDE/ATA-2 DISK support
  ...
  [*]    Generic PCI IDE chipset support
  ...
   [*]      PROMISE PDC202{46|62|65|67|68} support
   [*]         Special UDMA Feature
```

```
[*]        Special FastTrak Feature
...
<*> Support for IDE Raid controllers
<*>    Support Promise software RAID (Fasttrak(tm))
```

Once you have enabled support for the preceding options, execute *make* and copy the new kernel into your */boot* directory:

```
# make dep && make bzImage
# make modules && make modules_install
# cp arch/i386/boot/bzImage /boot/bzImage.ataraid
```

Reconfiguring LILO

Versions of LILO earlier than 22 do not recognize *ataraid* devices. So you will have to upgrade LILO before executing */sbin/lilo* to update the boot sector of a Promise array that uses the *ataraid* driver. Use the command *lilo -V* to determine which version of LILO you are using. If necessary, download the latest version of LILO from *http://ibiblio.org/pub/Linux/system/boot/lilo/* and install it before rewriting the boot sector.

Now that the new *ataraid* kernel is built and installed, add a stanza to */etc/lilo.conf*.

```
image=/boot/bzImage
    label=ataraid
    read-only
    root=/dev/ataraid/d0p2
```

Note that the root line contains a nonstandard device entry. The *ataraid* driver uses the */dev/ataraid* directory to organize the devices it manages. In this case, the *root* partition is located on the first array's (d0) second partition (p2). In general, *ataraid* devices use the format */dev/ataraid/dXpN*, where X is the array number and N is the partition number.

While you're editing */etc/lilo.conf*, check the boot line to make certain it points to the current system disk (*/dev/sda* or */dev/sda1*, in most cases) because at this point, you're still using the *FastTrak* driver. After you reboot the system, you can change the boot line to reflect the *ataraid* naming scheme, but for now, you need to be certain that the boot record is being written to the proper place. Since this is a new system, the installer might have created an */etc/lilo.conf* file with a boot line that refers directly to one of the component disks. That means you could unknowingly run */sbin/lilo* and write a boot sector that will hang the system on the next reboot. Don't forget to either change the default line in */etc/lilo.conf* to specify the new ataraid entry, or remove the default line altogether and make sure the *ataraid* stanza appears first.

You don't need to take any additional steps if you merely added support for a Promise RAID controller to an existing system. However, you will need to restart the system and use the *FastBuild* utility to define arrays. After you reboot, you can access any new arrays, using the naming scheme outlined earlier. Just create a filesystem as you would with any normal block device.

Additional steps for new systems

Change the */etc/fstab* entries for your system partitions if you are not using partition labels. If you're using partition labels, you don't need to make any changes to */etc/ fstab* right now.

Execute */sbin/lilo* and reboot the system. The system will restart, using the *ataraid* driver. If an error occurs, just reboot with the original kernel and double-check each step that I have outlined. After the system restarts, you can execute the *mount* command, without any options, to ensure that the proper driver is in use and that the partitions have been correctly mounted.

```
# mount
/dev/ataraid/d0p2 on / type ext3 (rw)
none on /proc type proc (rw)
/dev/ataraid/d0p1 on /boot type ext3 (rw)
none on /dev/pts type devpts (rw,gid=5,mode=620)
```

The proper device entries are listed in this output: */dev/ataraid/d0p2* for the *root* filesystem and */dev/ataraid/d0p1* for */boot*.

Next, edit */etc/fstab* and change your swap partition's entry to reflect the *ataraid* naming style. My original swap partition was */dev/sda3*, so I'll change its */etc/fstab* entry to */dev/ataraid/d0p3*. Since the change to the swap device was made after the system started, execute *swapon -a* to activate the swap space.

Finally, edit */etc/lilo.conf* so that the boot line references the *ataraid* device instead of the */dev/sdN* device used by the *FastTrak* driver. In this case, we'll change the boot line to *boot=/dev/ataraid/d0*, meaning that the boot sector should be installed onto the first array defined on the controller.

Converting an Existing Standalone Disk to a Mirror

Because there are so many problems associated with the Promise installation process, I recommend upgrading your system from a standalone disk to a mirror via a backup and restore procedure.

Post-Installation Array Management

There are no user-space management tools for Linux. While Promise does provide some Microsoft Windows management packages, they have unfortunately not been ported to Linux. To perform low-level array administration, you will need to reboot the system and invoke the *FastBuild* utility.

3ware Escalade ATA RAID Controller

3ware, Inc. sells several well-supported, multichannel ATA RAID controllers. Adam Radford developed an open source driver for 3ware. Joel Jacobson and Brad Strand of 3ware also worked on the driver, as well as Arnaldo Carvalho de Melo of Conectiva, Andre Hedrick of SuSE, and of course, Alan Cox.

The driver supports all 3ware controllers and has been standard in the stable Linux kernel since 2.2.15. Direct installation to 3ware controllers is simple and headache-free. You should have no issues when working with any distribution that uses a 2.4 or later kernel. I enjoyed problem-free installation using Red Hat, SuSE, and Mandrake.

Creating an Array and Installing Linux

The following steps outline the process for creating a new array and installing Linux onto a new system with a 3ware controller. The "Kernel Configuration" section later in this chapter outlines the process for adding 3ware support to the kernel on an existing system.

1. When the controller's startup banner appears, press ALT-3 to access the configuration screen. The main menu is split into a list of disks and a list of arrays. No arrays will appear during the first use.

2. Use the arrow keys to navigate and the ENTER key to select disks for inclusion in the new array. An asterisk appears next to each disk once it has been selected.

3. After the desired disks are selected, navigate to the Create Array button at the bottom of the screen and press the ENTER key.

4. An array properties screen appears. Use the arrow and ENTER keys to adjust the RAID level, cache type (write-through or write-back) and stripe size as needed. Select OK when finished, and you'll be returned to the main menu.

5. Press F8 to commit the new array to the controller's memory. Some additional warnings may appear, indicating that data on the selected disk will be destroyed. Confirm the warnings if you are certain that the disks contain no important data and you want to continue creating the array. If you created an array with redundancy, a synchronization process will start before the system reboots. When the system restarts, the new array appears in the controller's initialization banner.

When you install Linux, the array you created will show up as a standard SCSI device. If you created only one array and have no other disks, the array appears as */dev/sda* during installation. Create partitions as you would with any standalone disk and proceed with the installation as you would normally.

Converting an Existing Standalone Disk to a Mirror

I was not able to successfully import a single disk into a 3ware mirror without compromising the existing data. I recommend using a traditional backup and restore procedure if you have a single disk system that you would like to upgrade to a RAID-1 using a 3ware controller.

Kernel Configuration

3ware controllers use the *3w-xxxx* SCSI driver. If you installed Linux directly onto a 3ware controller, *3w-xxxx* support is already enabled (although it is likely a loadable kernel module). Follow the steps in this section if you are installing a 3ware controller into an existing Linux system or want to compile a kernel without the *3w-xxxx* driver as a module. Although I have used the 2.4.18 kernel throughout most of this book, I recommend using a later kernel (2.4.19 became available in August 2002) for this process because the 3ware driver code has been significantly updated. It's likely that the 2.4.19 kernel will not make it into any distributions for quite some time, so I recommend manually upgrading after the initial installation when possible. Readers who are already using a 2.5 development kernel should already have the most recent code.

Support for 3ware ATA RAID controllers is found in the SCSI support section of the Linux kernel.

```
SCSI support --->
  ...
 SCSI low-level drivers --->
  <*> 3ware Hardware ATA-RAID support
  ...
```

Enable support statically (as I have shown above) or as a loadable kernel module. Next, execute *make* and copy the new kernel into your */boot* directory:

```
# make dep && make bzImage
# make modules && make modules_install
# cp arch/i386/boot/bzImage /boot/bzImage.3ware
# cp System.map /boot
```

Now add an entry for the new kernel to */etc/lilo.conf*, updating global parameters as needed, and execute */sbin/lilo* to rewrite the boot sector. When the system restarts, access your 3ware arrays like any normal SCSI device. Before creating a filesystem, you'll need to partition the array like any normal block device.

3DM Disk Manager

3ware provides the proprietary 3DM software package for post-installation array management. 3DM runs as a daemon and monitors 3ware controllers, reporting any information (such as errors, status changes, and array health) via *syslog*. Email alerts are also available.

Administrators can use a web browser to access 3DM's built-in web management interface. From the web interface, users can configure spare disks, email alerts and array properties, and monitor arrays and disks.

Downloading and installing 3DM

Download 3DM from the support section of 3ware's web site (*http://www.3ware. com*). 3DM is also available on the CD-ROM that was included with your controller. Unpack the tarball and execute the installation script:

```
# tar xzf 3dm.tgz
# cd 3dm
# ./install.3dm
```

The script will ask a few questions about how to install the software.

```
Was RPM used to install the Escalade driver and/or 3dm? (Y/N) [N]

**** 3DM version being installed is: 1.13.00.015 ****

Please enter the location of the help documentation. [/usr/local/doc/3dm]

Would you like to have email notification enabled? (Y/N) [Y]

Please enter the name of your mail server.            \
    [bored.cynicism.com]: smtp.cynicism.com

Please enter the name of the user you want sending email \
    notification. [root]: 3ware-controller

Please enter the name of the user you want receiving    \
    email notification. [3ware_admin]: admin

Please enter the port number you would like to use for   \
    web monitoring. [1080]: 8080

Would you like 3DM connection security to limit          \
    connections to localhost only? (Y/N) [Y]

**** Starting 3dmd using configuration found in          \
    /etc/3dmd.conf ****

Starting 3ware DiskSwitch daemon:                        [OK]
```

Notice that I have changed the SMTP server used to email alerts, as well as the sender and recipient addresses. You can fine-tune the other portions of installation as needed. For security reasons, I strongly recommend keeping the default localhost-only option. Since port 1080 is also the default port for a socks5 proxy, I have decided to change the port number to 8080. Using port 1080 will likely generate errors with some web browsers and distributions.

Configuration and usage

After installation, the *3dmd* program executes. If you need to change any of these options, edit the file */etc/3dmd.conf* and restart *3dmd* using the *init.d* script */etc/init.d/3dm*. Of particular note are the PORT and REMOTEACCESS lines, which control the port that the *3dmd* web server runs on, and whether or not hosts other than the localhost can connect.

Once 3DM is installed and running, use a web browser to connect to the controller. I strongly recommend changing the default password as a first step. Click the *Settings* tab at the top of the browser window. You'll see a *Change Password* section with text input boxes for both a user and an administrator password. The difference between the two security levels is that users have read-only access. Change them by entering the current password (the default password is "3ware") and your new password, as well as a confirmation for the new password. You must manually change both the user and administrator passwords, even if you want to use the same password for each. After the passwords are changed, they must be enabled in the Password Enable section, located just below the Password Change boxes. Once the passwords have been enabled, the 3DM web interface will prompt you to enter the new passwords before you can proceed. Please also note that the passwords' ciphertext is stored in the */etc/3dmd.conf* file. As always, securing services like *3dmd* at the network level is a recommended additional safeguard.

Most of 3DM's other features are very straightforward, and its documentation is thorough and accessible via the web interface. Use the Configuration tab to perform administrative tasks without taking the system offline. From the Configuration tab, you can add spare disks, remove failed disks, rebuild faulty arrays, and schedule regular integrity checks. The Settings tab controls 3DM's settings, but it also contains options to change the write caching for individual arrays, as well as the amount of the controller's resources dedicated to background tasks such as media verification and array rebuilds. The Monitor and Alarms tabs display status information about the controller and its arrays. And configuration information about the controllers and arrays is provided under the Details tab.

Running 3DM is not a requirement, but it will provide some additional helpful information about your 3ware arrays and controllers. Even if you prefer not to use the web interface to manage and monitor arrays, 3DM still provides useful information via *syslog* for a more traditional approach.

LSI Logic (MegaRAID)

LSI Logic (*http://www.lsilogic.com*) sells a variety of SCSI and ATA RAID controllers, all of which are directly supported by Linux. I evaluated both the Elite 1650, a dual-channel SCSI controller, and the MegaRAID i4, a quad-channel ATA controller.

Working with these controllers is identical, except for some hard disk-specific configuration options. So the information in this section applies to both the ATA and the SCSI controllers.

Like some of the Adaptec controllers, LSI Logic RAID controllers have also shipped as OEM products with Dell systems. If you have a Dell system with a branded LSI Logic controller, you might want to take a look at Matt Domsch's page on the subject: *http://www.domsch.com/linux/*.

Creating an Array

Users have two options when creating an array for the first time. When the controller's initialization banner appears, a choice between the MegaRAID Configuration Utility (CTRL-M) and WebBIOS (CTRL-H) is presented. The difference between the two really boils down to ease of use. The MegaRAID Configuration Utility is a typical menu-driven utility, while WebBIOS is a mouse-driven GUI tool. WebBIOS is a bit slower, and since it does require a mouse, it might not be a good choice for some systems, despite its ease of use. On the other hand, the legacy configuration utility is a bit cryptic. Some of its navigation and menus are confusing, and it's sometimes not clear what changes you are making to arrays and disks.

Installing Linux Directly to a MegaRAID Controller

Since support for LSI Logic controllers is integrated into the Linux kernel, distribution support is common and straightforward. Arrays appear during Linux installation as standard SCSI devices, and no special driver disks are needed. I tested installation using Red Hat, SuSE, Mandrake, and Debian.

The MegaRAID Driver

LSI Logic controllers are supported by the *megaraid* kernel driver, which is found in the SCSI low-level drivers configuration submenu:

```
SCSI support  --->
 SCSI low-level drivers  --->
 ...
 <*> AMI MegaRAID support
 ...
```

There are no other configurable kernel options for the *megaraid* driver.

Converting an Existing Standalone Disk to a Mirror

Follow these steps if you want to replace your existing disk controller with an LSI Logic RAID controller and mirror your existing system disk.

1. Before physically replacing the controller, configure a new kernel with support for the *megaraid* driver. After the kernel is compiled, install it and add an */etc/lilo.conf* stanza for it. Don't forget to run */sbin/lilo* to rebuild the master boot record, too.

2. Power down the system and install the new controller in place of your original disk controller. Connect your existing disk and any new disks to the new LSI Logic RAID adapter.

3. After powering on the system, use CTRL-M to enter the MegaRAID Configuration Utility. (You can, alternatively, use the WebBIOS tool to perform the steps I have outlined here. However, I'm going to provide step-by-step instructions for the MegaRAID Configuration Utility because it's usable by everyone and is a bit more obtuse.)

4. Choose Configure and then New Configuration from the main menu. A list of disks, organized by channel, is presented. Use the arrow keys to move between disks and the SPACEBAR to include a disk in the array. Select your original system disk first and then the new disk. Once a disk is selected, it will be marked online.

5. Press the ENTER key twice, and a window containing RAID properties appears. Make certain that RAID-1 is selected, and tune the other options to you meet your needs.

6. Choose Accept (you will need to press the ENTER key twice) and a final confirmation dialog appears. Answer yes, and the configuration is written into the controller's memory.

7. At the main menu, choose Check Consistency. Use the SPACEBAR to select the array you just created and press F10 to begin the consistency check. The process could take some time, but when it is complete, your RAID-1 will be operational. Then reboot the system and run Linux as you would normally.

Managing Arrays

Like many other hardware vendors, LSI Logic does not provide a way to manage arrays from within Linux. Dell has ported the MS-DOS version of the MegaRAID Configuration Utility to Linux, but if you use it, don't expect support from LSI Logic or Dell. Since Dell only uses certain LSI Logic controllers in its servers, you might experience varied results when using Dell's MegaRAID management utility. I recommend searching the Web to read about other users' experiences with the controller you purchased to find out if an undocumented bug destroys the information on your disks, or worse.

Download the utility from Matt Domsch's Linux web page (*http://www.domsch.com/linux/*). Using the utility is very straightforward; it's a statically compiled binary and works the same as the BIOS utility.

Filesystems

Choosing and properly configuring a filesystem is as important as selecting an appropriate RAID level. *ext2* (*the Second Extended Filesystem*) is the standard Linux filesystem. Many users will be perfectly happy using ext2; it is reliable and can be fine-tuned to meet specific demands of file usage. But while ext2 might be suitable for end users, it doesn't fare as well for large, heavily used filesystems that have extremely large files or thousands of small files. ext2 doesn't provide any way to maintain filesystem integrity through system crashes. Also, ext2 is slowly making way for *ext3*, a journaling filesystem that I'll cover later in this chapter. Maintaining data integrity and availability has become an essential requirement for all critical systems. After all, this is one of the most recognizable benefits of RAID. Fortunately, there are a wide variety of filesystems for Linux that implement crash recovery and prevention features. These systems are collectively called journaling filesystems, and their main distinction from traditional Unix filesystems is that they don't require filesystem checks after a system crash. I'll cover journaling in greater detail later in this chapter. Even if you aren't interested in journaling filesystems right now, it's a good idea to begin learning about them. It won't be long before your need for increased data reliability or fast recovery may force you to make a change to a journaling filesystem.

There are several alternatives to ext2, in the event that it does not meet your needs. IBM has ported its *JFS* implementation to Linux. (Like many computer industry terms, JFS has a dual meaning. It refers generically to any journaling filesystem, but also refers specifically to the IBM implementation.) Silicon Graphics has released *XFS*, the longtime journaling filesystem of the IRIX platform, for Linux. And Hans Reiser has created *ReiserFS*, a journaling filesystem developed specifically for Linux. Finally, ext3 enhances the features of ext2 by adding journaling capabilities, along with many other features.

This chapter includes information about each of these filesystems, but a complete primer on the different filesystems is well beyond the scope of this book. I have provided enough information here so that you can make an informed decision about which filesystem to choose, how to patch your kernel, and how to build the filesystem. I strongly recommend reading more about each of the filesystems at their respective web sites (for which I've provided references).

Each of the filesystems that I cover in this chapter, including ext2, can be fine-tuned using filesystem parameters and mount options. In this chapter, I will explain how to make some adjustments that will improve overall system performance.

Basic Filesystem Concepts

This section provides some basic information about filesystems. While this overview is far from complete, it should help you decide which filesystem will best meet your needs.

If you're interested in learning more about filesystems, I recommend Moshe Bar's book *Linux Filesystems* (McGraw-Hill). William Von Hagen's book of the same name (Sams) also comes highly recommended, although I haven't had time to purchase and read a copy. There is an abundance of online resources about filesystems, both for Linux and for other operating systems. Without question, the site that stands out Daniel Robbins's Advanced Filesystem Implementor's Guide, available from the IBM DeveloperWorks web site at *http://www.ibm.com/developerworks/library/l-fs.html*. I've also pointed out online material that is specific to each filesystem throughout the rest of this chapter.

Blocks and Inodes

All Unix filesystems use two basic components to organize and store data: *blocks* and *inodes*. Just as a physical disk is organized into sectors, data on a filesystem is abstracted into *blocks*. Blocks have a fixed size, determined at the time the filesystem is created. The *block size* of a filesystem determines how many bytes are allocated to each block on the filesystem. Generally, block sizes are 1 KB, 2 KB, or 4 KB for 32-bit systems. A block size of 8 KB is also available on 64-bit systems.

Inodes are used to map blocks to physical disk locations on Unix filesystems. Every file created, whether it's a directory, normal file, or special file, is assigned an inode. Inodes work in much the same way as pointers do in programming languages such as C, Perl, and Java. Inodes also store information about a file, including its type, size, and parent directory. On traditional Unix filesystems, inodes are typically allocated when the filesystem is created. ext2, for example, allocates one inode for every 8 KB worth of data blocks when a new filesystem is initialized, although this value can be manually altered. That means an ext2 filesystem with a block size of 4 KB allocates a single inode for every two data blocks.

When a filesystem runs out of inodes, no new files can be created until existing files are deleted, thereby freeing up inodes that are already in use. For this reason, many new filesystems implement dynamic inode allocation, freeing system administrators from worrying about such limitations.

Space efficiency versus performance

Most filesystems use a default block size of 4 KB, but that size might not be efficient for all situations. Let's say that you have a partition that contains many files that are smaller than 4096 bytes. When those files are created, the remaining space in each block is wasted. So on a filesystem that contains many files that are smaller than the block size, you end up with a lot of wasted disk space. Tailoring the block size to meet the needs of your data helps you use disk space efficiently. A block size of 1024 or 2048 bytes on partitions that are expected to utilize many small files will help maximize disk usage, though files smaller than the block size will still waste disk space on some filesystems.

There is a trade-off when using smaller block sizes. Bigger block sizes mean that fewer I/O operations are required when reading larger files. For example, on a filesystem with a block size of 4096 bytes, only one block needs to be accessed to read a file that is 3 KB. On a filesystem with a block size of 1024 bytes, three different blocks must be accessed for I/O on that file. Now, consider a file that is many megabytes in length. The increase in the number of blocks that must be accessed to read that file is substantial when a smaller block size is used. In cases in which the blocks holding the data in the file are not contiguous, that also means that additional operations to locate the data blocks must also be performed.

Remember my discussion of sequential disk I/O from Chapter 2. Using bigger block sizes helps increase sequential data access for large files. Larger block sizes reduce file fragmentation by insuring that bigger chunks of files are contiguous. This translates into improved performance because the disk performs fewer seeks when reading or writing large files.

In general, use smaller block sizes when you anticipate creating many small files that could fit into single small blocks. Use a larger block size when you expect to be working with larger files. As a rule, you can safely use the 4 KB default block size on filesystems larger than a few hundred megabytes. Unless you have sound reasons for going with a smaller block size, 4 KB is likely to be a good choice.

Organization

Different filesystems implement different methods for organizing data. Traditional Unix filesystems relied on linked lists to organize inodes and data blocks. A table of inodes pointed to a physical disk block. This arrangement obviously doesn't scale well. So, newer filesystems have sought to optimize the process. ext2, for example, applies a block bitmap and splits up the inode table so that it is distributed across the entire disk. Rather than look up a data block from a single, large table, a filesystem such as ext2 needs to examine only a small subset of inodes to perform I/O.

As the complexity of applications and operating systems has evolved, so has filesystem design. Today, many new filesystems implement a data structure known as a B-tree to organize the filesystem. B-trees have been used in database design for many years. A B-tree is optimized so that it can be quickly accessed, even when it's stored on a hard disk. This usually means that the size of a leaf in a B-tree is equal to, or is some function of, the size of a filesystem data block.

A B-tree is similar to a balanced binary tree, with a few notable exceptions. B-trees have a large branching factor. Where a binary tree has only two leaves per node, a B-tree can have many, which makes the path to access data much shorter. In turn, the height of a B-tree is small, compared with a traditional binary tree. Some filesystems use B-trees exclusively, while others implement a combination with the traditional linked-list/block bitmap approach. A thorough discussion of data structures and algorithms is beyond the scope of this chapter, however. I humbly refer your to more learned texts on the subject, such as *Readings in Database Systems*, edited by Michael Stonebreaker and Joseph M. Hellerstein (Morgan Kaufmann); *The Art of Computer Programming*, by Donald E. Knuth (Addison-Wesley); and *Algorithms in C*, by Robert Sedgewick (Addison-Wesley).

Journaling Filesystems

Journaling offers improved filesystem reliability and fast crash recovery through the use of a transaction log, or journal. The journal is an on-disk log of metadata, or data about the filesystem, that is kept up-to-date as the filesystem changes.

Filesystems without journaling store changes to the updates in memory. These changes are periodically flushed from memory and written to disk. If a crash occurs before the buffers are flushed, data that has not been written to disk is lost. Instead of storing these changes in memory, a journaling filesystem writes a log of the changes to disk. The actual data is kept in memory until enough free system resources are available so that the full write operations can be performed efficiently. When the data is committed to disk, the journals are updated.

The journal allows a filesystem to instantly recover to the last good state after a system crash. After the system reboots, outstanding consistent entries in the journal are replayed (committed to disk), while any remaining inconsistent entries are discarded. This process is often referred to as a *log replay*. The benefit here is that you don't have to wait for a large filesystem to *fsck*. Journaling is especially helpful when working with RAID because arrays tend to be larger than single disks, which already take a long time to *fsck*. Imagine waiting for *fsck* to complete on a terabyte RAID partition that is using ext2. The downtime could be hours, or even days! With a journaling filesystem, the replay process generally takes only a few seconds, or at most a few minutes.

Doesn't journaling hurt performance?

Normally, the process of maintaining a journal would carry serious performance overhead. However, two factors help alleviate this additional load. First, journaling usually records only metadata, which has a very small overhead. Second, unlike traditional Unix filesystems, most journaling filesystems are designed with performance in mind. While a well-designed nonjournaling filesystem would outperform a similarly designed journaling filesystem, the new journaling filesystems available for Linux typically perform at least as well as legacy filesystems.

Just as RAID offers varying trade-offs between performance and reliability, so do journaling filesystems. While all journaling filesystems support metadata journaling, some support data journaling as well.

The Linux Virtual Filesystem (VFS)

The Virtual Filesystem (VFS) was developed to provide a common interface for many filesystems to interoperate with the Linux kernel. The VFS is an additional layer of abstraction between specific filesystem implementations and system calls. Figure 6-1 illustrates the relationship between filesystems, block devices, and the VFS.

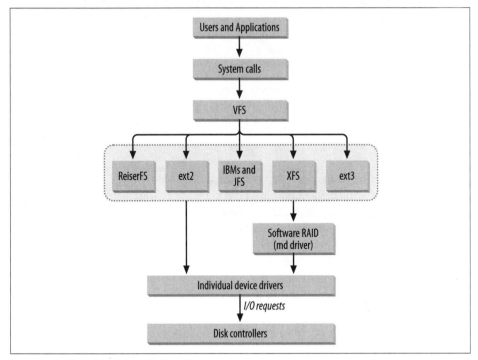

Figure 6-1. The Linux Virtual Filesystem.

The Linux kernel and the VFS impose some limits that affect the usability of any filesystem. Originally, the Linux file access API used a signed 32-bit value to represent file sizes on 32-bit systems such as x86 and PowerPC. This imposed a serious limit because file size could never be larger than a single 32-bit value. Using 32-bit values to store file sizes limits users to a maximal file size of 2^{31} (2,147,483,648) bits or 2 GB. Beginning with the 2.4 series kernel, this limit was raised to 1 terabyte (TB) or 1000 GB. Patches to correct the 2 GB limitation are available for 2.0 and 2.2 series kernels. Libraries and applications must also be patched if you want large file support. So even with a patched kernel, not all applications will support large file sizes natively. For more information on large file support, see *http://www.suse.de/~aj/linux_lfs.html*. Also note that many distributions that shipped 2.0 and 2.2 series kernels came with large file support already implemented. Check the specific distribution if you are unable to use 2.4, or later, kernels.

Limits on file sizes are also imposed by the filesystem, but these usually exceed the kernel API limit significantly. For general purposes, the maximum file size for any filesystem is limited to 1 TB, although filesystems could support larger sizes natively.

The maximum size of a filesystem on a 32-bit system is also limited by the kernel. Linux imposes a hard limit of 2 TB on any filesystem. In fact, the hard limit for just about anything running under Linux, as of version 2.4, is 2 TB. This 2 TB limit is much smaller than many filesystems are capable of supporting.

64-bit architectures

64-bit systems are not subject to the same limitations as 32-bit systems because they use a 64-bit value to represent file sizes. On 64-bit systems such as Alpha and IA64, files can be as large as 2^{63}, 8 exabytes (EB), or 8 million TB.

ext2

ext2, originally released in 1993, has a single advantage over the new, high-performance filesystems available to Linux users: it is the most widely implemented filesystem for Linux and has undergone seven years' worth of development and debugging. ext2 is not without its limitations. For example, unlike some newer filesystems, which can dynamically allocate inodes, ext2 allocates a fixed number of inodes when the filesystem is created. As a result, users must plan carefully when creating large filesystems because when all inodes are exhausted, no new files can be created. The only options at that point are to build a new filesystem or to erase existing files in order to deallocate inodes.

ext2 Organization

Each ext2 filesystem contains a *superblock*. The superblock contains general information about the filesystem, including its block size, the total number of inodes and

---

blocks in the filesystem, and information about the state of the filesystem. The super-block is essential for successfully mounting an ext2 filesystem. The superblock is stored at the beginning of a filesystem, at an offset of 1024 bytes from the start of the device. Because of its importance, backup copies of the superblock are stored throughout the filesystem in *block groups*.

Block groups are collections of blocks that further organize an ext2 filesystem. In addition to containing a fixed amount of blocks, each block group originally stored a backup copy of the superblock. However, this method wasted space, and now backup copies are stored only in block groups 0 and 1, as well as block groups that are powers of 3, 5, and 7. This distribution conserves space, while insuring that a usable copy of the superblock is always intact. In the event that the superblock becomes corrupt, a mount option allows system administrators to specify an alternate superblock location.

Each block group begins with a group descriptor, which contains a block bitmap, an inode bitmap, and an inode table. (The group descriptor follows the superblock backup on block groups that contain a backup of the superblock.) The block and inode bitmaps are simply bit patterns that identify which blocks and inodes in the current block group have been allocated. The inode table contains pointers to data blocks in the current block group.

Block groups help improve disk performance in two ways. First, because each block group has its own inode table, the time between looking up an inode and retrieving data blocks is decreased. Imagine if the inode table were centralized, for example, at the beginning of the disk. The time needed to move the actuator arm to the inode table and then back out to data blocks would significantly impact performance.

Block groups also help improve performance by keeping data in the same block group as its inodes and by attempting to store an entire file in the same block group. Overall, block groups help reduce the number of seeks a hard disk needs to make when locating and accessing files.

Creating an ext2 Filesystem

The *mke2fs* command is used to create ext2 filesystems on disk partitions or RAID devices. In addition, ext2 users have several other commands at their disposal to manage ext2 filesystems. Of particular note is *tune2fs*, which allows administrators to configure tunable ext2 parameters that don't require re-initialization of the filesystem. *tune2fs*, as well as many other useful ext2 utilities, is available as part of the *e2fsprogs* package, which is included with most distributions and is available from *http://e2fsprogs.sourceforge.net*.

By default, *mke2fs* creates a filesystem on the specified device, using a block size of 4096 bytes.

```
# mke2fs /dev/md0
```

Use the *-b* flag to change the default block size.

```
# mke2fs -b 1024 /dev/md0
```

Normally, the number of inodes is automagically computed by *mke2fs*, based on the block size chosen (8192 bytes for each inode, by default). However, if the values that *mke2fs* computes are inadequate, the ratio of inodes to bytes can be altered as well. Note that the ratio of bytes to inodes should never be smaller than the block size. As the number of bytes per inode increases, you are left with fewer inodes; as the number decreases (or approaches the block size), more inodes are created. Here is an example that creates an ext2 filesystem with a block size of 1024 bytes and an inode ratio of 2048 bytes per inode, or one inode for every two blocks:

```
# mke2fs -b 1024 -i 2048 /dev/md0
```

This arrangement might be useful for a system where you expect to find many small files, varying in size from 1 to 2 KB. *mke2fs* also lets you specify the number of inodes without attempting to compute the value. Use the *-N* flag to pass a fixed number of inodes to *mke2fs*.

```
# mke2fs -N 8960896 /dev/md0
```

Tuning ext2 Filesystems

As I mentioned in the previous section, *tune2fs* can configure variables associated with an already initialized ext2 filesystem. In addition, there are a number of other tactics that you can use to improve the performance of an ext2 partition: software-RAID-specific options for *mke2fs*, mount options, and filesystem attributes.

Reserved space

ext2 sets aside a fixed amount of space, by default, for the super-user. This reserved space is supposed to ensure that essential processes, usually running with a UID or GID of *root*, are able to continue writing data, even after the filesystem becomes full for normal users. In practice, nonprivileged users and processes are often able to unintentionally bypass this safeguard, so it's not really a reliable security mechanism.

By default, 5 percent of the total disk space is reserved when an ext2 filesystem is created. Using the *-m* flag, users can adjust this percentage to meet their needs. An integer value between 1 and 100 must be used. In this example, 10 percent of the total disk space is reserved:

```
# mke2fs -m 10 /dev/md0
```

It might also be useful to change the user who is allowed to write data to the reserved disk space. Since security is such a well-publicized issue these days, many programs no longer run as *root*. Therefore, you might find it useful to allow the user account under which your database runs, for instance, to have access to the reserved areas on certain partitions. Use the *tune2fs* command to modify the reserved blocks UID and group. It's safe to make this change while the filesystem is mounted.

```
# tune2fs -u mysql -g mysql /dev/md0
tune2fs 1.18, 11-Nov-1999 for EXT2 FS 0.5b, 95/08/09
Setting reserved blocks gid to 75
Setting reserved blocks uid to 75
```

There is some confusion surrounding the need for reserved space under ext2. Many administrators create ext2 filesystems without any reserved space, or with the minimum amount (1 percent), when working with extremely large partitions. Their reasoning is that when the reserved space option was introduced, even big partitions were small by today's standards. So reserving the default 5 percent on a partition typical for large systems, such as 40 GB, is perceived as a waste of valuable disk space. Generally, the super-user doesn't need that much reserved space because partitions that large are normally user partitions such as */home*.

However, reserved space is essential for minimizing file *fragmentation*. Fragmentation occurs as filesystems become increasingly full. As space on a disk decreases, it becomes more unlikely that large files can be stored in contiguous disk blocks. Because the file must be spread across different parts of the disk, the actuator arm needs to move more frequently to access those fragmented files. The result is slower disk performance.

Theodore Ts'o, an ext2 developer, advises:

> As the [filesystem] get[s] progressively full, the chance for fragmentation goes up. So it is appropriate to use a constant percentage of the total filesystem size for the reserved space. If you have a 500GB array, using 25GB of reserved space is therefore not necessarily overkill. It sounds like a lot of space, but it's still only 5 percent of the total filesystem.

The dangers of fragmentation present themselves only when a filesystem changes. Therefore, reserved space might not be needed at all when data is static. For example, an array serving large images that never change (perhaps from a popular space telescope), might require a filesystem that doesn't waste any space. Simply adding new images, without erasing old ones, isn't going to cause fragmentation.

RAID options

Using the *-R* flag to *mke2fs* sets options specific to software RAID during filesystem initialization. Currently, only one option is available—stride, which distributes metadata blocks evenly across an array so that an equal number of blocks is included in each chunk-size stripe. An array with a 64 KB chunk-size and an ext2 filesystem with a block size of 4 KB needs 16 blocks to fill a 64 KB chunk. In this case, a stride of 16 will yield optimal performance.

```
# mke2fs -b 4096 -R stride=16
```

The stride option increases the performance of any striped array (RAID-0, RAID-4, and RAID-5), but it has no impact on linear arrays or mirroring arrays.

Access time

Each file on an ext2 partition contains metadata concerning when it was created (ctime), the last time it was modified (mtime), and the last time it was accessed (atime). Whenever a file is written, its ctime and mtime are updated, and because these values are updated during write operations, the performance overhead is not noticeable. Keeping track of when files were created and modified is also quite useful for system administration, while access times are not often required.

Unlike modification and creation timestamps, *access time (atime)* is updated whenever a file is read or opened. This means that each time a file is accessed (read), a write operation, albeit a small one, is performed. On heavily used filesystems, this process can become an unwarranted burden. Is it really necessary to update the atime every time the *ls* command is executed? Certainly not. Likewise, the overhead needed to update the atime for files stored in news and mail spool directories, web caches, and *httpd* servers' document roots is also a waste of performance.

You can use the *chattr* command to set files and directories so that their atime is no longer updated.

```
# chattr +A /bin/ls
```

Using *chattr +A* on a directory automatically sets the noatime option for all new files created within that directory tree. But files that already exist under a directory structure must be manually changed after the command is issued. You can recursively set entire directory structures to cease recording atime information using the *-R* flag.

```
# chattr -R +A /usr/local/httpd/htdocs/
```

Modifying the *atime* flag is useful when you wish to continue updating access times for certain files and directories, while ignoring them for others. In some circumstances, it might be useful to ignore all atime updates for an entire mounted partition. For example, a machine that is hosting Usenet news might use a software RAID to store new articles. Passing the noatime option at mount time is better than issuing *chattr*, because storing the atime for any file on the news spool is unnecessary.

```
# mount -o noatime /dev/md0 /var/spool/news
```

A working example

To illustrate the ext2 features I have discussed so far, I'll create a RAID-5 array with a 32 KB chunk-size. This array will contain mostly compressed graphics files that are each about 100 KB in size. In this case, I'm not worried about the default number of inodes, because given the average image size, it's unlikely that all of my inodes will be exhausted before running out of space on the array. I'll create the filesystem with the following command:

```
# mke2fs -b 4096 -R stride=8 /dev/md0
```

Here, I've initialized an ext2 filesystem, making sure to include eight 4 KB blocks in each 32 KB array stripe. Because I'm working with large files, I've also chosen a block size of 4 KB—the maximum for the 32-bit system that I'm using. Since I plan to use this array as part of an *httpd* image server, I'm also going to modify my */etc/fstab* to automatically mount the array with the noatime option, so that I won't waste any time storing file metadata that I'll never use.

```
/dev/md0   /var/spool/news   ext2   defaults,noatime   1,2
```

ext3 Extensions for the ext2 Filesystem

ext3 is an attempt to add many of the features found in other journaling filesystems to the ext2 filesystem. Many users feel that this design approach will cause ext3 to inherit some problems that have arisen with ext2 over the years, and have instead opted to use a journaling filesystem that has been developed from the ground up, like ReiserFS. However, many also feel that by adding the journaling features onto ext2, users of ext3 are inheriting the time-tested reliability of the ext2 filesystem. And since ext3 is fully forward- and backward-compatible with ext2, users don't need to go through a tedious backup and restore process to upgrade older ext2 systems.

Regardless of whether you are ready to embrace ext3 or remain a skeptic, two things are certain. First, ext3 will become pervasive, simply because ext2 is so widely deployed. Second, ext2 is always being improved, so just because ext3 inherits its architecture from ext2 doesn't mean that there isn't room for it to develop as a filesystem.

ext3 supports journaling for metadata only, as well as combined journaling of data and metadata. That means users can improve the reliability of their filesystems by taking additional safeguards against data loss resulting from a system crash. ext3 inherits filesystem and file size limits from ext2. It also uses the same data structures and organization as ext2.

Support for ext3 has been included with the stable Linux kernel since 2.4.15. Users working with older kernels can apply a patch to gain ext3 support. As always, upgrading to the most recent stable kernel is advisable, when possible.

Patching the Kernel for ext3 Support

Patches for 2.4 series kernels are available from *http://www.zip.com.au/~akpm/linux/ext3/*. Download the patch that matches the kernel version you are working with and apply it to a clean kernel. If you don't find a patch for the kernel you are working with, upgrade. For example, if you are using 2.4.10, enter the following:

```
# cd /usr/src/linux-2.4.10
# patch -p1 < /usr/src/patches/ext3-2.4-0.9.10-2410
```

Patches for 2.2 kernels are available from *ftp://ftp.uk.linux.org/pub/linux/sct/fs/jfs/*, although using a 2.4 kernel is recommended.

Compiling the Kernel with ext3 Support

In 2.4 kernels, ext3 features are found under the Filesystems section of the kernel configuration.

```
Filesystems  --->
[...]
<*> Ext3 journalling file system support (EXPERIMENTAL)
[ ]   JBD (ext3) debugging support
```

The first option (CONFIG_EXT3_FS) turns on support for ext3 filesystems. It can be compiled statically (as shown above) or as a module.

 For 2.2 kernels, ext3 support is listed as *Second extended fs development code*, and not as ext3.

You can also enable debugging support (CONFIG_JBD_DEBUG) if you are trying to track a problem. When debugging support is activated, you need to set a debug level before any information is reported. Set the debug level by echoing a number between 1 and 5 to the file */proc/sys/fs/jdb-debug*.

```
# echo 5 > /proc/sys/fs/jdb-debug
```

The number indicates the verbosity level. A higher number means more verbosity. During normal use, you can leave debugging disabled by never setting the verbosity level. This way, you can keep its support compiled into the kernel without risking the performance degradation normally associated with such logging.

After the new kernel is compiled, installed, and running, you should see ext3 listed in */proc/filesystems*. If you compiled ext3 as a module, it won't appear in */proc/filesystems* until it is inserted.

Working with ext3

To successfully use ext3, you need a version of the *e2fsprogs* package that is newer than 1.25. As of this writing, release 1.27 is available. To determine which version of the toolset you have installed, execute *mke2fs* with the *-v* option:

```
# mke2fs -V
mke2fs 1.27 (8-Mar-2002)
    Using EXT2FS Library version 1.27
```

If you are using an older version, download a new one from the *e2fsprogs* home page (*http://e2fsprogs.sourceforge.net/*), compile, and install it. You may also be able to get an update from your distributor, although the tools can sometimes be a revision behind.

All of the traditional ext2 tools, like *tune2fs*, can also be used with ext3 filesystems. Be certain to check the manual pages to see which options apply; not all do. I've outlined some specific tasks in the rest of this section, but this information is by no means comprehensive.

Creating an ext3 Partition

You can create ext3 partitions by adding parameters to the *mke2fs* command. Executing *mke2fs -j* creates an ext3 filesystem. For example:

```
# mke2fs -j /dev/md0
```

The program *mkfs.ext3* is equivalent to executing *mke2fs -j*.

The size of the journal can be fine-tuned, but must be a minimum of 1024 blocks and cannot exceed 102,400 blocks. If you are using a block size of 2048 bytes, the minimum usable journal size is 2 MB and the maximum is 200 MB. By default, 8192 blocks are allocated (32 MB when using a 4 KB block size). The default block size for an ext3 filesystem, as for an ext2 filesystem, is 4096 bytes. Thus, the following example creates an ext3 filesystem with a journal size of 16 MB (4096 blocks * 4096 bytes per block).

```
# mke2fs -j -J size=16 /dev/md0
```

Converting an ext2 Filesystem to ext3

Perhaps the most convenient benefit of using ext3 is the ability to convert old ext2 partitions without destroying data or relying on a backup and restore process. Use the *tune2fs* command to add journal support to an existing ext2 partition. This method has been tested and proven safe by many users, but the paranoid should make certain they have backups.

```
# tune2fs -j /dev/md0
tune2fs 1.25 (20-Sep-2001)
Creating journal inode: done
```

While it's possible to upgrade a mounted ext2 partition, you will need to remount the filesystem as ext3 before journaling commences.

```
# umount /mnt/array
# mount -t ext3 /dev/md0 /mnt/ext3
```

Now that the filesystem has been upgraded, change your */etc/fstab* entry to indicate that the partition is an ext3.

Tuning ext3 Features

You can make a variety of performance-tuning enhancements to the ext3 filesystem. Remember that in addition to the changes I've outlined in this section, the performance tweaks associated with ext2 (like the `noatime` mount option) also apply to ext3 partitions. In fact, using `noatime` on any journaling filesystem is strongly recommended. Because all changes to the filesystem are logged, the impact of access time updates is amplified. This is especially noticeable on heavily used systems.

Data journaling

By default, only metadata journaling is enabled for an ext3 filesystem. To enable data journaling, mount the filesystem with the option `data=journal`. For example:

```
# mount -t ext3 -o data=journal /dev/md0 /mnt/ext3
```

While data journaling should slow down the overall performance of your filesystem, there has been some suggestion that in certain situations it could improve performance. I recommend testing each option. The default ext3 operations (`data=ordered`) specify that data should be written to disk before metadata. This is the default because it offers the best trade-off between performance and reliability.

The `data=writeback` option provides the best overall performance, but impairs reliability a bit. Unlike ordered writes, writeback mode places no constraints on the order in which data and metadata are written to disk. While filesystem integrity is maintained using writeback mode, it's possible that some data will not be committed to disk in the event of a system crash, meaning that you could be left with some old data. Still, this sacrifice is worthwhile on systems that require the highest level of performance.

Use the following command to mount an ext3 filesystem in writeback mode:

```
# mount -t ext3 -o data=writeback /dev/md0 /mnt/ext3
```

Once you've decided on the best journaling mode, add the mount option into your */etc/fstab* file so that it's always selected when the system restarts.

Using a separate journal device

To improve overall performance, try creating the journal for an ext3 partition on a separate device. For example, creating a journal on a small RAID-1 partition when the filesystem uses RAID-0 or RAID-5 for data adds some protection.

First, you need to create a journal device. This can be any block device attached to the system. The only requirement for the journal device is that it use the same block size as the ext3 filesystem for which it provides journaling.

```
# mke2fs -O journal_dev /dev/md0
```

Now */dev/md0* is a journal device usable by an ext3 filesystem. When a journal device is created, all the space available on the device is allocated for the journal, so it's important to repartition your disks appropriately. Using a pair of 9 GB disks for a journal device is overkill and will impact performance, especially when the system boots. Create smaller partitions and add them to your array. Next, create an ext3 filesystem that uses your journal device to store transaction logs. For instance, the following creates */dev/md1* and allocates the preexisting */dev/md0* as its journal device:

```
# mke2fs -J device=/dev/md0 /dev/md1
```

Further Information

For more detailed information about ext3, refer to the ext3 home page (*http://www.zipworld.com.au/~akpm/linux/ext3/*) as a starting point. The ext3 mailing list is also of particular interest:

> *https://listman.redhat.com/mailman/listinfo/ext3-users/*

Finally, the following paper describing some of ext3's features:

> *http://www.redhat.com/support/wpapers/redhat/ext3/index.html*

ReiserFS

ReiserFS is the brainchild of Hans Reiser, although today, a large cavalcade of developers is involved in its production. ReiserFS was the first journaling filesystem developed for Linux and has held its own remarkably well, considering that IBM and SGI have contributed impressive alternatives (the JFS and XFS filesystems, respectively).

Reiser began the ReiserFS project with an untraditional design that uses balanced trees[*] to manage and organize the filesystem, instead of a traditional linked list approach. Balanced trees have been used for quite some time in database architecture, but various disappointing attempts to create balanced-tree filesystems have led many in the operating system community to believe they are not suited to that purpose. Reiser, on the other hand, maintains that a proper implementation will eventually result in a better-performing and more reliable filesystem. While some other filesystems that have implemented the balanced tree algorithm used the tree to manage only metadata, ReiserFS stores both files and filesystem metadata in the balanced tree structure.

---

[*] A balanced tree is a tree where the lowest level of the tree must become full before a node is created at the next level. This arrangement ensures maximum efficiency in searching, because at most, half of the nodes in a tree must be examined for any given search. The trade-off lies in adding more overhead to each change in the tree. The balanced tree that ReiserFS uses has a maximum depth of 5, by default.

The ReiserFS design approach works very well for small files and for filesystem meta-operations, such as deletion. While ReiserFS used to struggle with performance on larger files, those issues have now been all but resolved, and some improved code for large files will appear in the 2.4.20 kernel, as well as in future development kernels. Performance continues to be a priority for Hans Reiser, and it's one of the main goals of ReiserFS version 4. Reiser writes:

> Most filesystems are able to run at close to disk bandwidth for large files unless data journaling is in use, and large files without data journaling on are not a good discriminator among filesystems anymore. Reiser4 will be unique in being able to run at close to disk bandwidth with data journaling on, and it will be able to run at close to disk bandwidth with medium and small files written in large batches. In version 3 we turn off data journaling by default, because for large files the performance is horrible due to needing to write the data twice. Wandering logs in V4 cure that, and data journaling will be the default. V4 is in alpha testing now.

ReiserFS originally provided metadata journaling only. In other words, the filesystem remembered after a crash that you wanted to move or delete a file, but did not remember how a file's contents might have changed. When kernel 2.4.20 is released, ReiserFS will support data journaling as well. Previously, users had to apply a patch, written by Chris Mason of SuSE, if they wanted data journaling under ReiserFS.

ReiserFS also implements a file packing approach called *file tails*. File tails allow unused portions of a filesystem block to be reused to store other files. That means that almost no disk space is ever wasted, making storage extremely efficient in ReiserFS. Despite this, many users, as well as Reiser, find that ReiserFS begins to slow down as disks become full. Reiser notes, "Once a disk drive gets more than 85% full, the performance starts to suffer," and that as you approach higher percentages, performance is seriously degraded. But he points out, quite correctly, that this is true for nearly all filesystems. Remember that ext2 reserves 5 percent of the total disk space, by default, to help alleviate such issues. Also, because of ReiserFS's use of file tails, 85 percent full is a more accurate reflection of actual data usage, as opposed to an indication of how many blocks are allocated.

Unlike traditional Unix filesystems, such as ext2, ReiserFS provides dynamic inode allocation, which means that users don't need to worry about creating a filesystem with sufficient inodes ahead of time. New inodes are automatically allocated as needed.

ReiserFS has suffered some bad press over the years. User reports complaining about mysterious filesystem corruption and interoperability problems with NFS have clouded many of its benefits. But the NFS issues have been resolved, and many users have been working successfully with ReiserFS for quite a long time.

I strongly recommend reading the white papers, FAQ, and documentation available at the ReiserFS web site (*http://www.namesys.com*). The ReiserFS version 4 white paper also provides a good road map for future development and outlines some of the proposed changes that seek to rectify some of the known performance issues when using ReiserFS. You might also wish to subscribe to the ReiserFS mailing list. To do so, send an email to *reiserfs-list-subscribe@namesys.com*. The archives are available at *http://marc.theaimsgroup.com/?l=reiserfs&r=1&w=2*.

Installing Directly to ReiserFS

If you want to install a new Linux system that uses ReiserFS for system partitions, you will need to choose a distribution that provides installation support for ReiserFS. Currently, SuSE and Mandrake both support out-of-the-box installation. If you use Red Hat, type `linux reiserfs` at the boot prompt. Reiser FS now appears as a filesystem choice in Disk Druid. (Cory Ellenson (*http://www.ellenson.org*) gets credit for pointing out this trick to me.) By starting Red Hat in this fashion, you can install directly onto a software RAID with ReiserFS.

Debian users who want to install directly onto ReiserFS should take a look at *http://kebo.vlsm.org/debian-extra/reiserfs/*. That is the best resource I could locate for Debian/ReiserFS boot media. I advise you to search for additional resources. If you have an existing system and merely want to add ReiserFS support, move on to the next section.

Compiling the Kernel with ReiserFS Support

Support for ReiserFS has been included in the stable Linux kernel since 2.4.1. Enable support for ReiserFS (`CONFIG_REISERFS_FS`) in the Filesystems section of the kernel configuration.

```
Filesystems  --->
<*> Reiserfs support
[ ]   Have reiserfs do extra internal checking
[ ]   Stats in /proc/fs/reiserfs
```

Depending on which sublevel release you are using, you might also need to activate support for development drivers (`CONFIG_EXPERIMENTAL`) because ReiserFS was not considered stable until 2.4.18. ReiserFS may also be compiled as a loadable kernel module.

After you enable support for ReiserFS, two more options appear. The first, `CONFIG_REISERFS_CHECK`, turns on debugging for ReiserFS. This option should always be disabled, unless you are experiencing problems and are planning to send in a bug report. In that case, turning on the extra internal checking might provide you with a useful error message that you can show to developers. Filesystem performance will be seriously hindered when this option is enabled, so don't forget to disable it after you have collected the error messages you need.

Enabling statistic reporting for */proc/fs/reiserfs* (`CONFIG_REISERFS_PROC_INFO`) will add some additional memory overhead to your kernel, but will provide you with statistics and internal data about your filesystem. The */proc/fs/reiserfs/* directory contains a subdirectory for each mounted ReiserFS partition and a file named *version* that contains the current filesystem driver version. Partition-specific subdirectories are named according to their driver and device major and minor numbers. For example, the directory *sd(8,6)* refers to */dev/sda6*. Each directory contains several undocumented files that report information about the filesystem.

/proc/fs/reiserfs support is generally used for development and testing. Few users enable statistics support because there are no user-space tools available to examine the data collected.

Patching older kernels

ReiserFS is not available for kernels prior to 2.2. Patches for the most recent 2.2 kernels are available from *ftp://ftp.namesys.com/pub/reiserfs-for-2.2/*. Grab the patch for the most recent 2.2 kernel and apply it to a corresponding unpatched 2.2 kernel source with commands such as the following:

```
# cd /usr/src/linux
# patch -p0 < /usr/src/patches/linux-2.2.19-reiserfs-3.5.35-patch.bz2
```

Now rebuild the kernel, turning on support for development drivers through CONFIG_ EXPERIMENTAL in the the Filesystems subsection and enabling ReiserFS support through CONFIG_REISERFS_FS, as described in the previous section. Compile the kernel as you would normally, install it, and rebuild your boot sector as required.

 There are several known issues with 2.2 kernels and ReiserFS, including one problem that affects the usage of disks larger than 32 GB. There are also compatibility issues with ReiserFS and Linux's software RAID subsystem in the 2.2 kernel. These issues prevent RAID-1 and RAID-5 from working properly with ReiserFS and a 2.2 kernel. You should be able to successfully use linear mode and RAID-0 with ReiserFS and a 2.2 kernel, but I recommend upgrading to the 2.4 kernel, if possible. Please consult the ReiserFS FAQ (*http://www.namesys. com/faq.html*) for more information.

Creating a Filesystem

Like other filesystems, ReiserFS requires a set of tools to create and maintain filesystems. Download and install the most recent toolset from *ftp://ftp.namesys.com/pub/ reiserfsprogs*.

```
# tar xzvf reiserfsprogs-3.6.2.tar.gz
# cd reiserfsprogs-3.6.2
# ./configure
# make && make install
```

An RPM is also available from the NAMESYS FTP server, if you prefer not to compile the tools yourself. Most distributors now provide a *reiserfsprogs* RPM as well. Debian users can simply enter:

```
# apt-get install reiserfsprogs
```

Use the *mkreiserfs* program to create a new filesystem on an unused partition. Remember that this process will destroy all existing data on the partition. The default options should be fine for most situations. To create a ReiserFS on */dev/sdb1*, enter:

```
# mkreiserfs /dev/sdb1
```

mkreiserfs generates some output describing the filesystem that was created. The default block size of 4 KB is the only block size currently supported. Additional block sizes are planned for future releases.

r5 is the default algorithm (hash function) that ReiserFS uses to locate files on disk. While two other hash functions (rupasov and tea) are available, r5 is the most reliable and performs best. rupasov should never be used, and tea should be used only when r5 presents problems, because the performance of tea is not as good. For more information about the particulars of each algorithm, including information about when to use tea in lieu of r5, check *http://www.namesys.com/mount-options.html*.

One option that may be useful with the *mkreiserfs* command is *--journal-device*, or *-j*, which specifies a separate disk partition for journaling. This is quite useful when you are working with a slower disk or array, but have access to a smaller partition on a faster disk. Thus, the following command creates a filesystem on */dev/sdb1* and uses */dev/sda6* for the journal:

```
# mkreiserfs -j /dev/sda6 -s 8193 /dev/sdb1
```

The *-s* option specifies the size of the journal (in blocks). If a size is not specified, *mkreiserfs* will use the entire partition for the journal, which is usually undesirable for large partitions. If you are using a separate journal device, it's wise to create a journal partition of the correct size ahead of time. The maximum size of a journal partition is 32749 and the minimum size is 513. The default size is 8193, and a 4 KB block size is assumed. Refer to the *mkreiserfs(8)* manual page for more filesystem options.

Mounting the filesystem

Mounting works the same way as in any other Linux filesystem:

```
# mount -t reiserfs /dev/sdb1 /mnt/reiserfs
```

ReiserFS has a number of mount options that affect its performance and behavior. Particularly interesting is the notail option, which disables the use of file tails and is reported to improve performance on systems with heavy random I/O—particularly systems with the type of activity that uses RAID-5.

 Craig Sanders originally reported this performance improvement on the Postfix mailing list. To read about it, see the thread *http:// archives.neohapsis.com/archives/postfix/2001-03/1071.html*, and specifically the message *http://archives.neohapsis.com/archives/postfix/ 2001-03/1148.html*. Related discussions have also taken place on the ReiserFS mailing list.

To disable the use of file tails, enter a command like the following:

```
# mount -t reiserfs -o notail /dev/sdb1 /mnt/reiserfs
```

The disadvantage of the notail mount option is that it eliminates the space efficiency gained through ReiserFS's method of file packing.

A complete list of options is available on the mount options web page (*http://www. namesys.com/mount-options.html*). In addition to options specific to ReiserFS, mount options like noatime (described earlier in this chapter in the "ext2" section, under "Access time") are also fair game.

reiserfsck, reiserfstune, and debugreiserfs

Despite its name, *reiserfsck* does not perform a traditional filesystem check, but rather replays transactions that might not have not been completed since the last unmount. This is usually done when the system boots (that's why the hard link *fsck. reiserfs* is also present), but system administrators can manually invoke *reiserfsck* in the following manner:

```
# reiserfsck /dev/sdb1
```

By default, *reiserfsck* performs a check and reports any errors found, but does not fix them. If no errors are detected, *reiserfsck* exits cleanly. To fix any fixable errors, try:

```
# reiserfsck --fix-fixable /dev/sdb1
```

reiserfstune and *debugreiserfs* perform additional administrative tasks on a filesystem. *reiserfstune* can be used to modify the filesystem's journal size and maximum transaction size (the number of journal updates possible without a commitment to disk). It's also useful for relocating a journal to another device. *debugreiserfs* displays the parameters of a ReiserFS and its journal. Without options, *debugreiserfs* displays the filesystem superblock. For further details, options, and examples, please refer to the *reiserfsck(8)*, *reiserfstune(8)*, and *debugreiserfs(8)* manual pages.

IBM JFS

IBM JFS was originally designed for the OS/2 Warp Server operating system. The filesystem was developed from the ground up for this operating system, not as an extended feature set for a nonjournaling filesystem. In addition to journaling capabilities, JFS also supports dynamic inode allocation. In February 2000, IBM began to port its JFS implementation to Linux.

JFS uses B+ trees to organize and manage large directories. B+ trees are similar to B-trees, but they use indexing to improve searches and data retrieval. Smaller directories—that is, directories with fewer than eight entries—use a traditional approach, storing directory information within the directory's inode. This two-pronged approach helps JFS perform well when working with heavily populated directories, as well as with sparse directories.

The maximum filesystem size under JFS is based on the chosen block size. With a 4 KB block size, a maximum filesystem size of 4 petabytes (4000 terabytes) is possible. With a block size of 512 bytes, a maximum of 512 terabytes is allowed.

Distribution Support

Recent versions of Red Hat, SuSE, Mandrake, and TurboLinux all support direct installation to JFS volumes. On Red Hat, the same trick that I mentioned earlier for ReiserFS applies. Although undocumented, typing *linux jfs* at the boot prompt causes JFS to appear as an option in Disk Druid. This allows you to install Linux directly to a software RAID, using JFS.

I am not aware of any boot media that allow Debian users to install a new system with JFS.

Patching the Kernel

JFS didn't make it into the official kernel releases until 2.5.6, so if you want to work with a 2.4 kernel, you will have to download and apply a patch. If you're confident using a development kernel, download the most recent 2.5 kernel and skip ahead to the next section, "Configuring the Kernel."

 IBM JFS was accepted into the 2.4 tree with 2.4.20-pre4. So users working with stable kernels later than 2.4.20 (which, at the time of this writing, is not yet released) won't need to go through the process of patching.

You can download a patch that matches your kernel version as well, as the most recent JFS core patch, from *http://www.ibm.com/developerworks/oss/jfs/*. Since I'm working with kernel 2.4.18, I downloaded both *jfs-2.4.18-patch* and *jfs-2.4-1.0.21.tar.gz*. After unpacking a clean 2.4.18 kernel, change into the source directory, apply the patch that is specific to 2.4.18, and unpack the jfs-1.0.21 archive.

```
# cd /usr/src/linux-2.4.18
# patch -p1 < /usr/src/patches/jfs-2.4.18-patch
# tar xzvf /usr/src/patches/jfs-2.4-1.0.21.tar.gz
```

The *jfs-2.4.18-patch* makes the necessary changes to the kernel configuration scripts. If no errors are encountered, the *patch* command outputs a list of the files that have been modified. If you encounter errors while patching, first ensure you are working with a clean kernel and then attempt to repatch.

Unpacking the file *jfs-2.4-1.0.21.tar.gz* creates the directories and files that comprise the JFS portions of the kernel source code. These files are created relative to the current path. So be sure to execute the *tar* command in the *root* directory of the kernel's source tree. Once the kernel is successfully patched and the JFS code has unpacked, you can begin configuration.

Configuring the Kernel

Turn on support for JFS (CONFIG_JFS_FS) from the Filesystems submenu:

```
File systems  --->
<*> JFS filesystem support
[ ]   JFS debugging
[ ]   JFS statistics
```

JFS support can also be compiled as a loadable kernel module. Debugging (CONFIG_JFS_DEBUG) provides some additional error reporting via the system log. It should normally remain disabled, although it has minimal overhead. Statistics support (CONFIG_JFS_STATISTICS) enables JFS statistics collection at */prov/fs/jfs*. It's safe to enable this option.

After you recompile, install, and boot the new JFS-enabled kernel, you should see JFS listed in */proc/filesystems*. If it does not appear there, make sure that you patched and compiled the kernel properly.

Installing the JFS Utilities

The JFS utilities let administrators create and manage JFS partitions. Download the utility archive that matches the JFS version you applied to your kernel from *http://www.ibm.com/developerworks/oss/jfs/*. In my case, I've downloaded *jfsutils-1.0.21.tar.gz*. Configure and build the JFS utilities as you would any standard GNU package:

```
# tar xzvf jfsutils-1.0.21.tar.gz
# cd jfsutils-1.0.21
# ./configure
# make && make install
```

Alternatively, an RPM containing the JFS utilities can be built using the command:

```
# rpm -ta jfsutils-1.0.21.tar.gz
```

You can also grab an RPM directly from your Linux distributor—many now provide one for *jfsutils*. Debian users may issue the command *apt-get install jfsutils*.

Always use a version of the utilities that matches the JFS kernel version. RPM and *.deb* users must double-check their utilities to ensure that they are up-to-date. Use *mkfs.jfs -V* to determine the current version.

Creating a filesystem

Use *mkfs.jfs* to create a new JFS filesystem:

```
# mkfs.jfs /dev/sdb1
mkfs.jfs version 1.0.21, 12-Aug-2002
Warning!  All data on device /dev/sdb1 will be lost!

Continue? (Y/N) y

Format completed successfully.

17920476 kilobytes total disk space.
```

The default block size, and the only one that is currently usable, is 4 KB. There are a few options for *mkfs.jfs* that are outlined in detail in its manual page. Mount the new JFS partition normally, using the *-t* flag to specify the filesystem type:

```
# mount -t jfs /dev/sdb1 /mnt/jfs
```

Several other utilities are also included with JFS that can be used to maintain and analyze the filesystem and the journals. *fsck.jfs* is used to replay transaction logs and ensure that the filesystem is clean. It is normally invoked automatically when the system boots, although system administrators can also invoke it manually. Also included in the *jfsutils* package are *logdump*, *xchkdmp*, *xchklog*, and *xpeek*. These utilities provide various low-level methods for examining and repairing the filesystem and its journals. Please read the associated manual pages before working with them.

Further Information

For more information about IBM JFS, consult the project web site at *http://oss. software.ibm.com/developer/opensource/jfs/*. Manual pages for each of the JFS utilities are also available. A short installation and overview document, created during the patch process, can be found in the sources under */usr/src/linux/Documentation/ filesystems/jfs.txt*.

You can also use Moshe Bar's JFS FAQ, located at *http://www.moelabs.com/modules. php?op=modload&name=FAQ&file=index&myfaq=yes&id_cat=1&categories=JFS*. In addition, there is a mailing list, complete with an archive, for JFS users. Subscription information is available at *http://oss.software.ibm.com/developerworks/opensource/ mailman/listinfo/jfs-discussion*.

SGI XFS

XFS has long been the default filesystem for SGI's IRIX operating system. It is a journaling filesystem designed with an eye toward performance and crash recovery. Since mid-2000, SGI developers have been working on a port of XFS for Linux. In May 2001, version 1.0 of XFS for Linux was released. Development continues, and version 1.1 is currently available.

Like the other filesystems covered in this chapter, XFS provides fast crash recovery through journaling. An XFS filesystem is divided into allocation groups not unlike the block groups used in ext2. Files, data, and free space within allocation groups are organized using B-trees. For a detailed overview of the XFS layout, refer to *http://oss. sgi.com/projects/xfs/design_docs/xfsdocs93_pdf/space_overview.pdf*.

XFS has been time-proven on the IRIX operating systems. Given that history, XFS's port to Linux is used by groups in the scientific community, such as Fermilab and the Sloan Digital Sky Survey. One of Quantum's NAS product lines is also based on XFS. So even though XFS is handicapped by its lack of inclusion in the standard Linux kernel and its lack of direct support across many Linux distributions, it is being used successfully in some high-demand projects.

Distribution Support

The most recent versions of Mandrake and SuSE support direct installation onto XFS. If you want to use another distribution to install directly onto XFS partitions, you will need to download and create XFS-compatible boot media. I recommend checking the XFS FAQ for a list of compatible distributions and links to alternative boot media that supports XFS. SGI keeps the list quite up-to-date, and it is an excellent resource.

SGI also distributes customized Red Hat CD-ROM images that allow you to install a new system directly to an XFS partition. You can use these images to burn a bootable Red Hat CD-ROM. Since Red Hat also provides installation onto software RAID partitions, you can use the custom SGI disk to install a new system that supports XFS and software RAID from the get-go, avoiding the headache of a post-installation upgrade.

You can download the install disk from *ftp://oss.sgi.com/projects/xfs/download/latest/ installer/*. i386 is currently the only architecture supported.

Obtaining XFS

XFS isn't included in any of the stable or development kernels. So you'll need to obtain and apply patches from the XFS web site or use CVS to get a prepatched kernel.

Using CVS to obtain a patched kernel

Since XFS is not included with any official kernel releases, CVS is by far the easiest way to obtain an XFS-ready kernel. To obtain a kernel with XFS support using CVS, execute the following commands:

```
# cd /usr/src
# export CVSROOT=':pserver:cvs@oss.sgi.com:/cvs'
# cvs login
(Logging in to cvs@oss.sgi.com)
CVS password: cvs
# cvs -z3 checkout linux-2.4-xfs
```

After the *cvs* command completes, you will be left with the directory */usr/src/linux-2. 4-xfs*. The *linux* subdirectory contains the XFS kernel, and the *cmd* subdirectory contains the user-space programs needed to manage XFS partitions. Skip ahead to the section "Compiling the Kernel with XFS Support" for instructions on enabling XFS features.

Patching the kernel

If using CVS isn't agreeable, you can download a patch and apply it to a clean kernel. Grab the file that corresponds to your kernel version from *ftp://oss.sgi.com/ projects/xfs/download/patches*. There is also a *patch-2.5* directory for those working with development kernels.

Decompress the patch and apply it to your kernel:

```
# cd /usr/src/linux-2.4.19
# patch -p1 < /usr/src/xfs-2.4.19-all-i386
```

A list of successfully patched files is printed on the screen. If errors are reported, it's likely that you didn't apply the XFS patch to a clean kernel. Download a new kernel and try to apply the patch again.

Compiling the Kernel with XFS Support

Whether you applied a patch or obtained an XFS kernel using CVS, XFS support (CONFIG_XFS_FS) will already be enabled under the Filesystems submenu. Note that development support is enabled, as indicated by the experimental options that appear. I'm using a 2.4.19 kernel in this example, as it is the kernel currently available via CVS.

```
File systems  --->
[...]
<*> SGI XFS filesystem support
[ ]    Realtime support (EXPERIMENTAL)
[*]    Quota support
[ ]    DMAPI support
[ ]    Debugging support (EXPERIMENTAL)
[ ]    Pagebuf debugging support (EXPERIMENTAL)
```

Quota support (CONFIG_XFS_QUOTA) is also enabled by default, but if you don't need disk quotas, you can disable this option. The remaining options provide support for additional features, and many of them are still experimental. If you don't require the specific support that these features provide, it's best to leave them disabled.

Real-time support (CONFIG_XFS_RT) allows the use of a data-only portion of an XFS partition. That means reduced overhead for metaoperations and results in increased data throughput. Real-time support is useful for streaming media. Refer to the *xfs(5)* manual page for more information.

DMAPI support (CONFIG_XFS_DMAPI) provides an interface for the Data Management API, which allows XFS to support hierarchical storage. (Hierarchical storage is an attempt to provide translucent access between filesystems and backup systems.) For more information on DMAPI and XFS, refer to *http://oss.sgi.com/projects/xfs/dmapi.html*.

Debugging support (CONFIG_XFS_DEBUG) is intended for developers and should never be used unless you are troubleshooting a problem and have exhausted other attempts at problem resolution. The same caveat applies to *pagebuf* debugging support (CONFIG_PAGEBUF_DEBUG).

Building the XFS Utilities

Once you have restarted your system with an XFS kernel, you will need to install the XFS tools before you can create and manage filesystems. If you obtained your kernel using CVS, you already have a copy of the XFS utilities.

```
# cd /usr/src/linux-2.4-xfs/cmd/xfsprogs
# make install
```

Alternatively, you can download a tarball containing the source code from *ftp://oss.sgi.com/projects/xfs/download/cmd_tars/xfsprogs-2.1.2.src.tar.gz*. SGI also provides an RPM file (*ftp://oss.sgi.com/projects/xfs/download/cmd_rpms/*). Debian users can use *apt-get install xfsprogs*.

The *mkfs.xfs* command is used to create a new filesystem; the *-b* flag specifies the block size of the new filesystem.

```
# mkfs.xfs -b size=4k /dev/md0
```

This command creates a new filesystem on */dev/md0*, with a block size of 4 KB. XFS supports block sizes ranging from 512 bytes to 64 KB in power-of-2 increments. However, the current implementation allows only a block size less than or equal to the page size of the resident system. That means 4 KB or less on 32-bit systems (i386, PowerPC) and 8 KB or less on 64-bit systems (Alpha, SPARC, IA64). By default, *mkfs.xfs* creates a filesystem using a block size equal to page size.

Further Information

For more information about XFS, please refer to the project's web site at *http://oss. sgi.com/projects/xfs/*. I'd specifically like to point out both the FAQ (*http://oss.sgi. com/projects/xfs/faq.html*) and mailing list (*http://oss.sgi.com/projects/xfs/mail.html*) as excellent sources of up-to-date information.

## CHAPTER 7

Performance, Tuning, and Maintenance

Keeping a system running, and running well, should be the desire of every system administrator worth their salt. This chapter covers a variety of topics related to this goal:

- Monitoring RAID devices
- Tuning hard disks
- Performance testing
- Installing directly to a software RAID

Monitoring RAID Devices

Monitoring is an essential part of working with RAID. Since most arrays can survive only a single disk failure, it's important to know when any failure occurs. That way, failed disks can be replaced before a second disk fails and causes data loss. The easiest way to monitor arrays is by modifying your existing scripts and monitoring platforms to look for information about the RAID subsystem in your system logs. You can look for keywords such as *md*, *raid1*, *recovery*, *resyncing*, *raid5*, *raid0*, *linear*, *RAID*, and *superblock*. It's a good idea to take a look at the information that the RAID subsystem reports to *syslog* so that you can get a good idea of how to custom-tailor monitoring for your specific needs.

RAID and syslog

The *md* driver uses the system logging daemon (*syslogd*) to report pertinent information and errors relating to the kernel RAID subsystem. *md* reports information using the *kern* facility (LOG_KERN). Table 7-1 outlines the priorities at which the RAID subsystem reports information to the kernel ring buffer.

Table 7-1. Software RAID log reporting

facility.priority	Information reported
kern.info	Status changes, including insertion and removal of member disks, resynchronization progress, and startup and shutdown notices. In general, any information about an array that does not affect performance or continuing operation.
kern.err	Error messages about problems that either prevent an array from being started, created, or modified, or affect array operation in a nonfatal manner. This includes disk failures and consequent insertion of spare disks, initialization and completion of reconstruction, and problems with the configuration file.
kern.alert	Catastrophic errors that prevent a running array from continuing to operate. Problems logged at this level usually result in the crash of a running array or the inability to start an array that is not running. These issues include memory problems, low-level device problems, and fatal errors that occur during the reconstruction process.

Many distributions log this information to some combination of */var/log/messages* and */var/log/warn*. The following line in */etc/syslog.conf* captures all kernel-level messages:

```
kern.*          /var/log/kernel
```

After adding this line, be certain to restart *syslogd*. You should also *touch* the file */var/log/kernel*, as well as any new files you reference in */etc/syslogd.conf*, if they do not already exist:

```
# touch /var/log/kernel
# kill -HUP `/var/run/syslogd.pid`
```

Since a lot of information is reported using the *kern* facility, it's a good idea to tune */etc/syslog.conf* to meet specific system needs. On high-volume systems, it is advisable to break out information reported by the *kern* facility into files of varying priority. This makes it easy to monitor the system for serious problems, while maintaining verbose information to retroactively diagnose persistent and unclear problems.

In general, search *log* files for the phrase " md:" to get a list of all software RAID-related messages:

```
# grep " md:" /var/log/kernel
```

You can also use *mdadm*'s monitor mode, combined with the *logger* utility, to dump messages that are generated specifically by *mdadm* into the system logs:

```
# mdadm --monitor --program='logger -p kern.crit -t md: $*'
```

The *logger* program creates system log entries. In this example, I report any message that *mdadm* generates using the *kern* facility at the *crit* priority. The *-t* option adds a bit of informational text to each entry (in this case, md:). You can also put the command used by the *--program* option in */etc/mdadm.conf*. In addition, *mdadm* reads its configuration file for a list of devices to monitor.

It's a good idea to run *mdadm* detached and in the background, as I described in Chapter 4. Remember that *mdadm* will report only limited information about critical problems. You should configure *syslogd* to capture *md* driver messages, even if you are using *mdadm* in Monitor mode.

BigBrother

Users of the popular monitoring tool BigBrother can use the *bb-mdstat.sh* script to monitor software arrays. Download the script from *http://www.deadcat.net/cgi-bin/download.pl?section=1&file=bb-mdstat.sh*.

SysOrb

SysOrb is a commercial system monitoring package developed by Evalesco Systems. It has complete support for Linux software RAID monitoring. The lead architect of SysOrb is Jakob Oestergaard, author of the Linux RAID HOWTO. You can demo SysOrb at *http://www.evalesco.com*.

Verbose SCSI Reporting

It might also be helpful to enable additional error reporting for low-level SCSI hardware. This is helpful for diagnosing SCSI problems that might affect array performance and stability.

When building your kernel, just turn on the Verbose SCSI Error Reporting (CONFIG_SCSI_CONSTANT) feature in the SCSI section.

```
SCSI support  --->
...
[*]   Verbose SCSI error reporting (kernel size +=12K)
...
```

Now SCSI messages that appear in the system logs will be more human-readable. For example:

```
Jun 27 18:15:53 apathy kernel: SCSI disk error : host 1 channel 0 id 2 lun 0 return
    code = 10000
Jun 27 18:15:53 apathy kernel:  I/O error: dev 08:61, sector 0
```

Managing Disk Failures

When a member disk of a RAID-1, RAID-4, or RAID-5 fails, the array enters into degraded mode. Degraded mode means that both performance and redundancy are impacted. RAID-0 and linear mode never enter into degraded mode because they do not support redundancy. If a disk in either a RAID-0 or linear mode configuration fails, the array stops. Unless the disk can be repaired, data will be lost.

RAID-1 can withstand at least a single disk failure. For a RAID-1 of *n* member disks, *n-1* disks can fail before service is interrupted. When all disks in a RAID-1 fail, the array is no longer functional. In addition, parallel read performance of RAID-1 is affected by disk failures. For example, a RAID-1 consisting of three disks can potentially achieve parallel reads of up to three times the throughput of a single member disk. If a single disk fails, parallel read performance is reduced by a factor of one. An interesting side effect of disk failures under RAID-1 is that write performance will actually improve during degraded operation. That's because the number of writes that occurs is multiplied by the number of member disks in the array. As a RAID-1 loses member disks, the number of writes per I/O operation decreases.

RAID-4 and RAID-5 deal with disk failures in the same way. They can each survive only a single disk failure. Disk failures in RAID-4 and RAID-5 considerably impact array performance. Each time data is read from the array, the system must perform parity reconstruction to access data from the missing disk. When working with software RAID, this means that a larger amount of CPU resources must be dedicated to array management. When you are working with hardware controllers, the controller handles the task of on-the-fly parity reconstruction, and the CPU is not affected. However, that does not mean I/O performance will not be affected.

Under software RAID, disk failures are reported at the *kern.crit* log level. In the following example, */dev/sdc1* has failed, but the array continues operating in degraded mode:

```
Jun 12 14:49:20 apathy kernel: raid5: Disk failure on sdg1, disabling device.
    Operation continuing on 5 devices
```

If you enabled Verbose SCSI Reporting (as I described earlier in this chapter), *syslogd* also reports low-level device information:

```
Jun 27 18:15:53 apathy kernel: SCSI disk error : host 1 channel 0 id 2 lun 0 return
    code = 10000
Jun 27 18:15:53 apathy kernel:  I/O error: dev 08:61, sector 0
```

In this case, the entire drive has failed and is no longer detected on the SCSI bus. (In reality, I have disconnected the drive from the SCSI bus to simulate a disk failure.) Note that the I/O error is returned when reading from sector 0. This information will aid in evaluating whether or not the disk failure is the result of data corruption (multiple sector I/O failures) or complete hardware failure. Usually, when the drive fails completely, only one error message, like the one above, is reported. Consequently, the system will slow down as the SCSI bus is rescanned and reset. During that period, I/O on that channel will be interrupted. On the other hand, data corruption would yield multiple errors at either single or multiple nonzero sectors.

Automatic Failover to a Spare Disk

Disk replacement can be handled automatically by the Linux kernel, or by RAID controllers, if hot-spare disks have been allocated to the array. Insertion of these disks should be fairly automatic. The *md* driver takes action immediately following the first read or write to an array in degraded mode and reports any changes via *syslogd*. When the hot-spare is introduced, reconstruction commences.

```
Jun 27 18:15:53 apathy kernel: md: updating md0 RAID superblock on device
Jun 27 18:15:53 apathy kernel: sde1 [events: 00000002](write) sde1's sb offset:
    17920384
Jun 27 18:15:53 apathy kernel: md: recovery thread got woken up ...
Jun 27 18:15:53 apathy kernel: md0: resyncing spare disk sde1 to replace failed disk
```

First, the *md* driver updates the RAID superblock for */dev/md0* to reflect the fact that the failed disk is no longer a member of the array and that the spare-disk is now an active member. Next, information about the new member's event counter is reported. (The event counter is simply a report of how many RAID configuration changes have been executed on the device.) Next, reconstruction commences and the *mdrecoveryd* process rebuilds the array. You can also examine */proc/mdstat* to monitor the reconstruction process.

When the process is completed, *syslogd* reports on the new status of the array:

```
Jun 27 18:35:33 apathy kernel: md: md0: sync done.
Jun 27 18:35:33 apathy kernel: RAID5 conf printout:
Jun 27 18:35:33 apathy kernel:  --- rd:3 wd:2 fd:1
Jun 27 18:35:33 apathy kernel:  disk 0, s:0, o:1, n:0 rd:0 us:1 dev:sdb1
Jun 27 18:35:33 apathy kernel:  disk 1, s:0, o:1, n:1 rd:1 us:1 dev:sdf1
Jun 27 18:35:33 apathy kernel:  disk 2, s:0, o:0, n:2 rd:2 us:1 dev:sdg1
Jun 27 18:35:33 apathy kernel: RAID5 conf printout:
Jun 27 18:35:33 apathy kernel:  --- rd:3 wd:3 fd:0
Jun 27 18:35:33 apathy kernel:  disk 0, s:0, o:1, n:0 rd:0 us:1 dev:sdb1
Jun 27 18:35:33 apathy kernel:  disk 1, s:0, o:1, n:1 rd:1 us:1 dev:sdf1
Jun 27 18:35:33 apathy kernel:  disk 2, s:0, o:1, n:2 rd:2 us:1 dev:sde1
Jun 27 18:35:33 apathy kernel: md: updating md0 RAID superblock on device
Jun 27 18:35:33 apathy kernel: sde1 [events: 00000003](write) sde1's sb offset:
    17920384
Jun 27 18:35:33 apathy kernel: (skipping faulty sdg1 )
Jun 27 18:35:34 apathy kernel: sdf1 [events: 00000003](write) sdf1's sb offset:
    17920384
Jun 27 18:35:34 apathy kernel: sdb1 [events: 00000003](write) sdb1's sb offset:
    17920384
Jun 27 18:35:34 apathy kernel: .
Jun 27 18:35:34 apathy kernel: md: recovery thread finished
...
```

Now the faulty disk can be replaced or repaired.

Remember that the reconstruction process affects overall system performance. In addition, ATA systems typically require longer reconstruction times and more CPU overhead than SCSI systems because intra-disk transfers are slower and more intensive. During reconstruction of ATA arrays, the CPU needs to handle not only the reconstruction process, but also array and disk management. This sometimes can be too much for a system to handle and can result in extremely long reconstruction times.

Sharing Spare Disks

While the *md* driver can't directly share spare disks between arrays, *mdadm* does support this feature through its monitor mode. When *mdadm* is in monitor mode, it will automatically move a spare disk from a working array to an array that encounters a disk failure, provided they are both marked as having the same spare disk group.

Manual Disk Replacement

Even if online spare disks are used, system administrators must physically replace failed drives. Replacement should take place as soon as possible to avoid the potential for a secondary disk failure that might incapacitate an array. A secondary disk failure, when no more spares are available, means that the array will operate in degraded mode until the disk can be physically replaced. It's also advisable to replace dead disks as soon as possible so they can be reallocated as spares in the event of another failure.

Remember that ATA does not technically support any hot-swap capability. Although some newer disk enclosures and controllers support this feature, disk manufacturers and reports from users discourage the use of hot-swap ATA. Therefore, set up hot-swap ATA equipment at your own risk.

Likewise, SCSI supports hot-swap only when working with SCA drives. Although some users have successfully swapped non-SCA SCSI disks out of running systems, this practice is not recommended.

If your system supports SCA disks, you can simply remove the drive and add a new one. The SCSI bus needs to be told that a new disk is present, because the Linux kernel or the hardware disk controller will have already marked the failed disk as nonoperational when it entered the reconstruction phase.

Using the */proc/scsi* interface, disks can be added and removed from a running system. To remove a failed disk from the bus (if the kernel hasn't already removed it), use the following command:

```
# echo "scsi remove-single-device 0 1 0 0" > /proc/scsi/scsi
```

This instructs the kernel to scan the first SCSI controllers for the disk with ID 0 and activate it. The *scsiadd* utility, available from *http://llg.cubic.org/tools/*, provides a command-line wrapper for this and other SCSI management functions. I encourage you to download and experiment with this utility.

There is no ATA equivalent for this function. On ATA RAID systems, you need to restart the computer to facilitate a rescan of the bus in order to activate disks that have been connected since the last time the system was started.

Don't forget that you also need to use either *raidhotadd* or *mdadm -a* to add replacement disks back into their respective arrays.

Problems with Hot-Swap and Disk Replacement

One of the biggest problems with hot-swapping or replacing devices under Linux (and many other Unix systems) stems from device naming. On an ATA system, Linux assigns the first drive on the first controller to */dev/hda*. Subsequently detected devices are named in the order in which they are detected, using the same naming scheme. Thus, the slave device on the primary channel is assigned */dev/hdb*, and the master and slave devices on the secondary channel are assigned */dev/hdc* and */dev/hdd*, respectively.

ATA is unique because of its legacy master and slave arrangement. If a device that was initially detected during installation suddenly disappears from a system, the naming order isn't affected. If */dev/hdb* suddenly dies, and the system reboots, */dev/hda*, */dev/hdc*, and */dev/hdd* will still be assigned the same device names.

One exception to this rule is systems that have add-on ATA channels via PCI cards. If an entire card is removed, or fails, the detection order will change. Let's say that a system has two ATA/100 PCI controllers, each with two channels. The first card, containing two disks that are assigned */dev/hde* and */dev/hdf*, fails. Naturally, users and applications will no longer be able to access data on those disks. The problem is further complicated when the system reboots and assigns device names. Because the first PCI controller isn't detected this time, the disks on the second controller now have their device names shifted down two positions. So while the disks on the second controller were originally assigned */dev/hdg* and */dev/hdh*, they will now be assigned */dev/hde* and */dev/hdf*. Not only will applications that are looking for data on disks connected to the failed controller complain, but filesystems associated with */dev/hdg* and */dev/hdh* will now look for their disks in the wrong place, causing another series of problems. Luckily, the advent of filesystem labels and UUID information helped fix some of the issues associated with device naming because arrays can now be started using parameters stored on disk, rather than based on their physical connections. Filesystems can be mounted in the same manner.

SCSI operates in almost the same way, except that the first four device names are not tied to onboard controllers. Although any onboard SCSI controllers will be detected first by the BIOS and Linux, the first device names are not reserved for them. On a motherboard with onboard SCSI and a PCI SCSI controller, the onboard controller is assigned a value of 0 and the PCI controller a value of 1. If the PCI controller has four disks connected and the onboard controller has no disks connected, then the disks on the PCI controllers are assigned */dev/sda* through */dev/sdd*. If two disks are added to the onboard controller, they will be assigned */dev/sda* and */dev/sdb*. The disks connected to the PCI controller would then shift to */dev/sdc* through */dev/sdf*. It's best to disable onboard controllers that you are not using to avoid any confusion or potential problems with device naming.

I advise you to consider using the Device Filesystem (*Devfs*) to help solve some of these issues. *Devfs* uses a device-naming scheme similar to the one used in many commercial Unix operating systems, such as Solaris. Devices' names are based on controller number and SCSI identification number, instead of simple device lettering. So a disk failure doesn't affect device naming within a single I/O channel. But failure or removal of an entire controller still has the same effect. Consult the *Devfs* FAQ at *http://www.atnf.csiro.au/people/rgooch/linux/docs/devfs.html*.

Configuring Hard Disk Parameters

Hard disks, like most computer components, are shipped with certain configurations that manufacturers have determined are ideal for the largest denomination of users. Unfortunately, these default settings often mean that disks are shipped with configurations that make them compatible with the largest number of consumer desktops, as opposed to making them perform as fast as possible. Luckily, many of these parameters can be tuned to meet specific system needs. With the help of system-tuning utilities, these parameters can be modified to increase overall array and standalone disk performance.

The performance tips covered in this section are meant to be performed on individual disks, not arrays. However, it is essential that you apply any changes uniformly to each component disk in your arrays. Tuning one or more disks and failing to tune others will result in poor, and probably bizarre, performance.

I strongly recommend that anyone who isn't already familiar with the basic tactics of performance tuning first carefully read *http://linuxperf.nl.linux.org/baseline.html*. It outlines quite a number of ideas that are essential to successful systems management and stability. There are also many other articles available from *http://linuxperf.nl. linux.org/* that make excellent complementary material to the disk I/O-specific information that I will provide in this section.

Tuning ATA Disks with hdparm

Written by Mark Lord, *hdparm* allows administrators to change low-level hard disk settings. Unfortunately, *hdparm* is really useful only for tuning ATA disks. (While *hdparm* can conduct a few operations on SCSI disks, most of those operations are purely informational.) SCSI users are left with quite a void in terms of low-level disk tweaking, compared with the number of features that *hdparm* can adjust. (Zealous proponents of SCSI would surely argue, of course, that SCSI needs no tuning because of its superiority!)

hdparm is usually found at */sbin/hdparm*. Because of the low-level hardware changes it can make, you must be *root* to use it. It's a good idea to make certain the most recent version is installed on your system. If you need to upgrade (version 5.2 is the most recent version, as of this writing), or if *hdparm* wasn't included as part of your distribution, you can download it at *http://www.ibiblio.org/pub/Linux/system/hardware/* or download a package from your distributor. Debian users may be able to run *apt-get install hdparm*, but as of this writing, the stable version is not the most recent.

With a device as its only argument, *hdparm* returns information about a hard disk's current settings:

```
# hdparm /dev/hda

/dev/hda:
 multcount     = 16 (on)
 I/O support   =  0 (default 16-bit)
 unmaskirq     =  0 (off)
 using_dma     =  1 (on)
 keepsettings  =  0 (off)
 nowerr        =  0 (off)
 readonly      =  0 (off)
 readahead     =  8 (on)
 geometry      = 2434/255/63, sectors = 39102336, start = 0
 busstate      =  1 (on)
```

The *hdparm* command can also be combined with the *-i* option to display identification information about the hard disk, as well as a list of its alleged capabilities. I use the word "alleged" because *hdparm -i* isn't always 100 percent accurate. Using the *-i* parameter is a feature supported only by disks that are relatively new (built within the last few years), so using it on older disk will have varied results.

```
# hdparm -i /dev/hda

/dev/hda:

 Model=ST320414A, FwRev=3.05, SerialNo=3EC0V5EG
 Config={ HardSect NotMFM HdSw>15uSec Fixed DTR>10Mbs RotSpdTol>.5% }
 RawCHS=16383/16/63, TrkSize=0, SectSize=0, ECCbytes=0
 BuffType=unknown, BuffSize=2048kB, MaxMultSect=16, MultSect=16
 CurCHS=16383/16/63, CurSects=16514064, LBA=yes, LBAsects=39102336
 IORDY=on/off, tPIO={min:240,w/IORDY:120}, tDMA={min:120,rec:120}
 PIO modes: pio0 pio1 pio2 pio3 pio4
 DMA modes: mdma0 mdma1 mdma2 udma0 udma1 udma2 udma3 *udma4 udma5
 AdvancedPM=no WriteCache=enabled
 Drive Supports : Reserved : ATA-1 ATA-2 ATA-3 ATA-4
```

Some of the tweaks I'm going to outline here can cause problems that include data corruption. Some of these problems may not necessarily be immediately noticeable. I advise testing thoroughly any changes you implement before moving your system into production. I'll point out some particulars and point you to additional information whenever it's available.

Enabling DMA mode transfers

All ATA disks transfer data using one of two modes: *Programmed I/O* (*PIO*) or *Direct Memory Access* (*DMA*). You'll notice in the *hdparm -i* output above that there are PIO and DMA lines, each with a list of more specific *transfer modes*. PIO support is deprecated at this point because it is much slower than even the original incarnations of DMA. There are also a few different iterations of DMA: *single-word*, *multi-word*, and *ultra*. (Multi-word DMA is also commonly referred to as bus-mastering.)

UltraDMA is the most modern and fastest implementation. On the DMA mode line in the last code example, there are three multi-word DMA modes and six UltraDMA modes listed. udma2, udma4, and udma5 correspond to the common UltraATA/33, UltraATA/66, and UltraATA/100 transfer speeds that I outlined in Chapter 2 (see also Table 7-2, below).

Table 7-2. hdparm -X values

Name	Speed (MB/s)	Value (-X#)
pio0	3.3	8
pio1	5.2	9
pio2	8.3	10
pio3	11.1	11
pio4	16.7	12
mdma0	4.2	32
mdma1	13.3	33
mdma2	16.7	34
udma0	16.7	64
udma1	25	65
udma2	33.3	66
udma3	44.4	67
udma4	66.7	68
udma5	100	69

You generally want to use the fastest mode available. The asterisk next to udma4 indicates that UltraATA/66 is currently selected. To change the transfer mode from udma4 to udma5, use the following command:

```
# hdparm -d1 -X69 /dev/hda

/dev/hda:
 setting xfermode to 69 (UltraDMA mode5)
```

The -X option uses a somewhat confusing syntax, so I've included Table 7-2 as an easy reference for all the integer and mode correlations. Each data transfer mode has a base numeric value: PIO (8), multi-word DMA (32), and UltraDMA (64). Single-word DMA is not used, because multi-word DMA has replaced it. (*hdparm* will allow the use of the base value 16 for single-word DMA, but I have not successfully used it, and it is undocumented.) To determine the correct value for the -X option, add a mode's base numeric value to the specific transfer mode within that particular type. For example, udma4 uses the numeric value 68 because the base value for UltraDMA (64) and the value for udma4 (4) equal 68.

The -d1 option ensures that DMA mode is enabled. Even though I just set my disk to UltraDMA mode 5, generic support for DMA is also required. Otherwise, the disk will operate in its default, archaic PIO mode. If you look back at the *hdparm /dev/hda* output that I showed earlier in the section "Tuning ATA Disks with hdparm," you'll notice that using_dma was already turned on. So I wasn't required to include it again with this command. However, I find that it's good practice to combine the -d and -X commands to be certain the transfer mode is properly set.

Most new disks ship with the best (fastest) mode enabled, but it's always a good idea to double-check. A lot of older disks typically shipped with PIO as their default transfer mode, even though they were capable of some level of DMA functionality. Therefore, it's especially recommended that you check the transfer mode if you are working with older disks.

32-bit I/O support

32-bit I/O describes the amount of data per cycle (remember my coverage of bus-width and bus-speed in Chapter 2) that the ATA controller sends over the data bus. It might seem obvious that hard disks should ship with 32-bit support enabled, but this isn't the case at all. I've found that while most manufacturers now have the good sense to enable the best transfer mode, few of them actually ship drives with 32-bit mode activated. If you look at the drive parameters I listed earlier in the section "Tuning ATA Disks with hdparm," you'll see that my Ultra ATA/100 disk was actually set to use 16-bit I/O:

```
I/O support  =  0 (default 16-bit)
```

Add the -c option to *hdparm* to enable 32-bit I/O:

```
# hdparm -c3 /dev/hda

/dev/hda:
 setting 32-bit I/O support flag to 3
 I/O support  =  3 (32-bit w/sync)
```

I've used I/O mode 3, which supports 32-bit data transfers and also implements a synchronization sequence that provides computability with the largest number of ATA controllers. Using mode 2 (*hdparm -c2 /dev/hda*) also enables 32-bit transfers, but doesn't provide the extra synchronization steps. This improves performance a little bit, but sacrifices some computability. If you do try using mode 2, please do adequate testing before putting the system into production. Use *hdparm -c0 /dev/hda* if you need to set the disk back into 16-bit mode.

Increasing multiple sector I/O

Multiple sector I/O (also called *Block Mode IDE*) allows the system to read/write more than one sector per interrupt. This tremendously increases the overall throughput of ATA disks and greatly reduces the CPU overhead required to perform I/O on ATA devices. My disk has a multiple sector I/O value of 16, as indicated by multcount = 16 (on) in the *hdparm* output I showed earlier in this chapter. That means that I/O occurs in 8 KB chunks (16 * 512 bytes per sector = 8 KB). This is actually a reasonably decent default value and the maximum value my disk will allow. You'll notice that in the output of *hdparm -i*, there is a maximum multiple sector I/O listed:

```
BuffType=unknown, BuffSize=2048kB, MaxMultSect=16, MultSect=16
```

On systems where this value is set below the maximum, increasing it doesn't necessarily mean increasing your I/O throughput, so I do recommend experimenting with different values. In fact, even if your disk is set to its maximum, as in my case, throttling down and running some throughput tests is still a good idea. The following command decreases the multiple sector I/O value to 8:

```
# hdparm -m8 /dev/hda

/dev/hda:
 setting multcount to 8
 multcount    = 8 (on)
```

There are quite a few caveats and computability issues surrounding the multiple sector I/O value. I recommend reading the *hdparm(8)* manual page for a complete discussion of these issues.

Interrupt unmasking

Normally when disk I/O is performed, the rest of the system must wait until the request is completed. On heavily loaded systems, it might be useful to allow other hardware to perform some tasks while waiting for disk I/O to finish. Interrupt unmasking won't specifically increase disk throughput, but it will increase the overall speed and responsiveness of a Linux system. Use the *hdparm -u1* command to enable this functionality.

```
# hdparm -u1 /dev/hda

/dev/hda:
 setting unmaskirq to 1 (on)
 unmaskirq    = 1 (on)
```

I must warn you that this feature has been reported to cause hazardous results with some hardware configurations, including filesystem corruption. Again, please consult the *hdparm* manual page for further details and use this option with caution. Use *hdparm -u0* if you need to disable interrupt unmasking.

Filesystem read-ahead

The filesystem read-ahead determines how many sectors are read, in anticipation that contiguous sequential blocks will be required by the current operation. The default value for this setting is 8 sectors (4 KB). Increasing it helps systems with a lot of sequential I/O, but a smaller value helps with random read performance.

To change the value to 4 sectors per read:

```
# hdparm -a4 /dev/hda

/dev/hda:
 setting fs readahead to 4
 readahead    =  4 (on)
```

To increase the value to 16 sectors per read:

```
# hdparm -a16 /dev/hda
```

Testing your configuration

After you have made some modifications to your disks, you can use the *-t* option to perform a rudimentary throughput test:

```
# hdparm -t /dev/hda

/dev/hda:
 Timing buffered disk reads:  64 MB in  1.65 seconds = 38.79 MB/sec
```

I recommend using one of the other benchmark programs, such as *bonnie++* or *tiobench* in lieu of, or in addition to, *hdparm -t*.

Saving your configuration

Most of the settings that can be altered using *hdparm* are not persistent through cold system reboots. Therefore, I recommend creating an initialization script that runs each time the system starts. Add one command for each hard disk that includes all the options you wish to modify. For example:

```
# hdparm -a16 -m16 -u1 -d1 -X69 /dev/hda
# hdparm -a16 -m16 -u1 -d1 -X69 /dev/hda
```

Tuning Disk Elevators

Linux tries to balance read and write operations on block devices to maximize performance. This helps ensure that heavily utilized systems aren't dominated solely by either read or write operations. The ratio can be tuned on a per-device basis, using the *elvtune* command.

Use *elvtune <device>* to get a list of the current settings:

```
# elvtune /dev/sdb

/dev/sdb elevator ID          246
        read_latency:         256
        write_latency:        512
        max_bomb_segments:    0
```

The *-w* and *-r* flags allow you to alter the read and write latency settings. The best settings really depend on system and device usage, so I recommend experimenting until you get an optimal setting. Try doubling each value, one at a time, and running some performance tests until you find a balance that works for you.

```
# elvtune -r 512 -w 1024 /dev/sdb

/dev/sdb elevator ID          246
        read_latency:         512
        write_latency:        1024
        max_bomb_segments:    0
```

Like settings altered with *hdparm*, *elvtune* settings should be added into your initialization scripts, so that changes are made each time the system starts. You need to use *elvtune* on low-level block devices, not arrays. So be certain to alter the settings for each array component, and not just one disk.

Performance Testing

I've already discussed using *hdparm -t* as a way of performing some elementary data throughput tests. But *hdparm* doesn't test a broad range of I/O operations, nor does it test performance over long periods of time, on large and small files, or on filesystem metaoperations such as file creation and deletion. For that reason, I recommend downloading and familiarizing yourself with some other performance test suites.

The two programs that I recommend are *bonnie++* (*http://www.coker.com.au/bonnie++/*) and *tiobench* (*http://tiobench.sourceforge.net/*). You can use either program to run a variety of throughput tests on both individual block devices, as well as arrays (software and hardware). I urge you to perform tests at each stage of array deployment and performance tuning to get a better idea of the overall effect of the various adjustments on your system performance.

Booting with Software RAID

One of the most frequently asked questions on the linux-raid mailing list is how to boot directly to software RAID. The answer depends on your situation. If you have an existing system and you want to move from a standalone, non-RAID situation to a software RAID system, you can use some very straightforward conversion steps that I've outlined below in the "Converting to Software RAID" section. If you are installing a new system for the first time, many distributions now support direct installation to a software RAID. I've listed some of these distributions here and outlined any noteworthy pitfalls that I've encountered.

Installing Directly to Software RAID

First, all /boot and / partitions must be on a RAID-1. So if you have only two disks, you can't create a RAID-1 for /boot and *root* and then create a few RAID-0 partitions for /usr, /home, and /var. While some installers and the *md* driver will allow this, it's strongly discouraged. There's no reason that you couldn't create non-*boot* and non-*root* partitions on separate arrays on a separate set of disks. However, considering the large size of even today's smaller hard disks, it would be quite a waste of space to house only /boot and *root* filesystems on a two-disk RAID-1.

Second, always use LILO in combination with bootable software RAID devices. Although GRUB provides some limited support, it's not as evolved as the support that LILO provides for *md* devices. Some installers might default to GRUB, so don't forget to manually select LILO as necessary.

There's also one drawback to direct installation to software RAID. Since RAID-1 is a requirement for booting, that means initial synchronization for every partition you create must occur in parallel with the installation process. This increases the time it takes to install the system. But the benefits of RAID-1 do provide a reward for this imposition.

Red Hat

Red Hat has supported software RAID directly in its installation process for some time. That means system administrators don't need to go through all of the extra steps that I'm about to outline when using Red Hat for a first-time installation onto software RAID.

The process for creating a bootable RAID-1 in Red Hat is very straightforward, but it does require using Disk Druid. Those of you who would like switch to a virtual terminal and use *fdisk* to manually create the partition tables should remember an important requirement: you must create the same partitions on each RAID-1 component disk. When Disk Druid executes, you can choose the *software RAID* filesystem type for each partition (on both disks). Next, use the Make RAID button to create each software array. If I wanted to create *root*, /boot, and swap filesystems for my new Linux machine, I'd create the same partitions for each filesystem on my first (/dev/sda) and second (/dev/sdb) hard disks.

Red Hat provides some good documentation for this process at the URL *http://www.redhat.com/docs/manuals/linux/RHL-7.3-Manual/custom-guide/ch-software-raid.html*. The documentation describes the software RAID installation process step-by-step, with screenshots. If you purchased a boxed copy of Red Hat, you should be able to find the same information in your printed manuals.

SuSE

SuSE now supports (as of 8.0) direct installation to software RAID, but I've noticed that it's buggy when compared with Red Hat's software RAID installation software. For example, *YaST2* complains that */boot* partitions cannot be created on a software RAID device. But clearly, this is an acceptable choice that is practiced by many users and other distributors.

Mandrake

Mandrake's RAID installation process (part of DrakX) is so seamless that it warrants almost no discussion. It is the most straightforward, and the most flexible, of all the installation-time RAID utilities that I have encountered. I used Mandrake 8.2 in my experiments. You should have no problems when using Mandrake to install directly to a software RAID.

Converting to Software RAID

The process for converting an existing system to utilize software RAID is simple and requires just a few steps:

1. Build a new kernel with software RAID support. Refer to Chapter 3 for details on how to include RAID support in the kernel. Be certain to include support for RAID-1, as well as generic RAID support. Remember, only RAID-1 works for boot partitions. In this tutorial, I'll assume that you are using RAID-1 for all system partitions, that your existing system partitions are on */dev/sda*, and that the new disk is */dev/sdb*.

2. After you reboot the system using your new kernel, create partitions on your new disk for each of the partitions (including swap space) on your existing system disk. So if you have three partitions on your existing disk (/, */boot*, and swap) create three matching partitions on the new disk. If you want to alter the size of any system partition, do so at this point by creating the new partitions using different specifications. Don't forget to mark each new partition *Linux RAID Auto* (that's type 0xFD).

3. After creating partitions on the new disk (*/dev/sdb*), create a new RAID-1 for each partition. Include a partition from */dev/sdb* in each array. If you use *mkraid*, you will need to create each array so that it has a `failed-disk` entry. The `failed-disk` entry corresponds to the existing partition on */dev/sda*. The `raid-disk` entry

for each array will be the new partition on */dev/sdb*. I prefer to use *mdadm* for this process.

```
# mdadm -C -n2 -l1 /dev/md0 /dev/sdb1 missing
```

missing is used as a placeholder for a disk that's not yet part of the array. In this case, we created a new RAID-1 in degraded mode (because only one partition, */dev/sdb1*, was used). Repeat this process for each new system partition.

4. Once you have created an array for each system partition, create a new filesystem on each array. Use *mkswap* to initialize the array that will act as the swap partition.

5. Bring the system into single-user mode and mount each new partition at an arbitrary mount point. I prefer to create some temporary mount points in the */mnt* directory (for example, */mnt/new-boot*).

6. Edit */etc/fstab* so that it contains the new RAID partitions instead of the existing partitions on */dev/sda*. I advise removing the use of filesystem labels in */etc/fstab* (LABEL=/home, for example) and using device names (such as */dev/md0* and */dev/md1*) instead. This will avoid any confusion. Don't forget to change the entry for swap as well.

7. Edit */etc/lilo.conf* and change the *root* line for the RAID kernel's stanza to reflect the new *md* entry. Don't change the *boot* line at this time.

8. Copy all the files from the current system partitions to the new arrays that will replace them. I find it best to use the *find* and *cpio* commands to accomplish this. First, change to the *root* directory of a filesystem. Then use the following command to copy all files to the new partition:

```
# cd /boot
# find . -xdev | cpio -pm /mnt/new-boot
```

The *-xdev* flag that I've passed to *find* instructs it to only return files that are on the current filesystem. This is very important because when we copy files from the *root* partition, we don't want files from */boot* to be copied, for example. The *-p* flag for *cpio* turns on pass-through mode, allowing another program to provide the list of files to copy—in this case, it's *find*. The *-m* option preserves modification times.

9. Repeat step 6 for each existing filesystem. When you're done, you should have populated each new array with the corresponding system partition.

10. Now run */sbin/lilo* and reboot the system into single-user mode. After the system reboots, you should notice that your degraded arrays are mounted (use *df* or *mount* to confirm this).

11. Next, add the old (*/dev/sda*) system partition to the new arrays, taking them out of degraded mode. If you're working with *raidtools*, use the *raidhotadd* command. For *mdadm*, use:

```
# mdadm -a /dev/md0 /dev/sda1
```

Repeat this command for each remaining partition and array until all of them are out of degraded mode. As you add partitions to the arrays, each one will begin reconstructing. So, the system might be a bit sluggish until the rebuild tasks have completed.

12. Use *fdisk* on */dev/sda* to change the partition types of *Linux Raid Auto*.

13. Edit */etc/lilo.conf* and change the *boot* line so that it points to the *boot* partition (for example, `boot=/dev/md0`). Now run */sbin/lilo* to rebuild the *boot* sector on your array.

For more information about booting using software RAID, I recommend the "Boot + Root + Raid + Lilo : Software Raid mini-HOWTO," written by Michael Robinton. You can find it at *http://www.tldp.org/HOWTO/mini/Boot+Root+Raid+LILO.html* or at any Linux Documentation project mirror.

Additional Resources

The following web sites, books, mailing lists, and magazines are valuable supplements to the material covered in this book.

Mailing Lists

The best resource for Linux RAID is the linux-raid mailing list. Many experts and developers read this list, and it's generally the best place to look for information. Be certain to check the archives before posting to the list. Archives are available at *http://marc.theaimsgroup.com/?l=linux-raid* or *http://groups.google.com/groups?group=mlist.linux.raid*.

To subscribe to the list, send a message to *majordomo@vger.kernel.org*, with the word "subscribe" in the message body (not the subject).

Web Sites and Online Resources

This section contains online resources that offer RAID and filesystem information, as well as hardware reviews.

RAID

Here are some web sites that provide information about RAID.

- The Linux Documentation (*http://www.tldp.org*) project provides a free, comprehensive library covering Linux and open source software. Of particular note are the following documents.
    - The Software RAID HOWTO provides a quick tutorial on configuring arrays, using *raidtools*. You can find this tutorial at *http://www.tldp.org/HOWTO/Software-RAID-HOWTO.html*.

— The Boot+Root+Raid+LILO mini-HOWTO provides cookbook examples for booting directly from a software RAID using LILO. You can access the document at *http://www.tldp.org/HOWTO/mini/Boot+Root+Raid+LILO. html*.

• "A Case for Redundant Arrays of Inexpensive Disks (RAID)," also known as the start of the Berkeley Papers, is available from the ACM web site (*http://www. acm.org/sigmod/dblp/db/conf/sigmod/PattersonGK88.html*), provided you have a subscription to their digital library.

• *http://www.nobell.org/~gjm/linux/ide-raid/* contains a case study of various ATA RAID setups.

Filesystems

The following web sites provide information about filesystems.

http://www.research.att.com/~gjm/linux/ide-raid.html
> The ext2 home page

http://e2fsprogs.sourceforge.net/ext2intro.html
> A technical paper authored by the developers of ext2

http://www.ibm.com/developerworks/oss/jfs/
> IBM's JFS for Linux home page

http://oss.sgi.com/projects/xfs/
> The XFS for Linux home page

http://www.namesys.com/
> The ReiserFS home page

http://www.zip.com.au/~akpm/linux/ext3/
> The ext3 home page

Hardware

Storage Review (*http://www.storagereview.com*) is an excellent resource that evaluates hard disks, RAID controllers, and standalone disk controllers.

Books

You might find the following reading material useful when building RAID systems. I'd like to specifically recommend *Advanced PC Architecture*, for those who need additional material to supplement what I provided in Chapter 2. *Advanced PC Architecture* covers many details that were beyond the scope of this book. I've also included *Readings in Database Systems* on my list. Although this book might seem out of place in the context of RAID, it provides a good introduction to many data structures, and I think that it can help readers to understand the interconnected relationships between applications, filesystems, operating systems, and hardware.

Bar, Moshe. *Linux File Systems*. McGraw-Hill Osborne Media, 2001.

Bovet, Daniel P. and Marco Cesati. *Understanding the Linux Kernel,* Second Edition. O'Reilly & Associates, 2001.

Buchanan, William and Austin Wilson. *Advanced PC Architecture*. Addison-Wesley, 2001.

Field, Gary and Peter Ridge. *The Book of SCSI: I/O For The New Millennium*. No Starch Press, 2000.

Schmidt, Friedhelm. *The SCSI Bus & IDE Interface: Protocols, Applications, and Programming*, Second Edition.Addison-Wesley, 1998.

Stonebraker, Michael and Joseph M. Hellerstein, eds. *Readings in Database Systems*, Third Edition. Morgan Kaufmann, 1998.

Thompson, Robert Bruce and Barbara Fritchman Thompson. *PC Hardware in a Nutshell*. O'Reilly & Associates, 2000.

Von Hagen, William. *Linux Filesystems*. Sams, 2002.

Hardware RAID Controller Vendors

This appendix contains a list of vendors who sell hardware RAID controllers.

Mylex (an IBM business unit)
6607 Kaiser Drive
Fremont, CA 94555
(510) 796-6100 (main)
http://www.mylex.com

Adaptec, Inc.
691 South Milpitas Boulevard
Milpitas, California 95035
(800) 442-7274
http://www.adaptec.com

Promise Technology, Inc.
1745 McCandless Drive
Milpitas, CA 95035
(408) 228-6300
http://www.promise.com

3ware, Inc.
Corporate Office
701 E. Middlefield Road
Suite 300
Mountain View, California, 94043
(877) 883-9273
http://www.3ware.com

LSI Logic Corporation
1621 Barber Lane
Milpitas, California 95035
(866) 574-5741
http://www.lsil.com

Highpoint Technologies, Inc.
5177 Brandin Court
Fremont, CA 94538 USA
(510) 623-0968
http://www.highpoint-tech.com/

Index

We'd like to hear your suggestions for improving our indexes. Send email to *index@oreilly.com*.

About the Author

Derek Vadala lives in New York City. He works for Azurance.com, an open source and security consulting firm that he cofounded. He has been published in *Sys Admin* magazine, *Linux Journal*, *The Perl Journal*, and *The Journal of Linux Technology*.

Colophon

Our look is the result of reader comments, our own experimentation, and feedback from distribution channels. Distinctive covers complement our distinctive approach to technical topics, breathing personality and life into potentially dry subjects.

Claire Cloutier was the production editor and copyeditor for *Managing RAID on Linux*. Ann Schirmer was the proofreader. Ann Schirmer, Mary Brady, and Jeffrey Holcomb provided quality control. Reginald Aubry wrote the index. Claire Cloutier, Genevieve d'Entremont, and Judy Hoer were the compositors.

The image on the cover of *Managing RAID on Linux* is a logjam. Emma Colby designed the cover of this book, based on a series design by Hanna Dyer and Edie Freedman. The cover image is a 19th-century engraving from the Trades and Occupations collection of the Dover Pictorial Archive. Emma Colby produced the cover layout with QuarkXPress 4.1, using Adobe's ITC Garamond font.

David Futato designed the interior layout. The chapter opening images are from the Dover Pictorial Archive, *Marvels of the New West: A Vivid Portrayal of the Stupendous Marvels in the Vast Wonderland West of the Missouri River*, by William Thayer (The Henry Bill Publishing Co., 1888), and *The Pioneer History of America: A Popular Account of the Heroes and Adventures*, by Augustus Lynch Mason, A.M. (The Jones Brothers Publishing Company, 1884).

This book was converted to FrameMaker 5.5.6 by Joe Wizda, using a format conversion tool created by Erik Ray, Jason McIntosh, Neil Walls, and Mike Sierra that uses Perl and XML technologies. The text font is Linotype Birka; the heading font is Adobe Myriad Condensed; and the code font is LucasFont's TheSans Mono Condensed. The illustrations that appear in the book were produced by Robert Romano and Jessamyn Read, using Macromedia FreeHand 9 and Adobe Photoshop 6. The tip and warning icons were drawn by Christopher Bing.

Other Titles Available from O'Reilly

Security

Practical UNIX & Internet Security, 3rd Edition

By Simson Garfinkel, Gene Spafford, & Alan Schwartz
3rd Edition February 2003 (est.)
1004 pages (est.), ISBN 0-569-00323-4

Updated for today's security and networking issues, *Practical UNIX and Internet Security*, 3rd Edition covers the four most popular Unix variants: Solaris, Linux, FreeBSD, and Mac OS X. In addition, the authors have added far more information about Linux, security policy, and cryptography, and have added new sections on embedded systems, biometrics, new authentication systems such as LDAP and PAM, and anti-theft technologies.

Building Internet Firewalls, 2nd Edition

By Elizabeth D. Zwicky, Simon Cooper & D. Brent Chapman
2nd Edition June 2000
894 pages, ISBN 1-56592-871-7

Completely revised and much expanded, this second edition of the highly respected and bestselling *Building Internet Firewalls* now covers Unix, Linux, and Windows NT. It's a practical and detailed guide that provides step-by-step explanations of how to design and install firewalls, and how to configure Internet services to work with a firewall. It covers a wide range of services and protocols. It also contains a complete list of resources, including the location of many publicly available firewalls construction tools.

802.11 Security

By Bruce Potter & Bob Fleck
1st Edition December 2002 (est.)
350 pages (est.), ISBN 0-596-00290-4

This book shows how to secure 802.11-based wireless networks focusing particularly on the 802.11b specification. Includes detailed coverage of security issues unique to wireless networking, such as Wireless Access Points (WAP), bandwidth stealing, and the problematic Wired Equivalent Privacy component of 802.11. You will learn how to configure a wireless client and set up a WAP using either Linux or FreeBSD. Controlling network access and encrypting client traffic are also covered thoroughly.

Network Security with OpenSSL

By John Viega, Matt Messier & Pravir Chandra
1st Edition June 2002
384 pages, ISBN 0-596-00270-X

OpenSSL is a popular and effective open source version of SSL/TLS, the most widely used protocol for secure network communications. The only guide available on the subject, Network Security with OpenSSLdetails the challenges in securing network communications, and shows you how to use OpenSSL tools to best meet those challenges. Focused on the practical, this book provides only the information that is necessary to use OpenSSL safely and effectively.

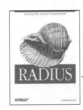

RADIUS

By Jonathan Hassell
1st Edition September 2002
206 pages, ISBN 0-596-00322-6

This new book provides a complete, detailed guide into the underpinnings of the RADIUS protocol, with particular emphasis on the utility of user accounting. Author Jonathan Hassell also provides practical suggestions for using an open-source variation called FreeRADIUS, giving the reader background in both RADIUS theory and practice.

SSH, The Secure Shell: The Definitive Guide

By Daniel J. Barrett & Richard Silverman
1st Edition January 2001
558 pages, ISBN 0-596-00011-1

SSH (Secure Shell) is a popular, robust, TCP/IP-based product for network security and privacy, supporting strong encryption and authentication. *SSH, The Secure Shell: The Definitive Guide* covers SSH in detail for both system administrators and end users, from the basics up to advanced case studies. You'll learn how to install and maintain SSH, configure servers and clients in simple and complex ways, apply SSH to practical problems, protect other TCP applications through forwarding (tunneling), and troubleshoot a wide variety of difficulties. Coverage includes SSH1, SSH2, OpenSSH, and F-Secure SSH for Unix, plus Windows and Macintosh implementations.

O'REILLY®

To order: *800-998-9938* • *order@oreilly.com* • *www.oreilly.com*
Online editions of most O'Reilly titles are available by subscription at *safari.oreilly.com*
Also available at most retail and online bookstores.

How to stay in touch with O'Reilly

1. Visit our award-winning web site

http://www.oreilly.com/

★ "Top 100 Sites on the Web"—PC Magazine
★ CIO Magazine's Web Business 50 Awards

Our web site contains a library of comprehensive product information (including book excerpts and tables of contents), downloadable software, background articles, interviews with technology leaders, links to relevant sites, book cover art, and more. File us in your bookmarks or favorites!

2. Join our email mailing lists

Sign up to get email announcements of new books and conferences, special offers, and O'Reilly Network technology newsletters at:

http://elists.oreilly.com

It's easy to customize your free elists subscription so you'll get exactly the O'Reilly news you want.

3. Get examples from our books

To find example files for a book, go to:

http://www.oreilly.com/catalog

select the book, and follow the "Examples" link.

4. Work with us

Check out our web site for current employment opportunities:

http://jobs.oreilly.com/

5. Register your book

Register your book at:

http://register.oreilly.com

6. Contact us

O'Reilly & Associates, Inc.
1005 Gravenstein Hwy North
Sebastopol, CA 95472 USA
TEL: 707-827-7000 or 800-998-9938
       (6am to 5pm PST)
FAX: 707-829-0104

order@oreilly.com
For answers to problems regarding your order or our products. To place a book order online visit:

http://www.oreilly.com/order_new/

catalog@oreilly.com
To request a copy of our latest catalog.

booktech@oreilly.com
For book content technical questions or corrections.

corporate@oreilly.com
For educational, library, government, and corporate sales.

proposals@oreilly.com
To submit new book proposals to our editors and product managers.

international@oreilly.com
For information about our international distributors or translation queries. For a list of our distributors outside of North America check out:

http://international.oreilly.com/distributors.html

adoption@oreilly.com
For information about academic use of O'Reilly books, visit:

http://academic.oreilly.com

O'REILLY®

Notes